D1118592

Management Theory in Action

Management Theory in Action

Real-World Lessons for Walking the Talk

Eric H. Kessler

MANAGEMENT THEORY IN ACTION
Copyright © Eric H. Kessler, 2010.

First published in 2010 by
PALGRAVE MACMILLAN®
in the United States—a division of St. Martin's Press LLC,
175 Fifth Avenue, New York, NY 10010.

Where this book is distributed in the UK, Europe and the rest of the world,
this is by Palgrave Macmillan, a division of Macmillan Publishers Limited,
registered in England, company number 785998, of Houndmills,
Basingstoke, Hampshire RG21 6XS.

Palgrave Macmillan is the global academic imprint of the above companies
and has companies and representatives throughout the world.

Palgrave® and Macmillan® are registered trademarks in the United States,
the United Kingdom, Europe and other countries.

ISBN 978–0–230–60758–3

Library of Congress Cataloging-in-Publication Data is available from the
Library of Congress.

Library of Congress Cataloging-in-Publication Data

Kessler, Eric H.
   Management theory in action : real-world lessons for walking the talk /
Eric H. Kessler.
      p. cm.
   Includes index.
   ISBN 978–0–230–60758–3
   1. Management. 2. Leadership. I. Title.

HD31.K4613 2010
658.4001—dc22   2009031257

A catalogue record of the book is available from the British Library.

Design by Newgen Imaging Systems (P) Ltd., Chennai, India.

First edition: March 2010

10 9 8 7 6 5 4 3 2 1

Printed in the United States of America.

To my parents, Nat and Lori, and my brother, Scott, who in their practical intelligence, uncompromising integrity, and unwavering authenticity are wonderful models for "walking the talk."

CONTENTS

Section III   Macro Management (=Us):
The Organizational

INTRODUCTION

We See It All too Often...

An eager young business student gets straight A's in school but fail miserably on her first internship. She just cannot figure out what her college courses have to do with this strange new world. To the casual observer, it would seem like she is completely unprepared for the challenges that face her in the workplace. Result: this stellar student is not offered any challenging assignments and not asked back next summer.

A freshly minted MBA graduate secures an interview at a prestigious firm but fails to impress the interviewer. During the talk he spouts a dizzying array of names, dates, and technical terminology but this does not make a positive impression. When given sample business scenarios to solve, the graduate cites research statistics and abstract theoretical models to support their generic cookie-cutter ideas but does not deliver specific actionable recommendations. Result: this high pedigree applicant does not get the job.

A high-potential new employee starts her first month at the office but becomes utterly lost in the day-to-day pragmatics of management life. When she retreats back to old textbooks for help, none of the actual items on their daily agendas can be found per se in the chapter indexes or tables of contents. It is as though her highly priced school lessons got lost in translation when being applied to her job, and she just cannot seem to link concrete problems with theoretical solutions. Her people don't respond to her actions and her groups seem to spend more time fighting with each other than accomplishing anything. Result: this promising individual earns poor performance reviews and falls off the fast track.

An upcoming middle-level manager is sponsored by his firm to return to school for a master's in business administration (MBA) degree but, when sitting in the classroom, is taken aback by the lack of connection between the professors' lectures and the "real" business world. He becomes extremely cynical of the textbook theories, tunes out the professor's lessons, and "sleepwalk" through what he considers to be a waste of his money and time. Result: this investment yields little return as the manager comes back to the workplace with no discernable improvement in his abilities and lacks the career bump he had hoped for.

An incoming management consultant is asked by a firm to help redesign their business model and eliminate inefficient practices. Despite the best efforts to motivate the workforce, the consultant cannot seem to grasp the logic of business structure and is constantly rebuffed by its deeply ingrained culture. The consultant's polished pitches fail to overcome employees' anxiety and make any headway with implementation as managers quickly regress back to old routines and perspectives. Result: the firm does not reverse competitive shortcomings and the expert-for-hire does not return or receive any referral business.

A long-time organizational veteran is becoming increasingly oblivious to new management techniques and technologies promoted by their organization. They cannot seem to keep pace with all of these buzzwords and, feeling that they should stick with what has worked in the past, they find that these old habits are not always useful in the modern workplace. When dealing with global subsidiaries, they cannot seem to get a handle on why they do so many things differently around the world than at the home office. Result: the employee spends ineffectual sunset years in a low-impact position with reduced opportunities to leverage their experience or contribute to the firm's success.

We see it all too often…but we do not have to.

What is the common thread here, the missing ingredient, the root cause of these frequent management failures?

Many readers will surely be familiar with the old saying, "Out of the frying pan and into the fire." Essentially the adage refers to a leap from a hot, difficult situation into a hotter, more difficult one. In the scenarios described earlier, the frying pan can be seen to represent the business school and the world of management theory whereas the fire is the actual business environment and the world of business practice. The classroom is meant to enhance people's abilities and prepare them for succeeding in the workplace. Students learn concepts and skills, and are thus assessed and graded, in this frying pan. However, the real "test" is whether they can successfully utilize them under fire. This is the ultimate goal of classroom teachers, research scholars, corporate trainers, management consultants, school administrators, corporate executives, and textbook writers—and it is the preeminent objective of business students—but it is hard to predict and even harder to measure. Unfortunately there is just no guarantee that the knowledge, skills, and abilities learned in the frying pan will ever successfully transition to the fire. A person's classroom GPA (i.e., book smarts) might literally be an "A" but his or her proverbial report card at work (i.e., life smarts) could very well be an "F."

Bottom line—All too frequently there is a fuzzy if not downright poor relationship between learning management theory and executing management practice. This gap is the missing link, or the broken bridge if you will, which explains the failures detailed in opening paragraphs and constrains people from effectively putting their knowledge to good use.

Rebuilding the bridge between management theory and action is the subject of our book.

The Problem

Let us begin with a simple truth—There is a difference between knowing something and doing something. This distinction goes back centuries, and it is grounded in both eastern and western intellectual as well as religious traditions that emphasize the importance of both seeing and actually walking along a right path. The idea is particularly well captured by the philosopher Aristotle, who clearly differentiates (a) intellectual sophia, a theoretically deep understanding of reality and (b) applied phronesis, or the practical skill and behavioral alacrity needed for succeeding in the real world. Relating the lesson to our modern business context, we might conclude that the recipe for success is to translate the former (reflective thought) into the latter (informed action). This book is primarily concerned with helping the reader bridge the theory-practice fissure in the business world.

Lamentably this is not an easy endeavor. There is a widespread and vocal stream of scholars and professionals bemoaning a considerable gap between, on the one hand the "frying pan" of business scholarship and education and, on the other hand, the "fire" of business reality. For example, in their discussion of a "great divide" between management theory and practice, Sara Rynes, Jean Bartunek, and Richard Daft[1] conclude that

> A substantial body of evidence suggests that executives typically do not turn to academics or academic research findings in developing management strategies and practices.

Moreover, as Nancy Adler and Anne-Wil Harzing[2] point out:

> Many leaders both inside and outside academia fear that universities today are no longer fulfilling their fundamental mission; business views business-school research as irrelevant...chief executives...pay little attention to what business schools do or say.

And this is echoed by past Academy of Management president Donald Hambrick[3] who in his address to the worldwide membership found a similar disconnect in management research:

> Each August, we (management scholars) come to talk with each other (at our annual conference); during the rest of the year we read each others' papers in our journals and write our own papers so that we may, in turn, have an audience the following August: an incestuous, closed loop...We must recognize that our responsibility is not to ourselves, but rather to the institutions around the world that are in dire need of improved management, as well as to those individuals who seek to be the most effective managers they possibly can be. It is time for us to break out of our closed loop. It is time for us to matter.

This is quite troubling. It means that the people charged with actually managing businesses and other organizations are not connecting with those who are empirically assessing, conceptually modeling, and actively developing guidelines for these very same types of activities. The obvious question therefore is "Why." Why does management theory have such a limited effect on management practice? Is it because business folk are stubborn? Uninterested? Too busy to be bothered? Caught within a here-and-now mindset? Or maybe academics are simply out of touch? Overly technical? Methodologically narrow? Caught within a self-serving loop? Perhaps there is some fault on both sides of the fence?

Warren Bennis and James O'Toole[4] focus on the latter, maintaining that this is partly because business schools have "lost their way," or more to the point, that

> Business schools are facing intense criticism for failing to impart useful skills...this scientific model is predicated on the faulty assumption that business is an academic discipline like chemistry or geology when, in fact, business is a profession and business schools are professional schools—or should be. Business schools must rediscover the practice of business.

So if our business students are not being imparted or encouraged to develop the skills and insights necessary to transfer theoretical to practical knowledge, then we need to know why this is the case. Now I am going to change the pace a bit and, instead of citing a noted scholar or famous executive, offer the words of a stand-up comedian (after all, what could be more real-world than standing on a stage and putting yourself on the line to instantaneously succeed or fail in front of a live audience!). Don

Novello, who on the show *Saturday Night Live* channeled character Father Guido Sarducci, offered the following thoughts[5]:

> I find that education, it don't matter where you go to school, Italy, America, Brazil, all are the same—it's all this memorization and it don't matter how long you can remember anything just so you can parrot it back for the tests. I got this idea for a school I would like to start, something called the Five Minute University. The idea is that in five minutes you learn what the average college graduate remembers five years after he or she is out of school...You see, you don't have to waste your time with conjugations and vocabulary, all that junk. You'll just forget it anyway, what's the difference.

This joke is funny because there is a certain amount of truth to it. Often students of business feel a low compulsion to internalize academic knowledge from classes or textbooks because they see it merely as instrumental in the short term for getting a good grade and do not fully appreciate its longer-term value for living the good life or building the good career. When reflecting on my personal experiences as a professor, I am simply amazed when my students have trouble recalling what they learned in their previous courses even one or two semesters prior. Grade over...lessons forgotten. What a lost opportunity for growth!

Now this problem would be bad enough if it was merely an educational dilemma. Yet numerous indicators seem to point to the fact that our theory-to-practice divide extends even farther than the classroom. The problem also inhibits the effectiveness of executives in the boardroom. Said another way, management theory is neither being sufficiently appreciated nor actively applied by its focal audiences—real-life managers! Jeffrey Pfeffer and Robert Sutton[6] identify this as a "Knowing-Doing Gap" as highlighted by the particularly pointed observation that

> Did you ever wonder why so much education and training, management consultation, organizational research and so many books and articles produce so few changes in actual management practice?

This is a significant problem. One so ironic that it might be worthy of a Jerry Seinfeld skit or Dilbert comic strip. If you close your eyes you could almost picture a stand-up comedian asking "Do you ever wonder why most of the theories and models about being a good manager are ignored by actual managers?" Or a cartoon character uttering "if you want to get ahead then forget about all the ideas you learned in business school and just do what the boss says."

This paradox was played out in a wonderful scene in the Michael J. Fox Movie *The Secret of My Success* in which a straight-A student is rebuffed for a job due to his supposedly inadequate preparation. When he protests that his business school training prepared him for the position he was told that he only had college experience, not "practical hard-nosed business experience." He asks then why he even went to college in the first place. The reply of the interviewer, "had fun, didn't you?" From this exchange we can see that not only are there different languages spoken in the classroom and boardroom, but on both sides of the fence it seems that there is a palatable distain for and patronizing attitude toward the other parties' language and methods. Oh those naïve scholars. Oh those superficial managers.

So how might we fix the problem? On the one hand there is an ample *supply* of good management theory and potentially useful ideas. On the other hand there is much *demand* for good management theory by organizations wrestling with the ever-evolving challenges of the modern business world. How can we get the two hands together? To clap so to speak? One way to remedy the proverbial knowing-doing gap is suggested by renowned psychologist Robert Sternberg[7] who draws from his extensive research to suggest the simple but penetrating insight that

> Teaching for successful intelligence involves helping students capitalize on strengths and compensate for or correct weaknesses.

This makes sense. People need to not only learn theories but also to actively embed themselves in these theories, develop the actual skills and competencies advocated by the frameworks, and apply them to specific situations in their personal and professional lives. Taking these steps would help them grow and become stronger individuals by making their newfound knowledge personal, productive, and useful. This notion is supported by Jonathan Gosling and occasional "rogue" (because he dares speak of the need for practical, problem-oriented education) management guru Henry Mintzberg[8] who argue that

> [management education so often fails]...because management is neither a science nor a profession, neither a function or a combination of functions. Management is a practice—it has to be appreciated through experience, in context...Management education should leverage work and life experiences...[and] the key to learning is thoughtful reflection.

Thus the gap between management theory and practice, and hence the need for better "bridge-building" and more "clapping," might begin with the realization that prospective as well as actual managers need to embed themselves in management theory in a reflective, personal, and applied manner to accomplish tasks and achieve results. But as the previous discussion suggests, this might not be the norm and is certainly not systemic or institutionalized in our mainstream approach to business education. It is a problem. And judging by the numerous high-profile failings of management practice across a broad swath of industries and environments—for example, corporate scandals, economic failures, bungled mergers, misguided strategies, short-sighted actions (just watch the news and cringe)—it is a critical problem at that.

But the situation is not as dire as it appears. The idea that management theory should be put into action within the context of management practice is a compelling one and provides a potential path for us to address the issue.

The Solution

The journey toward this book began over twenty years ago when I began my teaching career with the pie-eyed notion that it was my job to challenge students to apply theoretical ideas to develop their practical, real-world skills and actually improve their organizations. It seemed simply unacceptable for business students to exit the classroom wondering "what does this theory have to do with my job" or "how do I use these models in real life?" In fact I have often told my students that, if it was entirely up to me, they would not get a grade in the course for five years, when at that time I would find them and test the degree to which they have remembered and applied its lessons to become more effective persons and professionals. If you really think about it, might this be a more fair and accurate test of practical learning outcomes? Not just talking the walk on examinations...but actually walking the talk in actual business situations confronting the "tests" embedded in the everyday opportunities and problems of praxis.

As the seeds for this book began to grow, its ideas began to appear in several of my professional engagements. For example, in an address as the President of the Eastern Academy of Management, I stressed to the organization's membership of management scholars the importance of becoming more application-oriented our teaching and research.[9] Based on this premise, I later conceptualized and commissioned the EAM White Paper Series to apply important scholarly insights to critical business issues in a way that is specifically useful to managers.[10] The ongoing series supports the notion that educators should aim not only to deliver theories within the academic arena but also to look outward to improve actual management practice.

The idea of better applying knowledge took greater shape in the *Handbook of Organizational and Managerial Wisdom*, where I argued that we need to go beyond base theory and demonstrate through our reflections and actions what might be termed a higher-level management "wisdom." Wisdom means more than just knowing something; it also involves applying what we know to lead better lives and, in a manner particularly related to the jobs of managers, enable others to do the same. The distinction between knowledge and wisdom is a profound and important one. It is one thing to be a guru on a mountaintop, or scholar within an academic ivory tower, whereas it is a wholly different matter entirely to apply this knowledge within the ebb and flow of human activity to positively impact the world and make a real difference. Knowledge is passive and removed; wisdom is active and engaged. Management theory should therefore aspire to a more wisdom-based approach[11]:

> To be wise means more than merely to be knowledgeable. Surely, we all have witnessed our share of intelligent yet foolish individuals....Knowledge involves holding justified true belief, whereas wisdom uses this knowledge in the conduct of sound and serene judgment...Wisdom is inherently action oriented.

This application-oriented focus continued in a subsequent book on *Cultural Mythology and Global Leadership*, where I made the argument that we need to think about applying management ideas on an international scale. Not only must managers become more practically minded in their thinking; they must do so with an eye toward the many complexities that define the new realities of global business.[12] Attempting to hold myself and my home institution up to these standards, I directed an initiative to redesign the Business Honors Program at my university by breaking down traditional academic silos and overcoming standard departmental boundaries to focus on the development of cross-disciplinary, problem-based, and practically relevant knowledge.[13]

And so we arrive at the present time...

at book which you are now reading...

which represents the clearest and most direct path that I have found for bridging the gap between theory and practice.

Management Theory in Action: Real-World Lessons for Walking the Talk directly connects the world of ideas (management theory) with its execution (management practice) in a specific, concrete, and easy-to-relate manner. It communicates real-life accounts of how actual people have used classroom-taught theories to better understand and better perform at their jobs. From these stories it suggests tangible lessons for you, the

reader, to better make sense of your workplace events, grasp their implications, develop needed competencies, and use them to make a positive
difference in your organization. As such this book is at its core a vehicle
for practicing what is professed. And by doing this it offers you tools for
increasing your intellectual as well as behavioral acumen and becoming
a better manager.

Overall, in response to the problems discussed earlier in this introduc-
tory chapter, effectively applying management theory to practice will (1)
Better inform business executives in their jobs, (2) improve the quality of
business education, (3) extend the shelf-life of learning tools and models,
(4) produce real and productive changes in management, (5) facilitate
personal and organizational success, (6) leverage work/life experiences
in reflective growth and development, (7) enhance personal engagement
to better make a tangible difference, and (8) turn people's knowledge-
potential into actual wisdom. Indeed meeting these challenges will be
the aim of the following chapters. And it will be pursued not through
pontifications by some distant third-person authority but as directly evi-
denced by people like you who purposefully engaged in taking the theories to task.

It is important to note that what you are about to read is NOT a text-
book-or encyclopedic-like review of research studies and abstract conceptualizations. It does NOT seek to recreate step-by-step descriptions of
academic models, trace nuanced theorizations or statistical manipulations,
or provide painfully long lists of historical references and citations. If you
are looking for meticulously recounted and comprehensively documented
assemblages of "academese" then look elsewhere. Instead the chapters of
this book seek to capture some of the most essential insights and useful
recommendations of the management field in a reader-friendly format
that actual managers can proactively use to be more successful in their
pursuits.

To this end, the focus of the book is a broad collection of real-world
stories derived from actual business folk trying to put management theory into action. These people represent men and women, from teen-ag-
ers to golden-agers, occupying entry-level through upper-level positions
in the management hierarchy, employed in a broad gamut of industries,
and working in all corners of the world. The subjects of the stories vary
widely in their personality and family background, race and ethnicity,
and organization and geography. Their sole link is that they all embarked
on their own personal journeys of development and volunteered their
tales about how management theory related to "slugging it out" in the
real world. These reflections are used in this book to compose vignettes
that highlight both successful and unsuccessful examples of applying

theory to practice. Thus the reader will find that each section of the book is both firmly grounded in theory and fully embedded in real-world application.

Where Are We Going?: Objectives of the Book

There are three underlying, interrelated goals pursued in this book that you should be mindful of as you proceed forward.

(1) Understanding basic management concepts—(What are the key insights that I need to know?): The first goal of this book is to provide you with a basic familiarity of a body of knowledge that can help you to make sense of the organizational reality that surrounds you and help you manage it more effectively. I don't care if you memorize people's names, key dates, and technical terminology. I do care if you understand the major messages that emerge from established scholarly models. This book provides a road-map to help you relate management theory to the practice of management.

(2) Engaging in critical thinking and deep reflection—(Why do things happen the way that they do?): The second goal of this book is to challenge you to go beyond a general understanding of management theory and be able to analyze, synthesize, and evaluate it. Once basic knowledge is acquired, more complex reasoning skills can be used to assess and customize the theory. Analyzing management theory relates to breaking situations down into their component parts (e.g., what are the actual variables in play within the expectancy theory of motivation?). Synthesizing management theory relates to creatively combining information to link ideas and situations together (e.g., how might you construct a holistic approach to motivating different employees?). Evaluating management theory relates to assessing its usefulness in specific situations (e.g., which theory or theories of motivation might work for you in a given condition?). This book provides examples to help you reflect on and achieve a deeper mastery of management theory as it applies to the practice of management.

(3) Developing a "toolbox" of application skills—(How specifically do I use it to succeed?): The third and final goal of the book is to help you put the rubber to the road and increase your cognitive capabilities and behavioral repertoires. Said another way, this goal builds upon "what" (goal 1) and "why" (goal 2) issues by facilitating tangible actions that you can take for enhancing your personal and professional success. This book provides the prompts to help you formulate specific strategies and tactics for applying these tools to best achieve desired results.

In using this book, you can therefore expect to increase your ability to understand, evaluate, and apply management theory to develop core competencies and enhance practical skill-sets.

How Are We Getting There?: Structure of the Book

The book is divided into three sections that consider managerial dynamics at varying levels of analyses. In each section there are four chapters organized around a common theme. This structure is illustrated in the figure below.

Section I starts from the foundation of the individual person. The success of even the most complex organizations and institutions, no matter how big or powerful, is at the end of the day driven by its employees. Using an analogy from chemistry, we know that cells contain molecules that contain atoms that in turn contain quarks, and so on. Organizations similarly contain layers of divisions, functions, teams, and the like but are ultimately a function of their people. This first section of *Management Theory in Action* then offers real-world stories at the individual-level analysis to focus on the manager as a human being. Specifically it considers management issues relating to "Knowing Oneself Truly" (chapter 1), "Managing Time and Stress" (chapter 2), "Perceiving and Understanding Accurately" (chapter 3), and "Making Better and More Ethical Decisions" (chapter 4). The goal of these chapters is to help you develop and use core competencies for becoming a stronger person.

Section II builds on the prior discussion to address interpersonal issues. Indeed there is no escaping the fact that man is a social being. We do not

SECTION 1 *Managing the Individual (You)*	1	Knowing Oneself Truly	...For Becoming a Stronger Person
	2	Managing Stress and Time	
	3	Perceiving and Understanding Accurately	
	4	Making Better and More Ethical Decisions	

SECTION 2 *Managing the Interpersonal (+Them)*	5	Communicating Effectively with Others	...For Engaging in More Effective Interactions
	6	Motivating and Inspiring Others	
	7	Gaining Power and Influencing Others	
	8	Resolving Conflicts with Others	

SECTION 3 *Managing the Organizational (=Us)*	9	Forging High-Performance Teams	...For Building More Productive Workplace Environments
	10	Designing An Enabling Structure and Culture	
	11	Executing the Leadership Function	
	12	Developing a Global Mindset	

live in isolation or work inside of a bubble. No matter one's level of technical mastery and acumen, we simply cannot be effective and efficient in life's endeavors without some degree of interaction with others. Management is thus an inherently social endeavor insofar as it strives to achieve results through people. Therefore the second section of Management Theory in Action offers real-world stories at the interpersonal level of analyses as related to the practice of management. Specifically it considers management dynamics relating to "Communicating with Others" (chapter 5), "Motivating and Inspiring Others" (chapter 6), "Gaining Power and Influencing Others" (chapter 7), and "Resolving Conflicts with Others" (chapter 8). The goal of these chapters is to help you develop and use core competencies for engaging in more effective interactions.

Section III goes a step farther by examining some of the larger management challenges faced by organizations at large. The manmade constructions that we call organizations have evolved to become both important and ubiquitous elements of society, enveloping our personal and professional lives and enabling our very existence. On a typical day we may be scarcely aware of them, but it would be an interesting exercise to ponder the broad scope of the many commercial, social, political, religious, service, community, and other institutions that we encounter and the extent to which they touch different aspects of our lives. Therefore the third section of Management Theory in Action offers real-world stories at the organizational level of analyses as related to constructing the overall context for management. Specifically it considers management challenges relating to "Forging High-Performance Teams" (chapter 9), "Designing an Enabling Structure and Culture" (chapter 10), "Executing the Leadership Function" (chapter 11), and "Developing a Global Mindset" (chapter 12). The goal of these chapters is to help you develop and use core competencies for building more productive workplace environments.

The chapters can be read in the prescribed order, which follows a logical sequence of related issues and shared levels of analysis, or the reader can pick and choose chapters based on their personal interests and particular or pressing challenges.

In each of the twelve chapters, I present select issues and core management insights that relate to them. The issues will then be brought alive with "war stories" from actual people applying theory and developing skills to implement action in the real world. These stories go beyond common methods of instruction and training to actually link theory with practice. Next specific guidelines will be offered for the reader to apply these lessons to their circumstances. More specifically, following a general introduction of the chapter each of the topic discussions will be organized in the following manner:

Ask Yourself: First, I will prompt the reader to reflect on critical questions related to the managerial issue and its potential application to their personal and professional lives.

Management Theory: Second, I will share the most central insights of relevant management theory without getting bogged down in overly technical terminology, obscure jargon, long lists of citations, and complicated constructs or equations. What appears in this section is a distillation of major scholarly frameworks regarding the focal practical challenge. Throughout the book I draw heavily from a broad and diverse base of original research as well as published journals, readers, and textbooks too numerous to mention in order to provide an executive summary of key take-away templates that can be used to understand and guide action. Although we purposefully avoid diluting these core messages by lapsing into a journal-like presentation of individual research references, the reader should appreciate the solid theoretical foundation underlying the arguments and be aware that what appears is my enactment of the relevant academic literature's core ideas as they pertain to the subject at hand.

In Action: Third, I will present a real-world management story. It is important to note that all of these narratives are real and written from the perspective of the actual person applying management theory to practice. Some tales focus more on straightforward theory applications. In these cases the people describe their reflections on a specific management concept, discuss how it explained or guided a real-life experience they have had on the job, and evaluate actual "bottom line" implications on dimensions such as raising performance, increasing satisfaction, mitigating absenteeism, and reducing turnover. Other tales focus more on developing specific skills embedded in the theories. In these cases the people evaluate their need for developing the specific skill based on self-assessment and requirements for the select management skill in their job or career, present a specific plan for skill development, describe a timetable for implementing this plan, and offer a status report on the success of the plan as well as ideas for continued improvement.

Walking the Talk: Fourth, I provide guidelines for using these lessons to enhance the reader's management abilities and success—that is, walk the talk. In essence, they are presented to help you "deal" with actual situations. As such, and as a memory device, the steps correspond to the four letters in the word D-E-A-L:

1. **D**etermine where the theory fits with the situation
2. **E**valuate the relative effectiveness of your behavior

3. **A**nalyze why this happened and underlying reasons for this success/failure
4. **L**everage the insights and lessons for self-development to enhance your professional and personal endeavors.

In addition, following each set of DEAL guidelines a space will be provided where the reader will be challenged to develop at least one action that they will be willing to take in order to improve the discussed management competency and apply it to their lives. So be ready to make a commitment or two as you read through the book and think about what you will prepared to do in the next five days, five months, or five years to make it happen.

In summary, this book attempts to convey core ideas from management theory and show you how people have applied them in the real world to better execute management practice. In addition, it provides the tools to guide you in reflecting and acting on the lessons learned to develop core individual, interpersonal, and organizational level competencies. Herein lies the ultimate test of the book's contribution...not only that you read it but that you truly understand it, you personalize it, you apply it...in essence that you live it by effectively putting management theory in action to become a more successful person and professional.

SECTION I

Micro Management (You): The Individual

For Becoming a Stronger Person

You + Them = Us

CHAPTER ONE

Knowing Oneself Truly

Chapter one examines management theories about individuals' personalities and applying the foundational management skill of knowing oneself. We begin our conversation here for several reasons. First, despite what some might think, there is no ideal personality type. Some characteristics are certainly more useful on the whole than others but one would be hard pressed to identify a single personality attribute that is universally positive without any drawbacks or trade-offs. Therefore it behooves the effective manager to know himself or herself so that they can identify their different strengths as well as potential weaknesses. Second, the relationship between personality and success more often than not depends on situational factors such as the nature of their job, peculiarities of the task at hand, types of people they work and do business with, structure of the team in which they are assigned and organization in which they are employed, and overall culture of their firm and industry. Thus the effective manager will seek to establish a good "fit" with their surroundings. Third, the importance knowing oneself is multiplied because a person cannot know anyone else with any degree of accuracy if they do not know themselves. This is because managers see others only through the unique lens of their predilections and character. Generally, these points reinforce Western and Eastern philosophical traditions espousing the benefits of knowing oneself; for instance Plato's urgings toward self-examination, Shakespeare's lamentation to be true to oneself, Hindu inspirations directing us to reflect on the Atman or true self, and Sun Tzu's warning that without self-knowledge the probability of success is significantly reduced. Bottom line—you cannot manage and lead effectively if you do not know yourself. You cannot leverage assets and guard against exposures, optimize fit with your surroundings, or understand others with a high degree of accuracy. Therefore our first chapter looks at how one can know oneself truly.

1.1 Appreciating the Importance of Self-Knowledge

Ask Yourself: Who is the real "you"? Are you deeply and completely aware of your personality or instead sometimes find yourself surprised by how you behave in certain situations? Do you always see yourself in the same way that others see you or instead occasionally experience a gap between your and "their" images of who you are? How do you react when an employee's or coworker's conception of you differs from your own self-image? How do you handle feedback from others (say your boss) even if it takes the form of criticism, and do you ignore it or use it to learn about yourself and grow as a person?

Management Theory: Self-knowledge is the degree to which a person truly understands the fundamental characteristics about their personality. As people we all, by definition, have a personality—the relatively stable collection of characteristics and way of interacting with the world that makes us both unique and similar to others. Yet rarely do we take the time to reflect on our core self. Why? Perhaps it is just too much effort. Not making the time to look often results in a surface self-portrait with little reflection or deep consideration. Maybe we turn a blind eye to things that we do not like. Limiting ourselves to only desirable aspects often results in a picture that is incomplete and self-serving. Possibly we tune out social cues and criticism from others. Ignoring different viewpoints often results in a self-image that differs from the way in which others see us. Yet despite these potential pitfalls, the elusive goal of self-knowledge is critical to understanding our strengths and competencies, our learning opportunities and areas for improvement, and hence our well-being and continued growth. Moreover, in addition to the snapshot we take of ourselves there is also the cinema that represents the cumulative process in which we learn (or not) about ourselves. In this process, people have different degrees of sensitivity to feedback. We certainly go through life with ample reactions and responses from people such as bosses and teachers, colleagues and classmates, family and friends. These are potential vehicles for gaining personal insight but to use them we must maintain an open mind. On the one hand it is not advised to live completely by other people's opinions. On the other hand, if we shut out this information, perhaps by becoming too inflexible or defensive, then valuable opportunities for learning about ourselves are lost and our self-knowledge is reduced. Our story is by a manager who has worked on becoming more open to feedback from others and hence has started on an enhanced path of self-reflection.

In Action [Case Study]: When someone gave me criticism at work, I had the tendency to become defensive and often reacted by going into a protective shell and even insulting the person. At the time I knew it was bad to be overly sensitive. In the workplace, lashing out at others would be counterproductive to knowing myself better and would cause unnecessary tension in the office. I have really tried to not feel so defensive if I am criticized. The weird part is that I then started to do the opposite, just shrugging off someone's criticism, but ignoring feedback is not good either. To implement a plan for self-improvement, I had to take a deep look at myself and how I react to feedback. I evaluated those instances and seeing the point where I would become angry. What I have realized is that my outbursts were really unnecessary and actually unproductive. Another great help has been watching my coworkers and how they have handled criticism. Many have not done so in a mature and professional manner either. I have since learned that many times, an employee's reaction to different situations and defensive has to do with how they perceived the situation. *This theory made me realize how I used to perceive criticism. I used to feel it was a personal attack!* The emotion I felt was purely a reaction to me being "attacked." How I planned to continue to change my defensiveness is by changing my sensitivity. So far this has worked well. Now if I am criticized at work or in my personal life, I haven't become defensive like before. I now see it as a way of taking another step in growing as a person. To continue on the right path, I plan to continue use my new knowledge to help me reflect and to see any negative situation not as an attack, but as a learning opportunity to improve myself to succeed in my career. I plan to do this, by thinking first before I talk and react to criticism. Then by looking at myself from the outside to see how others would see my comments. Finally I'd like to take any negative criticism, unfounded or not, and try to see whether it would apply to me, then work to try to improve myself with it.

Walking the Talk: Select a situation in your life where you received criticism. (1) **D**etermine whether the criticism is a point of information that could help you in knowing yourself better. (2) **E**valuate whether your self-image was the same as the other person or persons. (3) **A**nalyze why the conceptions of you differed and if these different portraits provide useful information. (4) **L**everage these insights to develop an enhanced self-concept.

> To increase my self-knowledge and enhance my self-concept, I will...

1.2 Improving Self-Monitoring

Ask Yourself: Are you good at reading and adapting to situations? Do you know your audience and can you give them what they want? Are you ever seen as being too rigid or stubborn? Or alternatively do you change so often that people might see you as phony? Do you ever put on so many different "faces" that sometimes it is hard to remember who the real "you" is?

Management Theory: Self-monitoring is the ability to adapt ones behavior to the situation at hand. It is the proverbial "chameleon" characteristic. People who are high self-monitors do the following three things better than others: (1) Introspection: They know themselves and are aware of the image that they project to others; (2) Diagnosis: They are able to read the expectations of environment, including the people whom they work with and the projects that they are engaged in; (3) Flexibility: They can combine the first two aspects within a broad behavioral repertoire as to adapt their self-presentation to the situation needs. For example, high self-monitors can tell when a situation calls for a confident, unwavering personality and then project that exact image. Or conversely, they can switch to project the opposite image if followers in another organization, culture, or situation expect a more humble and adaptive personality. Research generally supports the usefulness of self-monitoring for managers. Said another way, successful managers tend to be more sensitive and adaptable to their situations. This skill is especially important since the workplace is getting more dynamic and complex. However self-monitoring is not without risks and these must be managed. For instance, high self-monitors might appear fake or "flip-flopping" (opportunistic, insincere, or dishonest) in their behavior. They might also lose touch with their true self amid their many images (hard to remember the authentic "self"). At the other end of the spectrum, low self-monitors tend to offer up a constant image no matter the situation. To use an analogy, they do not alter their wardrobe when the seasons change. This often results in poor performance and low satisfaction. Yet in some cases low self-monitors might be able to change the situation. Using the above weather analogy, perhaps they would move to a warmer climate that fits their preferences. The following story is by a low self-monitor addressing the challenges of fitting in.

In Action [Case Study]: The theory of self-monitoring applies to many parts of my professional life. In particular I can relate it to the very start of my career when I began by business studies. Looking back at when I registered to attend a small New England MBA program, I remember myself being very excited about the new adventure. As the semester began, I started having difficulty adjusting to the social mores among the student population. In the academic setting I started out on the Dean's List. There were very good professors at this school, and the classes were very informative. However, the prevailing student attitudes involved a heavy emphasis on partying and personal competition. In addition few, if any, came from my socioeconomic and religious background. In other words, I could do the "job" but had problems fitting in. Unfortunately I did not self-monitor well and was not able to adapt my behavior. *More than this, I refused to change my behavior or relax my attitude to adapt to the prevailing atmosphere.* As time wore on my performance in the program started to go downhill and I had little satisfaction. In turn, I looked for excuses to leave campus on weekends (absenteeism), which made it even harder to connect with others at the school. Eventually I ended up having to transfer to another institution (turnover). Fortunately at the new program I felt more comfortable because I took a more flexible attitude, and this enabled me to fit without having to change too much. As a result I became much happier and started getting better grades. I did not have to look for excuses to leave on the weekends and my desire to transfer was low. My fellow students even chose me for leadership positions in student organizations, and this enabled me to leave my mark on the school. Looking back it was fortunate that I was able to become less rigid and carve out a good niche for myself. I realized that sometimes you really have to be able to give and take to make the best of a situation. I am grateful to have learned this lesson early in my career because it has helped me outlast several bosses and cultural changes at my organization and rise to my current upper-management position.

Walking the Talk: Select a situation in your life where there is not a perfect "fit." (1) **D**etermine whether it is better to change yourself to fit the situation or change the situation to fit you. (2) **E**valuate, when changing the situation is not an option, if it would be better to adapt. (3) **A**nalyze how the theory of self-monitoring could guide you in doing this. (4) **L**everage these insights to better adapt across other situations while at the same time not losing sight of your true self.

To appropriately increase my self-monitoring while still remaining grounded, I will...

1.3   Expanding Emotional Intelligence

Ask Yourself: Are you in touch with your feelings and emotions? Can you master them or are you at their mercy? Is your job performance ever affected by your emotions? In a similar vein can you understand others' feelings and successfully deal with them? Would you perform better at your job if you could more ably manage your and others' emotional issues?

Management Theory: The scientific community, and many business organizations, have long assessed and evaluated people based on their brainpower or intellectual quotient (IQ). Relatively recently we have complemented these longstanding constructs of cognitive capability with the theory of emotional capability (EQ, or EI for emotional intelligence). Emotional Intelligence essentially refers to one's ability to understand and regulate ones own emotions as well as the capacity to see and deal with the emotions of others. Intellectual and emotional intelligence are distinct—surely you know of people who have a high IQ but very low EQ or vise versa. In general, there are four broad clusters within EQ, each representing specific emotional competencies: self-awareness, self-management, social awareness, and relationship management. The first two competencies are derivative of deep reflection and self-control—getting in touch with ones emotions and not letting them dominate you. The latter two competencies are more in line with what we commonly term empathy and social skills—being receptive to others' emotions and responding to them appropriately. Indeed a person's emotional intelligence is often a better predictor of managerial success than is a person's intellectual acumen. Studies show that EQ is a critical factor underlying individual and organizational performance, with superior competencies linked to a plethora of bottom-line metrics. That is to say, much evidence supports the usefulness of EQ in management. It is especially important in situations that involve a heavy interpersonal and social element such as sales. Our story is by a manager who used her knowledge of EQ to improve the hiring and placing of workers.

In Action [Case Study]: A few years ago, I was a department manager in a Chinese trade company. At that time, the general manager of the company felt that it was necessary to recruit some new employees to enhance our ordinary office and trading work so that we would expand the business. I was told to participate in the recruitment of these individuals with the Human Resource Department. There were two types of open positions. One was office clerk (secretary) position whose main duty was to do word processing, statistics, and keeping touch with old customers in the office. Another was a salesman position whose main duty was to seek business opportunities and develop new customers to improve sales. Five young men were finally recruited after they had been interviewed. In the past we decided on a candidate based on his or her intelligence, skills, abilities, education, and work experience. But this time we did something very different. We asked the prospective employees to take the EQ tests first, and then we determined their job field mainly on their respective EQ test results rather than those conventional factors. We believe that a successful salesperson should have good positive personalities and emotions. They should have strong abilities of self-awareness, self-management, self-motivation, empathy, and social skills. They can work under pressure and feel easygoing when coping with the different kinds of people or strangers because they have strong interpersonal awareness. *So we chose those who were with high EQ scores especially in the parts of self-knowledge and social skills to be trained as salesman, and the others to do the office work. Six years passed, the subsequent fact testified our decision is right.* All of these five people do their jobs well in their respective field; they feel satisfactory with their job; they are seldom absent; and they still work in company up to now. It's a true example that EQ can be applied as an effective tool to improve employee job performance and satisfaction and to reduce his or her absenteeism and turnover.

Walking the Talk: Select a situation in your life where your emotions played a part in your work. (1) **D**etermine whether you were able to understand your emotions. (2) **E**valuate the degree to which you were able to manage them well. (3) **A**nalyze why and how Emotional Intelligence relates to your performance in the situation. (4) **L**everage these insights to develop your overall EI competencies and become more reflective and empathetic as well as demonstrate better self-control and social management.

> To expand my emotional intelligence, I will...

1.4   Clarifying Personal Values

Ask Yourself: How often do you think about what you want out of life? Does your current job and long-term career path support these values? Do you ever wonder whether the way that you spend your energy at work is consistent with, tangential to, or worse yet gets in the way of, the things that are deep down the most important to you? How can you better align personal values and professional engagements?

Management Theory: Personal values are the standards that govern what goals we pursue and how we pursue them. The former, regarding what we want from our professional and personal lives, refers to terminal values and the desired end-states or outcomes that we esteem. The latter, regarding the conduct of our behavior, refers to instrumental values and what actions we deem right and wrong. Knowing your values and achieving a fit between them and your work engagements play an important role in an individual's level of success. If you are able to identify them then it will be easier to set goals, prioritize your actions, live consistent to your code, and take steps toward fulfilling your plans and achieving your dreams. From a professional standpoint, people need to be aware of their values to determine whether they are compatible with their organization, job, and career path. If a person's values clash with their work, then it will be difficult to be satisfied or successful in the long run because they may not be positioned to achieve their objectives and thus there is a greater chance that they will feel alienated and be unproductive. We focus here on terminal values because they most directly provide the picture of a person and that which they want to become. As such a keen awareness of terminal values enables a more measured and proactive approach to achieve harmony between how one spends their time—if you think about it, approximately half of our waken adult lives are spend at work—and what one feels is most desirable. Matching our values to our actions begets a much more productive and satisfying experience, whereas a mismatch is more likely to hinder our performance (e.g., cannot do it) and enjoyment (e.g., just feels wrong). Our story is by a manager working toward pursuing a more rewarding job and career strategy that is better in sync with their personal values.

In Action [Case Study]: I feel that I tended to lose sight of my terminal values and their priorities. As a result, I was not making the best professional choices. For example, about five years ago I made the jump from a nonprofit firm to a large multinational company. The opportunity was tremendous and promised many perks and benefits. However I soon discovered that it was not the best fit for my core values. In my race to climb the corporate ladder, I forgot why I got into the work in the first place. I am very cause-driven and never really got the same satisfaction working in the commercial sector than I did serving the larger public interest. Anyway time seemed to go by quickly and I made the best of the situation. I worked hard and just last year was offered a promotion to head up our entire division. The new position offered much more prestige and salary so of course I took it. But it did not take long to see that this was again a giant mistake. Long hours and endless meetings kept me away from dealing with actual customers and helping people. There was also less time available to be home with my family. I found that I was feeling distant from my work, started losing my focus, and was taking short cuts instead of performing to the best of my ability. *To better get a handle on my values, I decided to define a list of long-term goals and committed myself to restructuring my career so it contributed to my personal definition* *of success.* I feel that my plan is successful because I have already taken action to be consistent with my terminal values. I decided to resign my position and have taken a job in the service sector working with children and promoting the environment. The opportunity definitely would not have presented itself, if I was not focused on my terminal values. Since a person's priorities and values can change over time, I think that going forward it will be necessary to review my goals each year. That way I will be better able to prioritize my actions and be sure that I don't make the same mistake as in the past. If I allowed myself to continue in my old firm, the inconsistency in my position and values would have continued to lead to unrealized goals, a lack of enthusiasm, low morale, and decreased performance. With my new career plan, I hope to reenergize myself by being in constant synch with my long run values and get myself better positioned to attain them.

Walking the Talk: Select a situation in your life where values are important. (1) **D**etermine what your long-term terminal values are. (2) **E**valuate the degree to which they are consistent with your behavior in this specific situation. (3) **A**nalyze where there is better and worse fit and why. (4) **L**everage these insights to better clarify and act in a manner that supports your terminal values.

To better clarify and act in accordance with my personal values, I will…

1.5   Internalizing Locus of Control

Ask Yourself: Are you in control of your workplace success and career progression? Or instead do you believe that your level of performance is determined by forces beyond your control? When you do well is it because you are good or that you just got lucky? When you fail is it because you performed poorly or the chips just did not fall your way? How can you examine your personal role in loss of control and work to change it?

Management Theory: Locus of control is the attitude an individual takes to a situation in determining the reasons for their success or failure. Management theory shows us that a person can attribute outcomes more so to internal (themselves—personal reasons) or external (others—situational reasons) factors. At one end of the spectrum, some individuals feel that they are the proverbial masters of their fate. These people are called "Internals" and tend to believe that their actions can influence their workplace performance in a real and meaningful way. They are not big on luck, good or bad, and instead think that people can create their own professional opportunities and shape their own destiny. At the other end of the spectrum, "Externals" tend to attribute the outcomes of their actions mainly to chance and contextual factors such as the behavior of other people or the nature of the organizational circumstances that they find themselves in. They are usually more deferent to outside influences, such as bosses and markets, and tend to accept situations rather than proactively affect them. Generally speaking research has found that internals tend to do better in terms of workplace performance and career success. However this is not an absolute because there are some jobs that are a better fit (i.e., those requiring initiative) and worse fit (i.e., those requiring compliance) with an internal locus of control. Our story is by a worker who changed their locus of control to more effectively navigate his professional path.

In Action [Case Study]: For the first thirty-one years of my life, I was an unconscious "external," not knowing that I believed my fate to be controlled by others but, looking back on that period now, that's exactly how I perceived my life to be. In particular, I look back first at my decision to major in education. I realize now that it wasn't a desire within myself that led me to that decision but, rather, it was uncertainty about the job market combined with the fact that a teacher had once told me that I'd make a good teacher myself that led to the decision. Following graduation, I repeated that same pattern, accepting a full-time position at the real estate consulting firm where I had worked for the past five summers without really testing the market. I felt the decision was a given. In the larger scheme of things I felt as though there was nothing I could do about it and that this was the only option open to me. When my company began to face financial difficulties and was clearly heading toward insolvency, I took the "What can I do about it?" approach and stayed with the sinking ship. When it finally submerged, I was finally forced to reexamine my life and the direction I was headed. *Through this examination of myself, I was able to discover both what I want to do with my life and that I was in control of getting there.* As a result, I changed paths and began to pursue a new course of both formal and informal education, working toward my MBA in Information Systems and taking the initiative to teach myself the technical "ins & outs" of operating systems. By finally taking personal control of my career I have managed to become a Certified Systems Engineer, working for one the fastest growing firms in the country and am being groomed for a spot as a project manager within the Engineering group here in its New York headquarters! I am now better equipped and more capable of handling difficult and complex types of work, which are characteristic of "internals." My performance has been higher since realizing that whether I succeed or fail is ultimately under my control because I take the steps to ensure success. I am also happier now than anytime in my career and rarely miss a day at work.

Walking the Talk: Select a situation in your life where you have an unclear amount of control. (1) **D**etermine whether you hold internal or external control beliefs about your level of success. (2) **E**valuate the degree to which your actions or uncontrollable elements in the situation are the primary determinant of performance. (3) **A**nalyze why this is the case and if there are specific steps that you could take to alter the balance. (4) **L**everage these insights to increase your sense of control of this and other aspects of your life.

To appropriately internalize my locus of control, I will...

1.6   Improving Agreeableness

Ask Yourself: How well do you get along and work with colleagues? Would you categorize your personality as a "team player"? Are you generally more cooperative or competitive in professional situations? When working with others is it very important to get your way and personally do well (i.e., be the winner or best performer) even at the expense of group harmony? Do you ever have difficulty trusting and deferring to others ideas and viewpoints?

Management Theory: The "Big-Five," or five-factor, Model is one of the most widely known and best corroborated management theories that measures personality characteristics. Utilizing sophisticated statistical techniques, the model empirically combines various research frameworks to derive common categories of traits. As its name implies, the resultant theory describes five primary dimensions of an individual's personality: extraversion, agreeableness, conscientiousness, emotional stability, and openness to experience. We focus here on the dimension of agreeableness, which is particularly relevant to management because it is profession inherently embedded in organizational contexts marked by people working together for common objectives. Agreeableness relates to the degree to which a person is trusting, good natured, cooperative, values harmony, is pleasant and easy to work with, exhibits empathetic understanding, is prone to forming strong working relationships, and can even on occasion defer to others when needed. As such people higher on agreeableness tend to be seen as better partners, coworkers, and "team players" so to speak. Individuals lower on agreeableness more frequently come across as stubborn, suspicious, and even intolerant. As we see the modern workplace evolving to a point where workers spend more and more time in work teams as well as increasingly engaged in professional networks and global relationships, it stands to reason that agreeableness would become even more important to the success of a manager. Our story is by a person who is trying to enhance this aspect of her personality.

In Action [Case Study]: Based on my self-assessment, I came to the conclusion that I need improvement on being more "Agreeable." The theory says that people who are low on agreeableness prefer having their say on issues and doing things their own way. To be perfectly honest I am low on agreeableness. This problem was very evident to me because I have a tendency to be very stubborn and interrupt others in the middle of their conversation to push my conclusions. My way of correcting this drawback was to concentrate on being more of a team player, not interrupt coworkers as much, and be more open to their ideas of how to do things. I also started recording the frequency of these behaviors on a weekly base. When I reviewed my weekly log on my results, I observed somewhat of an improvement. But lately there has been sort of a breakthrough on this. My greatest improvements happened during the last week of November and the beginning of December when I was working on a major team project and preparing for a formal presentation of our office. I really saw how my interrupting of team members and being overly competitive alienated me from the others, reduced everyone's satisfaction, and harmed my performance. *From this enlightenment, I have turned the corner and become more agreeable when I converse and discuss issues with my coworkers.* I am trying to practice what I preach on the idea that everyone is entitled to complete his/her ideas. And since your personal life can spill over to the job, I am also going to practice this with family members and show a little more time and patience with them when we disagree on things. I have also worked on being more agreeable with my boyfriend. Throughout this whole process he has been very supportive and patient with me and being less competitive has definitely strengthened our relationship. I will not become a rubber stamp and simply go along with what others think, but I will continue to expand my overall level of agreeableness.

Walking the Talk: Select a situation in your life where you experienced disharmony with others. (1) **D**etermine your level of agreeableness in the situation. (2) **E**valuate the degree to which you valued competitiveness versus teamwork and whether the balance was appropriate. (3) **A**nalyze why this happened and, if appropriate, any ways in which you could have been more supportive or good natured. (4) **L**everage these insights to increase your general capacity for agreeableness and your long-term ability to promote true cooperation.

To improve my capacity for agreeableness and cooperation, I will...

1.7 Discovering Your Cognitive Style

Ask Yourself: How do you process the daily information that come at you? Are you very detail oriented? Do you focus mainly on the facts of the specific case in point? Or instead do you prefer to take a broader view and look at the big picture? Tend to focus mainly on the general patterns and overall nature of the situation? Is there ever a disconnect between your style and requirements of the task at hand?

Management Theory: Cognitive Style refers to the intellectual patterns of how people use their brains and process information. A widely used method for assessing someone's thinking style is the Jungian Myers–Briggs theoretical framework. It considers, among other things, how individuals prefer to approach and attempt to understand their environment, for example, through detailed observation or a broader reflection and overall scan. This characteristic is particularly relevant in our "Information Age" where managers are constantly bombarded with streams of data competing for their attention. Management theory describes how people demonstrate different patterns and strategies for processing information. On the one hand, individuals who have a Sensing preference tend to focus on details and specific facts. They are meticulous and practical while emphasizing what is tangible and observable—that is, in front of their face. They like to deal with the here and now, looking at bottom-line issues, and process this information in a very practical, matter-of-fact manner. On the other hand, individuals who have an Intuitive preference tend to focus on the big picture and overall tendencies. They are abstract thinkers who emphasize what is emergent and possible—that is, in the scope of possibility. They like to deal with conceptual relationships, looking at overall trends and future outcomes, and process this information in a very broad, insightful manner. Of course achieving fit with ones environment is critical insofar as each characteristic has its strengths and weaknesses and can be more or less suitable to different workplace challenges. Our story is by a manager who wants to change his style so to better match job requirements and increase performance.

In Action [Case Study]: After conducting a self-assessment and thinking about the way I gather and process information at work, I realized I focused more on the sensing strategy. I would like to develop more of an intuitive strategy. At my job I encountered large amounts of data and experienced information overload and personal stress due to my current cognitive style. There are many times when I spend so much time focusing on the details that I never got to look at the general picture. The need for attention to details in my job is critical and time consuming, but I needed to develop the skills necessary to look at and understand the overall relationships among the various elements of data. I feel that by developing more of an intuitive strategy, I can learn more and have a better understanding, which is critical when speaking with management who are interested in the overall impact on the firm. I needed to develop more of an intuitive strategy to develop the skills necessary to advance my career and one day be part of a successful management team. The plan that we developed was for my group to hire a person under me to assist me with the daily workload. This would free me up to concentrate more on the broader scope of my job and the connections between departments. The plan has been very effective and it has allowed me to develop more of an intuitive strategy. *By developing more of an intuitive strategy approach, I have been able to develop a better understanding of the nature of my job and how it affects the whole company.* I am now better able to do my job by being able to look at and understand not just the details but also the strategic picture. A big milestone in my skills development came two weeks ago. My boss and I felt so confident about my grasp of the position that I spoke in place of her in the annual meeting and we both felt I did extremely well. I feel much more confident about my grasp of the material that in turn makes me more confident while speaking to others. I have realized that the need to develop my intuitive strategy has helped me improve my management skills, which in turn will help me advance my career.

Walking the Talk: Select a situation in your life where you need to process information. (1) **D**etermine whether you used a sensing or intuitive strategy. (2) **E**valuate whether the strategy was suitable to the task at hand.

(3) **A**nalyze why you chose it and how you might complement it with the opposite strategy to gain a better understanding of both the specifics and big picture. (4) **L**everage these insights to more effectively process information across the many challenges in your personal and professional life.

> To better discover and apply my cognitive style, I will...

1.8   Identifying Machiavellianism

Ask Yourself: Is it more important "whether you win or lose" or "how you play the game"? Given the choice would you rather lose nobly or win shadily? Are there times when the most important thing is getting the job done regardless of what you have to do or how you have to do it? Or alternatively do you generally feel that your level of output is not as important as conducting yourself with honor and dignity? Which of these types of people would you rather work for—the "just win baby" or "do it right" manager?

Management Theory: Derivative of the ideas espoused by fifteenth-century Florentine thinker Nicolo Machiavelli, the personality dimension of Machiavellianism refers to the belief that "the ends justify the means." Even though Machiavelli did not say these exact words per se, arguments in his book *The Prince* referred to various methods of a questionable nature for gaining, using, and keeping power. Thus the individual characteristic of Machiavellianism embodies an emphasis on outcomes over process. People vary in the range of actions they will find acceptable to reach their goal. High machiavellianists put more emphasis on practical issues involved in winning and thus will go to greater lengths to triumph. They tend to be more pragmatic, maintain a cool detached disposition, utilize a broader array of persuasion and manipulation tactics, prefer face-to-face interactions, and like situations that are not black and white but instead governed by fewer rules and standards. In other words, win at all costs and by any means available. Alternatively low machiavellianists put more emphasis on acting consistently within accepted standards of behavior. Which personality characteristic is better for a manager to possess? The answer to this question will depend on the individual's moral code as well as its fit with the larger environmental, cultural and professional requirements (would a

Machiavellian's performance thrive in some positions and less so others—say politics, finance, medicine, military, law, engineering, education?). Our story is by a person who suffered negative effects from working for a highly Machiavellian manager.

In Action [Case Study]: A few years ago, I was faced with the challenge of working with an individual who had a high Machiavellianism personality. This person was the team leader of a very high profile project that I was assigned to support. During the year or so that I worked with this team leader he continuously, and many times ruthlessly, forced his views, plans, opinions, methods, and directions on the rest of the team, even when we were all in total disagreement with him. My team leader never listened to my or anybody else's recommendations or opinions, no matter what negotiation or persuasion tactic we relied upon. As a true high Mach individual, he only wanted to get the project finished, even if that meant cutting comers and going against established procedures. The latter was particularly worrisome and frustrating because I had to constantly fight with him since our regulated industry demanded that we follow and meet all the establish procedures and requirements. He was blatantly disregarding standards and manipulating people on the team just to make the schedule. Finally, my team leader never seemed to loose his cool—he was always calm and artificially pleasant through many of the highly charged disagreements I found myself having with this individual. Dealing with this team leader certainly proved to be a frustrating challenge and took so much time that the energy we had left over to deal with the actual technical requirements of the job was severely decreased. *I realized that no matter how good you are, Machiavellianism will eventually come back to hurt you because of the shady practices that it promotes, the energy that it drains from the work, and lack of loyalty that it inspires.* During the year I had to deal with the individual described earlier, my level of technical performance on the team suffered. As one might expect, my level of satisfaction with my job was very low. Due to the constant conflict I had with my team leader, I found myself skipping some team conferences and always avoiding meetings where I had to deal with this person alone. Finally, at the end of one year, I took a transfer to another department vowing that if when I was a team leader I would never be like him.

Walking the Talk: Select a situation in your life where you faced a choice between means and ends. (1) **D**etermine whether it was more important how you did the job or what the outcome was. (2) **E**valuate the degree to which you were comfortable with the actions that you pursued and the results that you obtained. (3) **A**nalyze why you took this position and whether the right trade-off was achieved between means and ends. (4) **L**everage these insights to better navigate similar challenges in your life.

To better identify and balance Machiavellianism, I will…

1.9   Enlarging Tolerance of Ambiguity

Ask Yourself: How comfortable do you feel in uncertain and ill-defined situations? Can you function well when information is incomplete and the environment is frequently changing? Do you like to work on problems that do not have an obvious answer or clear method? Would you ever take a job in a country, climate, or industry that you have no experience with? Or instead do you like prefer structured and familiar tasks where things are well organized and clearly spelled out?

Management Theory: People vary in their tolerance of ambiguity, or the degree to which they feel comfortable performing in vague and uncertain situations. Those individuals with a high tolerance for ambiguity are more at ease with, and hence more adept at their jobs, when they are faced with frequent and unpredictable changes, multiple alternative solutions to problems, unclear or incomplete information, new and unfamiliar conditions, or complex and confusing circumstances. These types of people like the challenges that these circumstances bring and would tend to thrive as managers within emerging, entrepreneurial, cross-cultural, and fast-moving workplace environments. In contrast, people with a low tolerance for ambiguity have a greater need for structure and direction in their lives. These individuals would prefer, and tend to perform best in, more stable and predictable jobs and when working for organizations such as established bureaucracies and those in regulated industries. Therefore it is important to achieve a fit between tolerance of ambiguity and job characteristics. Notwithstanding this contingency relationship, because the modern workplace is becoming increasingly complex and dynamic, it stands to reason that the capacity to function in "fuzzy" and ill-defined arenas is becoming increasingly important to a manager's success. Our story is by an individual initiating some wonderfully creative and quite successful attempts to increase her tolerance for ambiguity.

In Action [Case Study]: Vague requests and change caused me to experience discomfort and I used to find it difficult to execute tasks that were new and lacked detailed instructions. From management theory, I recognized the need for better tolerance of ambiguity in today's dynamic environment. Change is inevitable and unpredictable, unclear, and complex situations constantly have to be addressed. I formulated a plan to facilitate development of this skill that involved three strategies: attending more weekend gatherings with less familiar faces; reading non-work related magazines and articles in my spare time and lastly, embracing new and difficult tasks at work. For example, I recently accepted responsibility for a new project, a project that I was invited into a year ago but was disinclined to accept because it involved a lot of activities that I did not understand and was uncomfortable reaching out and asking for direction. *Embracing what seemed like a threat really turned out to be an opportunity to increase my knowledge and skill as a professional. I was really surprised at how my plans successfully increased my tolerance for ambiguity and how much I learned when I was willing to try new things.* From my experience, I believe that the key strategies for developing this skill are to be more accepting of change through simple recognition that there is the opportunity for learning and through constant acquiring of knowledge from various sources. I also believe that there is great power in taking the time out to think about the possible solutions that might exist to solve a problem, before resorting to apprehension. Another example, about three weeks ago I attended "Latin Night" at a lounge in the city with some coworkers. This was truly different for me and I was very hesitant to go for fear that I would not fit in. I was so used to attending functions with close friends where I could mingle easily, that I felt a little out of place and threatened in this new environment. However, before the end of the night, I actually learned a few steps in the Salsa and also made some new friends. This reinforced how change is really a tool for learning new things, and the importance of embracing change as an opportunity for growth. I will therefore continue to challenge myself with new possibilities.

Walking the Talk: Select a situation in your life where you faced ambiguous circumstances. (1) **D**etermine the types and sources of uncertainty, change, and complexity present in the situation. (2) **E**valuate the degree to which you demonstrated tolerance of ambiguity and the effects on your performance and satisfaction. (3) **A**nalyze why you were more or less comfortable in this situation and what if any factors could increase tolerance levels. (4) **L**everage these insights into specific strategies for becoming more tolerant of ambiguity that would increase your overall capacity for succeeding in these types of situations.

To enhance my tolerance for ambiguity, I will...

CHAPTER TWO

Managing Time and Stress

Chapter two examines management theories about stress and applying the management skill of stress and time management. To appreciate the importance of this topic, pause for a moment to make a list of all the people that you know who are completely and utterly "stress-free"? This is probably a very short list indeed. If you are alive and engaged in the social sphere then you most probably experience some degree of time pressures and other forms of stress. Of course some of us manage these better than others. Make no mistake about it, poor time management is a widespread cause of stress in the workplace, and this stress can affect people in a myriad of ways—physically, psychologically, emotionally, and behaviorally. The mismanagement of time and other forms of stress can be an individual handicap at the least and, if it persists over an extended period, become personally debilitating. When time and stress are poorly managed lots of bad things can happen—your body breaks down, your mind power is constrained, negative emotions cloud your ability to make decisions, job satisfaction ticks down, and work performance suffers. Therefore in this second chapter we look at how one can better understand and deal with the causes, alter the processes, improve the outcomes, and develop better approaches to managing time and stress.

2.1   Appreciating the Importance of Managing Stress

Ask Yourself: Do you ever feel stressed? How does this stress affect you? How does it affect your work? Could you or your organization do anything to manage this stress better? Is there any real payoff for doing so?

Management Theory: The potential for stress is all around us, and this has never been more evident than in these complex and fast-changing times. Whereas there is no universally accepted definition of stress, most theoretical models agree that it represents a response to forces in either the external environment or internal person that act on an individual to cause physiological, emotional, or mental tension—often resulting in feelings of being overwhelmed and losing control—which in turn are capable of affecting their behavior capacity and overall well-being. Generally if something is simultaneously uncertain and important to a person, then it has a potential to cause them stress. Of course some degree of stress is natural and this is not always a bad thing—moderate levels of stress can impel individuals to learn, grow, make improvements, and achieve results. This positive effect is termed "eustress." Yet if stress is poorly managed, takes negative forms, or is left to grow beyond reasonable levels it can turn into "distress," causing people significant problems and even trapping them in vicious cycles that can ultimately do significant harm to both the employee as well as their organization. From the perspective of the individual, we know that people have varying tolerances and exposures to stress and that some people handle stress better than others. Unfortunately for a large portion of the population, it may be more accurate to say that stress handles them. If left unchecked, sustained stress can lead to individual burnout that reduce performance and satisfaction while elevating employee absenteeism and turnover. Given that stress is so widespread and potentially disruptive to the bottom line, managers need to be aware of ways to mitigate it or channel it more effectively. Our story is by a manager who contrasts high and low stress work environments and traces their very different effects on their behavior, attitude, and overall health.

In Action [Case Study]: Over the course of my career, I have experienced varying levels of stress and the consequences of those stresses have been evident throughout. Specifically, I think back to a time just a little more than a year ago when I was in a position rife with stress. I was working for a demanding, often unreasonable, erratic, and inconsiderate boss. His behavior was also inappropriate for the workplace, as his strong views on politics, race, and religion were daily topics of conversation. My position also had some ambiguity in terms of job responsibilities and this provided additional stress. It is also important to note that, while the intensity level of this stress would rise and fall, this was an ongoing problem that began the day I started and did not end until I left this job. Specifically, I remember two incidents that illustrate this quite well. First there was the penchant for assigning work at 4:45pm that could have been, and often should have been, assigned at 9:00am. Second, I recall an incident in which I was called out of my office and publicly berated for submitting a $2.50 bridge toll as part of an expense report for a recent business trip I had taken. Despite having both a receipt and a valid, business related reason for crossing the bridge, the boss deemed the expense unwarranted and infuriated me by removing it from my expense report. Contrast that with my current situation, in which I not only love what I do, but I genuinely like the people I work with and they appear to both like and care about me as a person. Physiologically, these stresses have manifested themselves in much the same manner as is stated in the theory. During the period of high, negative stress, both my blood pressure and frequency of headaches and back pain were high, and each has been dramatically reduced since changing my work environment. Likewise, the psychological symptoms of stress have also followed the constructs of the theory, with significant increases in anxiety, irritability, and procrastination during the former period described and being nearly eliminated during the latter. Finally, in terms of behavioral symptoms, my actions have essentially mirrored that described in the theory, including increased smoking and consumption of alcohol in the first job and little of this now. So, how has stress affected my PSAT's? As the stress level increased in both intensity and duration, so too did my dissatisfaction with my employment situation. *Likewise, as stress has been managed down in the new job, my satisfaction has increased.* In addition, both performance and absenteeism have dramatically improved as the stress has been reduced, and turnover is less likely to occur now.

Walking the Talk: Select a situation in your life where you felt stressed. (1) **D**etermine what was creating the stress. (2) **E**valuate the degree to which the stress affected you. (3) **A**nalyze why a better awareness and management of stress levels could have made a difference. (4) **L**everage these insights to enhance your appreciation for the role of stress in your personal and professional success.

To better appreciate the importance of managing personal stress, I will...

2.2 Addressing Workplace Causes of Stress

Ask Yourself: Is your job a source of stress for you? Do you ever feel overwhelmed at work? Tasks ill-defined and hard to pin down? Treated poorly by your boss? Stuck in a bad position with little joy or mobility? Unhappy with work conditions in general?

Management Theory: If you feel stressed because of your job then you are not alone. Work-related stress can come to individuals from many sources. Management theory points to several factors at work that may contribute to individuals' stress levels. First people can get stressed out by their immediate task and role demands, which is to say the specific things their jobs require them to do. Jobs can be poorly defined and too ambiguous, overloaded and too intense, and poorly integrated or too far removed from a person's ability, values, or expectations. Individuals can be stressed by the larger organizational structure and climate, including the overall state of the business, relationship with their boss, and strategic direction of the firm. Individuals can be stressed by bad working relationships and clashes with coworkers. Individuals can be stressed by poorly managed career ladders, promotional or transfer moves, and job-security issues. Individuals can be stressed by the actual physical demands of their jobs, including layout, noise, air quality, workspace, travel, hours, privacy, and the like. These are certainly a lot of potential job-related stressors out there, and their effect is exacerbated by the fact that people are spending a large and growing portion of their lives either physically at the workplace or tethered to work with electronic PDAs, Internet, and cellphone leashes. Therefore it stands to reason that increasing our understanding of how workplace stressors in particular can affect us can help in better managing or mitigating them in our job and career decisions. Our story is by a worker reflecting on some stressful jobs that they have held and the factors which have contributed to this stress.

In Action [Case Study]: Throughout my career as a manager, stress related to organizational factors has proved a constant challenge for me. A series of lay-offs, restructurings, downsizing, and constant changes in organizational goals and leadership have created highly stressful work environments in all three of the fortune 500 companies I have worked for. *I realize now that the lack of clear roles and responsibilities has yielded situations in which I have been expected to take on tasks and roles that were, in some cases, beyond my scope.* Perhaps the single most stressful example of this was the job I held at my second company. In this particular job, I was brought in as a midlevel engineer with the added role and responsibilities as a department director. I was expected to provide constant support to highly technical, regulatory, legal, and clinical situations in which many times I had very little experience. The lack of leadership or support from my absentee boss who was always traveling did not help the matter. Adding to this situation, the company underwent a series of significant organizational leadership and goals changes, including multiple lay-offs and restructurings. In hindsight the people who were let go were the lucky ones. As a "survivor" of the leaner workforce my position was saddled with additional vice president roles. The combination of all the unrealistic technical and organizational demands drove my stress to a level I had never experienced before. What effect did I see from my stress? Negative for sure. Now I am more aware of how organizational stress affects my performance, level of job satisfaction, absenteeism, and turnover. Whenever I find myself in stressful situations, I try to combat them by building a support structure among my coworkers. I am very clear to others about our roles and what I am expected to do so that my performance and level of job satisfaction is not compromised. I find that today I am less inclined to "ride out" stressful jobs. Instead I look for other opportunities that will change the situation or take me to a less stressful work environment.

Walking the Talk: Select a situation in your life that was stressful. (1) **D**etermine what aspect of work was the source of your stress. (2) **E**valuate the degree to which this stressor influenced workplace performance and satisfaction. (3) **A**nalyze why this stressor arose and whether you could have acted to reduce it or even eliminate it. (4) **L**everage these insights to manage workplace stress to appropriate levels.

To better address workplace causes of my stress, I will...

2.3   Addressing Personal Causes of Stress

Ask Yourself: How much of your stress do you personally manufacture? Are you constantly in a rush and moving from task to task? Do you take the perspective that there is always too much to do and too little time to do it? Ever just "go with the flow" and separate what you can and cannot impact? Is it difficult for you to relax and take it easy?

Management Theory: Not all of our stress comes from work. In fact we create much of it ourselves. Type-A personality is the chronic, incessant drive to accomplish more and more tasks in less and less time. Alternatively people can be classified as Type-B to the extent to which they prefer to do things at a more measured pace with a more deliberate and quality-focused approach. Each style has there positive and negative aspects, but it is important to point out that Type As are becoming more common in today's go-go business world. Type-A individuals are typically hard workers whose incessant drive can impel them to achieve high levels of performance. On the downside these individuals are frequently impatient and hasty, feel guilty and have difficulty relaxing, become easily frustrated, demonstrate free-floating hostility and explosive behavior, and often experience increased amounts of stress and related problems that can impede their long-term productivity. One of the chief strategies for mitigating these dangers is to focus our energy only on things that we can effect with hard work and determination—that is, "concerns" such as specific aspects of workplace performance that can be changed by working harder or smarter. However much of what people actually stress about are circumstances beyond their scope and could not change even with the best of intentions—that is, "worries" such as larger corporate, geopolitical, or natural events. Concerns are thus more deserving our attention and can be worth the stress whereas worries…not so much. Our story is by a manager who is admittedly Type-A, who discusses the implications for himself and those around him.

In Action [Case Study]: Many of the people that I work with have Type-A personalities, including myself. In fact I perfectly fit the Type-A description. I usually wake up very early in the morning and arrive at work to start at approximately at 7:00am. I never leave the office throughout the day and rarely come home before late in the evening. I have a poor diet because I am always on the go and do not feel as if I have enough time in the day to break for lunch. It is a rare occurrence if I am not doing at least two or three things at the same time. If my daily tasks are not completed, then I become very edgy and can be difficult to deal with. I constantly worry about everything and anything and find it difficult to sleep with so many "disaster" scenarios swirling around in my head. This affects my performance at work. I remember one recent incident where one of my new employees was not accomplishing what he expected. I impulsively took this new employee into a conference room and harshly reprimanded him as if he were a child. Later I found out that my voice was so loud that people near the conference room were able to hear everything that was said. *I feel that this was indicative that my Type-A behavior was leading to burnout. The theory is exactly right when it describes how operating like this for a long time can really take its toll on a person.* As a result of being Type-A, I recently suffered a heart attack. This shocked me into the realization that I needed to change my personality. I could not allow it to cause so much stress in the workplace and affect my health in such a major way. At this point in time, it is unclear whether I will return to my position. Because my position was very important to a key project, my absence could cause stress throughout the division. I also noticed that before this incident, there was a great amount of turnover in the people I supervised. I feel that my personality might have caused many of the employees under me to look for other employment. The absenteeism and turnover seen in this example no doubt has cost valuable time and money to the organization.

Walking the Talk: Select a situation in your life that was stressful. (1) **D**etermine whether you brought this stress on yourself. (2) **E**valuate the degree to which this stressor influenced short-term and long-term performance and satisfaction. (3) **A**nalyze why this occurred and how you could better balance A- and B- like characteristics in your approach and focus only on controllable aspects of the situation. (4) **L**everage these insights to manage personal stress to appropriate levels.

To appropriately mitigate my Type-A tendencies, I will...

2.4 Facing the Consequences of Stress

Ask Yourself: Can stress physically harm you? Affect you in real and measurable ways? Make you sick? Hurt your performance? Dampen your spirit and effect your satisfaction?

Management Theory: The effects of stress are indeed very real and its detrimental consequences can range from the behavioral and performance-based, to the psychological and emotion-based, to the physical and health-related. Simply stated, stress can cost people in their productivity, happiness, and wellness and therefore costs organizations in their bottom line. Let us review some of the main insights about the effects of stress embedded in management theory. First, poorly managed stress has actual physiological and medical implications. Although the relationships are complicated we can generally say that high levels of stress have been linked to coronary and heart disease including stroke, headaches and body aches, intestinal and stomach disorders including ulcers, skin conditions, and a host of other illnesses as related to the immune system and respiratory systems. Second, there are mental consequences of poorly managed stress. These include life and job dissatisfaction, negative work attitudes, tension and anxiety, and, if prolonged, psychological burnout that is manifest in feelings of low personal accomplishment and emotional exhaustion. Third, there are behavioral implications of poorly managed stress. These include loss of productivity and job performance, increased absenteeism, deceased loyalty and higher turnover rates, changes in eating and health habits, as well as sleep and other related disorders. In the broader scope of things, these widespread individual consequences have implications for organizations in terms of employee morale, heath, quality of work, and overall efficiency and output levels. Our story is about a manager's experience with harmful consequences of stress and the lessons learned.

In Action [Case Study]: Stress has physical and emotional effects on us and can create positive or negative feelings. Mild forms of stress can act as a motivator and energizer. However, having too much stress damages our performance, and can lead to unhappiness, exhaustion, burnout, and serious illness. Four years ago, when I worked as assistant production manager in a textile manufacturing company, I was put under stress. It was caused by organizational and personal factors. It began when my company underwent downsizing, several staffs were laid off, and my workload was dramatically increased. To meet the deadlines, I had to cut back the lunchtime and work overtime. At the same time, I had to report to three bosses whose different points of view brought me into conflict. Frustration, time pressures, and deadlines kept me exhausted. Fatigue and overwork forced me to choose quantity rather than quality. In fact, I no longer liked my job and the industry that once I liked. However, two months later, the combined effect of organizational and personal factors drove me to a complete breakdown. Personally, I broke up with my long-time girlfriend. I was so depressed and stressed out. It seemed they were the darkest days in my life. I felt like I was such a loser that I was not good at anything. *The stress level was so high that it affected me emotionally and physically. I can see now how it was the cause of my headaches, lack of sleep, and overeating problems that combined to make me so sick.* It ended up half the time I either had to leave early from work or take medical leave. Finally, my family urged me to see a doctor who advised me to take some time off. Therefore, I quit my job. During the "healing" process, I talked to my family and friends and met a counselor. They helped me to reflect on personal goals and acknowledge that by reducing my stress level I can again achieve useful and important things. As a result, I decided back to school to complete a masters degree and moved to a company with a more supportive environment. Looking back, I learned a lesson that once there is stress one should try to reduce it and not wait until it does serious harm to you.

Walking the Talk: Select a situation in your life where stress had a real impact on you. (1) **D**etermine whether the stress was a positive or negative force. (2) **E**valuate the degree to which the stress affected you physically, psychologically, and emotionally. (3) **A**nalyze why its effects grew to such a level and how the impacts of this stress could have been managed. (4) **L**everage these insights to directly address the harmful effects of stress.

To better face the consequences of my stress, I will...

2.5   Improving Your Attitude toward Time Management

Ask Yourself: Do you have too much to do and too little time to do it? Is time a major source of your stress? Ever wish you had more hours in the day to get everything done? Is there any way of scheduling and prioritizing your time to make this more manageable?

Management Theory: One of the primary stressors facing managers, as well as one of the more prevalent challenges of employees that require managers' intervention, involves the management of time. At the most fundamental level, managers are charged with scheduling tasks and establishing routines in the workplace that create predictable patterns of interaction and process efficiencies to generate results. Thus an important part of a manager's job is organizing their employees' time. Poor coordination and prioritization can result in stressed-out workers and operational inefficiencies that hurt the bottom line. Moreover the modern manager is themselves faced with a daunting set of challenges that require a management of their own time. Here it seems that for most managers that the numbers of tasks accumulating in their proverbial "inbox" have expanded at a much greater pace than the time and resources that they have for getting them done. When tasks-to-time ratios are imbalanced, available resources are outstripped by their demands, and schedules are overwhelmed by numerous deadlines, then the result is unhealthy stress levels. It should therefore be no surprise that sound time management is the hallmark of the high-performing manager and is one of the most resonant practices differentiating successful individuals from their lower-achieving counterparts. Said another way, managers who are able to effectively set priorities and allocate time to accomplish them are typically less stressed and more productive. Think about it—we all have the same number of hours and minutes in the day but the more successful (and happier) individuals just seem to manage them better. Our story is by a manager refocusing his attitude to managing time and as a result reaping the rewards of less stress.

In Action [Case Study]: For a long period, I was experiencing a lot of stress in my life. Time stressors had become the major source of my stress. It was getting so bad that I felt like I needed at least twelve extra hours a day. Time stressors were also causing me a lot of frustration, a lot of losing of sleep, and most of all, losing enjoyment of my life. I started using time management theory to work on this. Thank goodness because I am proud of what I have achieved. Here are some of the things that rethinking my attitude toward time management did for me. I do not procrastinate as much. I got into the habit of writing in my calendar at work of what I wanted to accomplish during the day. My motto became, "Don't put off until tomorrow in what can be done today." I was able to carry the list and it worked great. I am better focused. Instead of reading every single page of the newspapers, I am only reading special sections that are more related to my career so that I no longer spend endless time to read all these newspapers before I go to bed, but I am still able to obtain the knowledge that I need. I delegate better. I have been trying to identify the importance of different details that are in the projects and letting my subordinates take on each part in accordance to each individual's ability. I then review the finish project as a whole and go from there, which is much more manageable. I take the time to relax. When I come home from work, I either wash up first or recline for thirty minutes. What an amazing difference! That half-hour of mentally diffusing slows me down enough that I can refocus my thoughts for productive means. *I think the important thing is that I know bad time management habits can be changed even though it might take some effort.* I have to admit that it feels so much better not having so much stress and that I no longer have black circles under my eyes constantly, only occasionally. Also, I feel that things are getting done much more organized in accordance to their importance. Lastly, I feel like I have a lot more time to do other things that are equally important in my life, like exercising, spending good quality time at home, going to ballets, show, and so forth. I think, though, I need to reinforce these new habits continuously because I know how easy it is to fall back to the old trend.

Walking the Talk: Select a situation in your life where you felt overwhelmed and did not have enough time to get things done. (1) **D**etermine whether you approached the situation with an eye toward time management. (2) **E**valuate the degree to which better time management might have made a difference. (3) **A**nalyze why you did or did not bring a "can-do" time management attitude to the situation. (4) **L**everage these insights to better appreciate the role of time management in personal success.

> To rethink my attitude toward time management, I will...

2.6   Developing Effective Time Management

Ask Yourself: Are you focusing your time, attention, and efforts on the really significant aspects of your work and life? Are the big-impact items getting your largest blocks and best quality time? Do you prioritize your tasks by the degree to which they relate to your life goals and career objective? Can you say "no" to those things that are not central to and distract you from these? Said another way, is your time management effective— are you doing the right things?

Management Theory: The most successful time management strategies share two qualities, they are simultaneously effective and efficient. Regarding the former, effectiveness is about doing the right things. Effective time management therefore involves prioritizing and allotting ones time based on an individual's most central values and deeply held objectives. Ideally people should spend the most time, and their best time, on the core issues that have the greatest impact on their personal, professional, and organizational goals. Focus on the major items which drive performance and success. Concentrate on the things that matter the most to us. Yet too often individuals act as if they are puppets controlled by the daily (or hourly) stream of demands instead of carefully organizing them and sorting out what really matters and merits their attention. Our agendas tend to be externally driven by whatever pops up on the proverbial radar (or e-mail and handheld) screen and, to use slightly more technical terms, dominated by what is urgent rather than what is fundamentally important. By contrast successful managers tend to clearly define their mission and spend their time on the big-ticket items that bear most on their achievement. In a word, they do the right things. Our story is by a worker gaining insight into what is important to them and learning the ever-important skill of how to say no to the other stuff.

In Action [Case Study]: The problems I had on time management are that I used to spend my time on urgent or pressing activities and left the really important activities behind. I always felt guilty saying no to people even if the requests were not congruent with my core principles and values. To improve my time management, I did the following: (1) sat down and determined what's really important to me, (2) made a commitment to spend more time on these important activities, and (3) learned to say "no" to activities that are not suitable for my personal values and principles. During the last two months, since have been so stressed lately and many projects are coming due, *I really started to clarify my principles and values, and that helped me to see what I really needed to do rather than just responding to what other people asked me to do.* I now think about what important activities I should do for today and plan how much time I should do for those activities. I have been trying to work on the most important activities early in the morning because this is my best time and least open to distractions. And eliminating urgent activities that disturb my time plan such as phone calls or talking with coworkers. Now every time something comes up through e-mail or memo, or whenever the cell phone rings when I am at a meeting or having dinner with my children, I screen them first to determine the degree of importance and then urgency of engaging in those activities. I also started to say no to those activities that are not related to these important projects. However, it remains a most difficult thing to me to say no to people, like a bad habit, but I am getting better at it. The results of this have really been great so far. I am getting more done and my performance and peace of mind have improved. In my personal life, I also feel that I am making more time for the important people like family and friends. To keep improving my time management, I will spend a few minutes to determine the importance of activities and their results each time a project comes to me. I will also practice feeling comfortable saying "no" to those activities that do not fit my main goals.

Walking The Talk: Select a situation in your life where you experienced a disconnect between your priorities and actions. (1) **D**etermine whether you spent your time on the big-ticket items that really mattered. (2) **E**valuate the degree to which you were working on important or merely urgent tasks. (3) **A**nalyze where and why this schism occurred and how it affected your level of success. (4) **L**everage these insights to better focus your time on what is truly important to your values and objectives.

> To be more effective in my time management, I will...

2.7 Developing Efficient Time Management

Ask Yourself: Do you accomplish your goals with minimum time and effort or do they tend to drag on and on? In a typical day how much time do you waste? Once you identify a goal, do you usually choose the most logical and sensible path for getting there? Said another way, is your time management not just effective but also efficient—are you doing things right?

Management Theory: Whereas the previous story is focused on effective time management and aligning time and values, efficient time management is acting smartly in their pursuit. It is a measure of means or process—how well-organized and/or proficient you are in the talk at hand. Even if an individual keeps focused on the proper ends, he or she still could be wasting much time and effort in execution. As a trip to the self-help section of the bookstore will attest, there is an abundance of frameworks that profess the secrets of managing ones time more efficiently. However it is possible to cut through the fluff and discern several underlying themes that form the theoretical foundation of sound time management approaches. For example, Individuals should utilize agendas as tools for understanding, organizing, prioritizing, and scheduling their tasks. Since no two people work exactly alike, they should also customize these agendas to fit their cognitive and work style. Individuals should combine tasks that have similar demands or requirements so that they can be completed together with minimum down time. Individuals should minimize distractions and low-value activities to streamline meetings and similar processes so that they focus on actionable items and get to their objective quicker. Individuals should delegate as many responsibilities that are appropriate as to build a strong support team and free up personal time for other tasks. Individuals should set deadlines and milestones for accomplishing projects and monitor their progress to increase their productivity. With these types of best practices, people would be better able to manage their time and get things done with greater speed and precision. Our story is by a manager who embraces several of these approaches in their attempts toward becoming more efficient at time management.

In Action [Case Study]: I recognize now that time management is an important function that if used effectively can minimize the amount of stress I experience in my personal and work life. My job places several time constraints on the work that I am solely responsible for. School and parenting place additional stresses on my already busy schedule. I have felt the particular need to address my time management skills because I believe I can function at a more productive level if I were to become more organized. My specific plan for becoming more efficient in my time management skills consisted of the following: (1) Keeping track of my daily tasks, meetings, deadlines, and so on through the use of a daily planner. (2) Organizing the work on my desk through the use of a filing system and labeling, and creating an "inbox" for things to be done. (3) Reserving a time during each day in which I will not be interrupted so I can perform some of the duties that need more of my attention than others. (4) Run my meetings so that they get right to the main points and focus on solutions. I now track each day's activities on my desktop calendar. In fact, this has become a habit for me. At the end of each day, I create a "To-Do" list for the next day, which includes returning phone calls/e-mails, as well as payroll submission and month-end close. Keeping track of my daily activities is now much easier. To become more organized, I have created folders on my computer to group my e-mails according to the subject. This has enabled me to double-check certain issues faster and with increased efficiency because the chance of me overlooking an e-mail is significantly reduced. For example, I have started keeping all my payroll issues in one stack. Also, I have assigned various parts of my desk/drawers for different items. I have made my counterparts and subordinates aware of where certain items belong. Overall, this helps prevent others or myself from misplacing important papers on my desk. On a daily basis, usually first thing in the morning, I review e-mails and respond to the ones that do not require much research. The other e-mails requiring more time are printed and/or forwarded to a member of my staff to do the research. This frees up time for me to focus on the highest-priority items. At our afternoon staff meeting I do not tolerate side issues or endless talk and keep the agenda focused and moving forward. *Since beginning this approach, I have found that I have more time in my day to do actual work and am not so overwhelmed with outstanding issues when the payroll submission time comes.* I have found that the changes that I have made have been very effective. In an effort to continue improving my time management skills, I am hoping to adopt even more principles of efficient time management. You can definitely say that I am now a believer.

Walking the Talk: Select a situation in your life where you might not have gotten the most return for your time investment. (1) **D**etermine whether you spent your time in well organized and executed ways. (2) **E**valuate the degree to which you were working not just hard but also smart. (3) **A**nalyze exactly why and how efficient time management principles could have made a difference. (4) **L**everage these insights to become more productive and efficient in your work.

> To be more efficient in my time management, I will…

2.8   Building Resiliency through a Better Life-Balance

Ask Yourself: Are you a workaholic? Do your overall stress levels mirror the daily ups and downs at the office? Alternatively are you able to find a healthy level of stability and peace between various aspects of your life? Would people consider you well-rounded? Do you achieve a good balance between work and personal activities?

Management Theory: Some of the preceding stories illustrate individuals' attempts to eliminate stress through effective and efficient time management. However it is rare that people can completely remove all of the stress from their lives. Therefore management theory advises that people supplement this strategy with the development of a hardier, more resilient way to deal with any stress that makes it through their defenses. That is to say, the effects of stress will be less severe if a person's ability to withstand them, their stress-amour or stress-shield so to speak, is strong. For example, research documents the positive impact of having a social support structure on an individual's ability to handle stress. A key strategy for obtaining this is enhanced resiliency through life balance. When individuals engage in a broad array of relationships and engagements, their more diverse (i.e., balanced) portfolio of activates acts as a hedge against stress in any one area. Therefore it is important to reduce vulnerability to stressors in one part of life by developing a well-rounded outlook. This is especially evident for the so-called workaholics of the world. These people spend the lion's share of their energy on their job and career, and often to the neglect of family, friends, spirituality, aesthetics, and cultural pursuits, and the like. Think about it, how often has someone on their deathbed lamented that they wish they had spent more time at the office?! And more than this, aside from value mismatches to which imbalance leads, from a functional perspective it has been demonstrated that well-rounded individuals are often more refreshed, productive, creative, intrinsically satisfied, and less vulnerable to stress-related sickness that can cause unnecessary absenteeism and turnover. Consider yourself forewarned—cheat sleep, skip vacations, and chain yourself to the office at your own peril. Our story is about an overstressed employee's plans to reduce the amount of energy devoted to work and develop a better balance across a broader array of pursuits.

In Action [Case Study]: My work week is now more than sixty hours with little leisure time and filled with emotions from sadness, depression, fatigue, and frustration. To combat this, I prepared a timetable, which detailed the steps that I would take in achieving a more balanced life: (1) Start to get to bed earlier so I feel more alive in the morning. This will also enable me to use the morning commuting time of one hour and a half to read the material for my job. I have made a conscientious effort in getting to bed at a reasonable hour. I was even able to do this a few times at the beginning of the month when work deadlines are heaviest. (2) Begin to attend church service again with my mother on Sunday mornings. This will fulfill my need for religious beliefs and allot time to spend with my family. I have already gone a few times since I recognized this activity as a stress managing tool. It has given me an opportunity to grow spiritually and spend time with family. I need to concentrate on incorporating this event into my life permanently. (3) Schedule "girls night" again. This is important because it allows me the chance to spend time with a group of my girlfriends; getting together once or twice a week for dinner and drinks. I am happy to report that I have a "girls night out" every two weeks and the benefits of this social support network surfaced immediately. We all shared our horror stories from work and rallied around anyone who seemed down and burned out. (4) Restart relaxation techniques such as Yoga as a method of alleviating pressure. The techniques have been an added bonus to my day. I must continue to maintain the momentum with the steps I have outlined and move forward with other alterations that will assist me in further attaining a balanced life, such as (a) Build and sustain an exercise regimen and healthy eating habits, and (b) Create a money jar for one monthly subway-free day (taking a nice car service to work). The results that I have seen so far have been very encouraging. *I have been successful in integrating many of these activities into my daily routine and really see the importance of using these stress managing tools to better balance my life and for the first time in years feel like a "whole person" again.* It also does not hurt that since doing this I have never been more productive at work.

Walking the Talk: Select a situation where you were overly engaged in one specific part of your life. (1) **D**etermine whether your myopia was temporary or something more systematic. (2) **E**valuate the degree to which this narrow focus limited the development of other aspects of your life and increased your dependence on, as well as stress sensitivity to, this one area. (3) **A**nalyze where and why this imbalance occurred and if it could have been better managed. (4) **L**everage these insights to develop a more supportive and balanced life.

> To increase my resiliency to stress through a better life balance, I will…

2.9 Improving Stress-Coping Strategies

Ask Yourself: Do you ever feel the need to escape? Does stress ever build to such a dangerously high level that it threatens to get the best of you? Do you have in your "toolbox" healthy methods for quickly and temporarily giving yourself some relieve without doing longlasting harm? Are these temporary techniques your last resort or primary method for dealing with stress?

Management Theory: The best way to deal with stress is to proactively eliminate its causes (e.g., through effective and efficient time management) and then build up resiliency to it (e.g., through social and support and life balance). But what happens when these strategies do not work entirely and stress simply overwhelms our defenses? We cannot always eliminate or shield ourselves from all stress every day. Paraphrasing the poet Burns, people's best laid plans for stress-management often go astray. When this situation occurs then individuals need a stop-gap. Sometimes people require emergency stress management tools to make it through a situation—to cope as it were. Coping is a short-term technique for temporarily eliminating or alleviating the effects of a particular stressor or the long-term accumulation of stressors that have built up to a dangerous point. Coping is most appropriate only when stress levels spike above optimal levels and immediate action is necessary to preserve ones performance capability and mental or physical health. Management theory clearly indicates that coping should NOT be a person's primary strategy. This is because it is inherently temporary and does not reduce the underlying sources of stress. Notwithstanding managers need the tools so that, when necessary, they can shift into survival mode. It is also important to know that there are better and worse coping methods based on the degree to which they build up (e.g., positive imagery and healthy exercise) or deteriorate (e.g., binge eating and drinking) physical and mental resiliency. Our story is about a manager in the fast moving and highly charged financial industry exploring ways that they can practice more effective stress coping strategies.

In Action [Case Study]: Working at the stock exchange can be very stressful. I am working with large amounts of money and markets move extremely quickly. I try to use this stress to stimulate myself and perform better. However, there are times when I get overwhelmed or frustrated at work, and it can harm my ability to do my job. These are the times that I feel I could improve my temporary stress-reduction techniques. Normally when this happens, I find myself turning to food for comfort. I must admit, the foods I like most are all high in fat, cholesterol, calories, and are generally just not good for you. I also consumed more alcohol, sugar, and caffeine and that can also do harm. As a result, my ability to cope with stress and mitigate its impact was compromised. Among other things, my absenteeism due to illness was quite high and my energy level plummeted from all those extra pounds. Obviously there are smarter ways to cope with stress. *Management theory suggests a number of healthy coping techniques to reduce stress temporarily. I have tried several of these.* I now use the muscle relaxation technique to reduce stress, and I feel that it works particularly well for me. When stress gets out of control I tighten each muscle for five to ten seconds and then relax. This eases the tension in the muscles themselves. I also use deep breathing, taking slow deep breaths and then holding them for five seconds and exhaling completely. Rehearsal is used everyday by walking through a situation before the real thing attempting to find the best scenario. I also focus on imagery and reframing by mentally escaping a situation and optimistically redefining it to focus on the manageable parts. These both have worked well for me. The subconscience has an unbelievable power, and I feel that people can use it to their advantage. Thinking positively for example, or imagining yourself getting what you want, helps when a person tells themselves to do something or sees themselves doing something because our body and mind somehow begin to work toward that goal. I would also like to expand my physical reactions. Growing up, whenever something was bothering me I would go and shoot baskets by myself. It would always help to clear my head and help me to gain my composure. Although I do not have a hoop, I plan to start using the swimming pool at my gym and finding a local court to make some alone time to think through what is bothering me. I consider this temporary only because the activity does not make my stress go away, but gives me a healthy way to put things into perspective and survive the really rough spots.

Walking the Talk: Select a situation where you were overly engaged in one specific part of your life. (1) **D**etermine whether your myopia was temporary or something more systematic. (2) **E**valuate the degree to which this narrow focus limited the development of other aspects of your life and increased your dependence on, as well as stress sensitivity to, this one area. (3) **A**nalyze where and why this imbalance occurred and if it could have been better managed. (4) **L**everage these insights to develop a more supportive and balanced life.

> To increase my resiliency to stress through a better life balance, I will...

CHAPTER THREE

Perceiving and Understanding Accurately

Chapter three examines management theories about perception and applying the management skill of understanding and sense-making. Perception is not something we do only sometimes; it is a constant and natural process to all people that is endemic in all walks of life. Perception refers to the practice of selecting what information in our environment we will process and then using it to make sense of these phenomena to take action. Yet our senses simply cannot take in all possible information, so by definition we are selective sense-makers. In addition, people do not always form identical pictures of our surroundings, so we are also subjective sense-makers. These selective and subjective perceptions of the world influence individuals' attitudes, actions, and outcomes. It also stands to reason that how other people feel about and treat us are based on their selective and subjective perceptions. And because of all these differences, managers can disagree about the nature of the challenges and opportunities that they and their organizations face. So what are we to do about this? I suggest three general approaches in the application of perception theory to practice: (1) Crystallization—Better understand the biases and traps in perception to improve the accuracy in which you see things, (2) Reconciliation—Work to integrate your and others different perspectives to develop enhanced understandings of complex issues, and (3) Capitalization—Use your knowledge of perceptual patterns (e.g., in meetings, negotiations, or speeches) to influence others and facilitate the successful completion of your goals and objectives. Therefore in this third chapter, we look at how one can utilize sense-making strategies to perceive more accurately and subsequently crystallize, reconcile, or capitalize on people's perceptual imperfections.

3.1   Appreciating the Importance of
Perceptual Differences

Ask Yourself: Do you always notice each person and every event that happens around you? Of these people and things that actually make it onto your radar screen, do you see them completely objectively and accurately? Do your perceptions ever misrepresent an issue or object? Do they ever differ from those of other people? How do you react when your perceptions are challenged?

Management Theory: Perception is the active process by which individuals select, organize, interpret, integrate, retrieve, and respond to sensory input—impressions and other available information—to give meaning to their environment and make sense of their world. Due to the incomplete (we cannot see everything) and fickle (we are not totally objective) nature of this process, people are unavoidably selective and subjective perceivers. It stands to reason then that people will often see the same things in very different ways. More specifically, as applied to the workplace, we should expect to find differences in perception between managers and their employees, coworkers, bosses, customers, suppliers, partners, regulators, and other individuals who are involved in their job and bear upon its success. Management theory suggests several variables that may underlie these differences. For example, we tend to see things and assess their nature based on such factors as our training and education, values and attitudes, motives and interests, experiences and stereotypes, personality and abilities, affiliations and organizations, as well as goals and positions. Thus an individual in marketing might see a problem differently than someone in accounting. Same for individuals who prioritize achievement versus comfort. Same for individuals raised in the city versus country. Same for seasoned versus novice workers. Same for risk-seeking versus conservative types. Same for Republicans versus Democrats. Same for workers versus managers. You get the picture. Our story speaks to this last example and is by a banker disagreeing with his boss about performance evaluations.

In Action [Case Study]: When I was employed with a bank as a product administrator, my supervisor and I formed different perceptions of my work and, as a result, I believe I was wrongfully evaluated during my performance evaluation. In January, my supervisor took over a new area within the company, and a gentleman from another area took over our group. The first few months were spent bringing him up to speed with the department and our responsibilities and we seemed to work well together and get along. Over time, my supervisor began to get overwhelmed with the position and his responsibilities. When problems arose, there were a lot of finger pointing and constant bickering about minor issues. Our working relationship became strained and our communication suffered from it. I believe I was never given credit for my work and was blamed for things that were either out of my control or not my responsibility. The attempts we made to discuss our issues with one another did not help the situation. In October, our department was split into two areas, transaction processing and client-reporting. I joined the client-reporting group and was under a new supervisor. During our year-end performance evaluation, I was informed that since our group was new, our previous supervisors would handle the evaluations. As I expected, I disagreed with the review I received from my former supervisor and was very concerned since this would affect my pay raise, bonus, and any possible promotion. *Fortunately I documented my own job performance throughout the year, keeping track of many examples to support it, and was able to show how my actual performance contradicted what my supervisor had perceived.* I was content that I was able to show some proof to back up my work achievements. My performance was significantly affected due to such a negative work relationship I had with my supervisor, especially since I was treated poorly even though I did my job well. It was very frustrating to not get credit for my work. I was happier in my new group, but other coworkers who remained with my former supervisor had similar issues with him and a few decided to leave the company.

Walking The Talk: Select a situation in your life where your perceptions were difference from someone else. (1) **D**etermine what your and "their" perceptions were of the issue at hand. (2) **E**valuate the degree to which the perceptions were similar or different. (3) **A**nalyze why certain perceptual factor might have been influencing each perspective in a certain direction. (4) **L**everage these insights to enhance your perception, reconcile the views, and/or influence their view to advance your goals.

> To better appreciate the importance of perceptual differences, I will…

3.2   Seeing the Halo Effect

Ask Yourself: What things about a person do you focus on when forming perceptions of them? Are there some factors that are more important to you and drive your impressions? Can a single characteristic dominate how you see someone? Do others ever judge you by a single characteristic?

Management Theory: The halo effect refers to a tendency of individuals to judge a person or thing based solely on one characteristic or aspect. Certainly people and the business environments in which they operate are complex. Hence they are often difficult to understand and assess. Halo provides an easy way out. It zeroes in on a single feature and allows a person to form an overall impression entirely from this small piece of the puzzle. When we overgeneralize specific characteristics to judge a person's entire character, whether to their benefit or detriment, we are guilty of the halo effect. What are typical halo factors? Frequently they are easily seen (i.e., salient) factors such as dress and appearance, articulation and vocabulary, or even such actions as a handshake or eye contact. Why do people use the halo effect? Often when they are uninformed or unaware of the complexities of the target being perceived, or are in a rush, or are extremely emotional about the halo issue. When do we see the halo effect in action? Perhaps when a manager hires an applicant based only on their looks. Or when a person votes for a candidate based on a single issue. Or when someone evaluates a subordinate or supervisor solely on whether they are friendly and nice. Or when an individual invests their money based solely on the broker's affiliation or manner of speech. Our story is by a high-tech worker observing how a strong developmental manager was seen negatively by others because of a single characteristic.

In Action [Case Study]: At my high-technology firm, people frequently base their judgments of others based on the halo effect. As an example, when I first started there I worked directly for the vice president/general manger, Newton. People who knew him well described him as a person who is willing to bring people into the company and help them get started. I always felt comfortable asking him for help or advice when I needed it. Newton is a very friendly person who works hard and is willing to help out when necessary. However, there is one quality about him that people tended to focus on—his presence is intimidating. Some employees tended to overlook his positive qualities and view Newton negatively solely because of this one aspect of his personality, a typical case of the halo effect. One day, I was helping one of the secretaries with a computer problem. Newton walked past the room and the secretary made a comment about how she is afraid of him and he is a bad manager. I did not understand why, since he brought me into the company and did a lot to help me adjust to the work environment. I started to talk to other and they all had the same feelings. I realized that the way Newton looked and talked might be seen as intimidating to some people and that they might be judging him completely based on this. He is very smart, knows a great deal of information, and is willing to help others, but sometimes he comes across as intimidating even though he does not mean to. For example, once when he assigned a project to me he assumed I knew the information required to do it. I told him that I did not know what he was looking for because I had not learned about it yet. He was very understanding and found someone to teach me the ropes. He was really an excellent manager and did what he could to accommodate me and help me grow. *Maybe this person comes across as a very intimidating at times, but he is an excellent manager and a great person to work for. Unfortunately some people will not see beyond this one characteristic and benefit from his expertise.* Newton's career advancement might be derailed as well if people do not look past his intimidating presence.

Walking the Talk: Select a situation in your life where you have used a single attribute to judge a person. (1) **D**etermine what factor you emphasized in forming the perception. (2) **E**valuate whether the factor is truly representative of the entire person in all of their complexity. (3) **A**nalyze why you may have opened up yourself to perceptual error and if there were any other factors that you could have considered to lessen this bias. (4) **L**everage these insights to better utilize multiple characteristics to minimize halo errors and form a more accurate and complete perspective of people.

To reduce my vulnerability to halo errors in my perception, I will…

3.3   Guarding against Contrast Effect

Ask Yourself: Do your impressions of people ever change depending on whom you happen to compare them with? Or do your perceptions of someone stay the same regardless of their company or context? Would you see someone in a more positive light just because they were next to a weaker other (or vise versa, more negative just because they were around somebody who was very good)? Are people comparing you to colleagues and associates when forming their impressions of you?

Management Theory: People's perceptions tend to be influenced by cues in the environment that can make something look better or worse by comparison. This is known as the contrast effect. It is a bias of perception that occurs when an individual's perception of a person or thing is distorted by comparing them to other cases in their context. For example, many have probably come across perceptual tricks that make certain lines or shapes look bigger depending on how they are embedded into the background. Two sides of a hat could be identical but one might look smaller if positioned cleverly. Two people might be of equal weight but one seen as smaller if they were standing next to a sumo wrestler. In the workplace we might evaluate someone as a higher quality employee simply because they were hired at the same time as a poor or average performer. They just looked better by comparison. The contrast effect occurs in a variety of circumstances, for example, when two people interview for a position, make a speech, or perform a similar task. In the former case, an applicant could receive an inflated rating simply if, by the luck of the draw, they interviewed for the position immediately following a poor applicant. On the flip side, a manager might evaluate someone in too negative a light if they happened to be in a high-level cohort. Say being an above-average worker within a department full of superstars. A high-potential employee (or "A" level student) is exactly that...no matter if they happen to be sitting in a room next to a bunch of Kindergarteners or Einsteins. Yet we tend to loose perceptual objectivity and accuracy depending on the context. Our story is by an intern who saw how contrast effects tainted the evaluations of himself and a colleague.

In Action [Case Study]: This past summer I had the opportunity to rotate through several departments when interning for a major insurance company. This process served the purpose of introducing me not only to the various aspects of the insurance industry, but also to the various lines of insurance that the company writes. I spent a week in each department, doing underwriting exercises, learning the more technical aspects of certain lines of business, going on agency visits, learning departmental work flows, and so on. Unfortunately, I did not make this rotation alone. I was paired with another employee, Ann. Each week we were evaluated on our work in and contribution to each department. *It became obvious after the first week that not only we were comparing ourselves, but that we were being evaluated in comparison with each other, however subtly.* The fact that we were thrown together for the entire rotation program and that our evaluations reflected contrast effects will affect both of our futures with the company. I feel that Ann and I both performed well in the program. However, it became evident that I picked up new skills, absorbed new concepts, and finished projects a bit quicker than Ann did. In isolation, I am sure that my performance would still have been viewed as very good, but in comparison, I looked like an all-star. I derived a great deal of satisfaction from my work. I am positive that a great deal of that satisfaction was derived from the fact that I had a lower "benchmark" for my performance. Unfortunately, Ann did not thrive on the atmosphere of competition. As the program wore on, she resented the fact that her solid performance was being viewed negatively because it was being compared with my slightly better work. She soon quit and expressed her dissatisfaction with the organization. Absenteeism was an area that most likely would have gone unnoticed for both of us in isolation. However, because we constantly worked together, Ann's occasional absences were immediately remarked on when I would be seen hard at work, alone. The company did not seem to perceive that the turnover of this particular intern would be a great loss, but in my opinion they lost a good employee with a solid future. Contrast effects served to taint our evaluations and actually altered both Ann's and my performance, levels of satisfaction, perceptions of absenteeism, and eventual turnover.

Walking the Talk: Select a situation in your life where you have judged a person based on a comparison to someone else. (1) **D**etermine the benchmark that you used when forming the perception. (2) **E**valuate whether it was an appropriate comparison and if it might have unfairly biased your perspective. (3) **A**nalyze why you did this and how you could have used different or multiple comparison points, or a more objective process, to improve the accuracy of this picture. (4) **L**everage these insights to develop more evenhanded perceptions of people that are less influence by the choice of comparison points.

To guard against the contrast effect in biasing my perception, I will...

3.4   Reducing Projection

Ask Yourself: Do you ever assume that other people want the same things out of life that you do? Hold identical values as you or see things just like you? Have you ever "projected" your feelings onto someone else? Thought that they would or should act just like you did in a situation? When trying to understand others' actions do ever you superimpose your standards and priorities onto them?

Management Theory: People's perceptions tend to be influenced by their personal preferences and biases. More specifically, individuals tend to attribute their own characteristics to others when trying to make sense of them. Management theory identifies this tendency as projection. Formally defined, projection is an individual's ascription of their own personal attributes to others while essentially disregarding the characteristics of these other people. In a word, projection denies others individuality because you see everyone as similar to yourself. For example, believing that, because you are a hard worker who does not mind coming in on weekends, your employees naturally feel the same way. Or that, since you have no problems with the new corporate policy, feeling that neither should anyone else. Perhaps even reasoning that, because you want more money and power, your coworkers must feel the same way. Projection could manifest itself in inaccurate perceptions such as "I want my boss' job so my subordinates are probably all gunning for my job." It is important to note that projection is becoming increasingly problematic as the workplace becomes more diverse. Quite frankly, in our age of globalization people are less likely to be "just like you" so projecting oneself onto others is less likely to result in an accurate assessment. Our story is by a Peace Corps volunteer realizing this on her mission to the country of Botswana.

In Action [Case Study]: As an expatriate service manager in a country much different than my own, I found myself wrongly using projection to evaluate my colleagues, superiors, and reports. *I tended to expect way too much from the employees because I was basing my opinions on my own characteristics.* I tend to be someone who likes to take charge and get things done as quickly as possible. But in this area of the world, these characteristics are not emphasized or found in many of the people. It was easy for me to become frustrated with the local workers, who I thought were very lazy, and my fellow managers, who tended to sit back and not demand too much. After a few months in this office, I learned to adapt to the differences in character between myself and the people around me. I now realize that if I had not used projection in my evaluations, I would have begun enjoying my time in this assignment a lot sooner than I had. In terms of performance, I feel that because I wrongly projected and often became frustrated when my colleagues or the employees did not meet my personal standards or value efficiency the same way I did. This prevented me from performing to my best abilities and getting my employees to do the same. My satisfaction level at first was very low, I was constantly upset about the situation. Things were not getting done as I would have like them to have. But once I adapted and learned to live with these differences in character between the people and myself, and accept them for who they were instead of whom I wanted them to be, I became very satisfied. I put much more effort into the job, and we were much more successful in accomplishing our goals. Although I was never absent from work, I did take very long breaks and definitely took my time returning to the office after these breaks. This was all due to the fact that I had at first wrongly used projection to judge the workers and my colleagues. There were even a few times that I really felt like throwing in the towel and quitting. I could definitely see that distorted perceptions from projection would make people unhappy with their jobs.

Walking the Talk: Select a situation in your life where you may have projected yourself onto others. (1) **D**etermine whether you saw the person as a distinct individual or as an extension of yourself. (2) **E**valuate the degree to which this perception was an accurate portrayal of the person. (3) **A**nalyze where and why your sense-making strategy led you astray in terms of key differences between you and them. (4) **L**everage these insights to develop a perception of others that is less dependent on your characteristics and more determined by theirs.

To reduce projection bias in my perception, I will...

3.5   Limiting Self-Serving Bias

Ask Yourself: How do you determine what factors are responsible for your level of performance? When you perform well (or win) do you credit yourself? When you perform poorly (or lose) do you blame the situation or other people? Are your attributions of credit and blame ever self-serving? Does playing the "blame game" ever get in the way of your personal development and sense of responsibility?

Management Theory: The self-serving bias is an all too-frequent error of perceptual attribution. It is the tendency for individuals to take credit for their successes and blame others for their failures. When people perform well, they tend to form an internal ("it was me!") attribution for this positive result, claiming personal recognition and praise due to their level of skill or hard work. Alternatively when people perform poorly, there is a countervailing tendency to form an external attribution ("it was NOT my fault!") for this negative result, denying responsibility due to unfavorable conditions or other people's errors. This self-serving pattern of perceptual distortion might make you feel better, and in some instances may indeed be politically helpful, but it can hinder a person from accurately perceiving events, understanding situations, identifying problems, learning from mistakes, and embarking on needed self-improvement. From a social perspective, this self-serving tendency can hurt the morale of those who are blamed. Moreover the bias can create a counterproductive and even dangerous culture where people do not share a sense of individual accountability and spend more time playing the "blame game" than addressing issues and getting things done. Indeed this is a common lament of those with a high sense of personal responsibility and negative view of personal gamesmanship. Our story is by a university employee who has observed the self-serving bias in their educational setting.

In Action [Case Study]: It is human nature to take credit for oneself but pass blame on to others or external factors. I myself admit that I have passed the blame onto lower level employees when it was not entirely warranted. Back when I was working as a residential assistance for my university, we were subjected to a performance evaluation every semester. When the staff has done a good job and performance levels were rated high, I attributed it to my leadership style, qualities, and abilities. On the other hand when any report was unsatisfactory and/or performance level was rated low, then I blamed the staff and extenuating circumstances. I also saw this same self-serving bias occur in other areas of the university. Later on, when working at the admissions office, when a particular procedure was implemented successfully I noticed that upper management praised themselves on their ability to design that piece of work. On the other hand, when a different procedure had failed and this was clearly due to them leaving out vital information in the redesign of applications, they blamed the computer technicians or support staff who actually had no responsibility for the particular application system. *In both instances, the self-serving bias made us play the blame game instead of taking responsibility for our actions and trying to improve performance.* If blame is passed on a consistence level, this can distract people's effort and lead to a decrease in productivity. Getting blamed for something you did not do also decrease our morale.

Walking the Talk: Select a situation in your life where you altered perceptions in a self-serving manner. (1) **D**etermine the extent to which you took credit for successes and passed the buck for failures. (2) **E**valuate whether these were accurate attributions or in fact they distorted the perceptions. (3) **A**nalyze why you did this and how you could have been more objective in the sharing of credit and responsibility for blame. (4) **L**everage these insights to develop a more accurate approach toward determining cause and assigning accountability.

To limit the self-serving bias in my perception and playing the "blame game," I will…

3.6 Minimizing Perceptual Laziness

Ask Yourself: Do you tend to take the easy way out by making quick assessments about things rather than looking at them carefully? Do you ever rely on "rules of thumb" that have worked for you in the past instead of examining things on a case by case basis? Have you taken shortcuts in judging others? Gotten into trouble because of a fast and easy assessment rather than detailed diagnosis of a situation?

Management Theory: Individuals often adopt shortcuts, also called heuristics, in perceiving others. This is largely because it is hard work to perceive and fully examine everything that we come across. There is just too much stimuli to process for our limited perceptual faculties. Perceptual shortcuts are therefore, in a sense, necessary techniques to deal with information overload and survive in a complex world. However many of us take this simplification too far and superficially process much of what we see without expending the effort to probe deeper. We often overuse these "rules of thumb" even when there is ample ability, time, reasons, and resources to make a more thorough assessment. We get lazy, and this laziness opens us up to systematic perceptual biases that can result in distorted sense-making. For example, people tend to overestimate how often something happened if the event is particularly vivid and easily remembered (this is called "availability"). People also tend to overestimate how appropriate someone would be for a position or how useful an action would be for a situation when it fits their mental prototype or a success story (this is called "representativeness"). Mental laziness occurs much more than many managers realize and can be seen when employees mentally check out of work and sleep-walk through their daily assessments and assignments. We might be able to get away with our simplifying perceptual strategies much of the time but they open us up to mistakes that could skew our understanding of situations, especially when they change and are moved outside our usual comfort zone. Our story is by a particularly reflective manager who seeks to remedy this bias in time for the next performance evaluation.

In Action [Case Study]: I sometimes have a "bias against thinking" and take the easy way out when perceiving other people. For example, when noticing a subordinate staring out the window, the first thing that came to my mind was that they were idling their time. *I tend to close my mind and go on automatic pilot when I see something different that I am not used to, immediately generalizing it as a waste of time, a waste of company resources, and so on.* Maybe he was thinking of something that I am not aware of, or simply needs a mental rest to stimulate productivity, or is in the middle of a creative idea that could save the company millions. But why did I just jump to conclusions? By reflecting on the theory and in particular the representative bias it brought to my attention the depth of this issue and I need to do something to change. I begin to think, hey—why couldn't it be the other way around, a different point of view? Why does the present have to be just like the past? Why do all of my employees have to fit my notion of the perfect worker? If I think about things from other viewpoints, maybe I would understand more of the whole picture and see different angles. How do I change this mental laziness in my perception? Instead of looking to a subordinate and imposing my past standards on them, I should try and find out in what is causing their behavior in the particular situation. I have to find out the root cause and not merely scan the surface. The organization that I work with has an annual performance evaluation system coming up soon wherein various aspects of ones character and behavior are analyzed and evaluated. It is the perfect time to put my new way of thinking into practice in a very real way that would mean a lot to my staff, to the organization, and to me. During the time since I read about this theory, I have been more open and probing about issues and situations that I did not see before. Just because it is different than my model of success does not mean that it is bad. This I feel is a change in my thinking bias, a start of a long battle against perceptual laziness.

Walking the Talk: Select a situation in your life where you might have been lazy in your perception. (1) **D**etermine whether your view of things matched the complexity of the things themselves. (2) **E**valuate whether perceptual shortcuts were used and to what extent they oversimplified the situation. (3) **A**nalyze where and why corners were cut and how you could have formed a more realistic picture of the situation. (4) **L**everage these insights to develop more balanced perceptual strategies that do not overwhelm you but at the same time do not obscure your sense-making through oversimplification.

> To minimize laziness and oversimplification in my perception, I will…

3.7   Avoiding Stereotyping Based on Appearance

Ask Yourself: Have you ever judged a book by its cover? Do you feel that the way someone or something looks is a good indication about their character? Has there been an instance where you have grouped someone together with others just because they had similar appearances? Do people who look alike also think and act alike?

Management Theory: Stereotyping is the process of judging someone based solely on a perceived group to which they belong. Similar to projection, stereotyping denies people their individuality. Only here you are seeing others not like yourself but like everyone else in their "category." A simplified model of stereotyping from management theory identifies three general steps in a self-perpetuating cycle of perceptual bias: (1) Put people in a group, (2) Make generalizations about the group, (3) Confirm generalization and apply them to all of its members. This process leads us awry in several respects. People are all members of multiple groups so any single identifier used to group them is destined to be incomplete and arbitrary. Also inter- as well as intra-group differences prevent any generalizations from being completely accurate or universally applicable. Finally closing ones mind to alternative viewpoints propagates automatic acceptance and devotion to stereotypes and freezes out disconfirming information, alternative viewpoints, and opportunities for learning. Yet stereotypes in the workplace persist and continue to distort individuals' accurate perception and sense-making strategies. One of the most frequently invoked categories of stereotyping is appearance. How people look, dress, and present themselves. And thus such stereotypes are formed that make sweeping generalizations about "beautiful" people, "overweight" people, "short" people, "flashy" people, "long-haired" people, or even "dirty" people. If left unchecked stereotypes can lead to prejudices that reinforce individuals' beliefs about the superiority or inferiority of certain groups merely based on their appearance. Our story is by a person forming negative stereotypes about a male partygoer with unkempt clothes and long hair.

In Action [Case Study]: I remember attending a party talking with some friends when an older gentleman wandered in. He had long dirty hair and it looked like he had not changed his clothes in about two months. I thought he was one of the town's alcoholics crashing the event. I turned to my friend John and said, "Is that one of the townies that should be at the local bar. John turned to me and said, "No, that's Karl, my friend's dad!" He went on to tell me that this was no bum; it turns out that he had a doctorate in Computer Science from M.I.T., and he was a leading scientist at laboratory that my company occasionally does business with. *Boy, was the egg on my face! It* *taught me an important lesson, never judge a book by its cover.* I perceived Karl to be one of the local winos, and it turned out that he was one of the smartest people in the business! Since that experience, I have always tried to judge people on their merits and not their appearance. Not to say that appearance is not important, it can have merit in the business world. I'm sure that Karl would not show up to a job interview dressed the way he was at that party. (Who knows, maybe he would and because of this I would not hire him.) The bottom line is that people definitely make snap judgments about people based on appearance and, we have to realize that. People will perform based on how their managers perceive their performance. There was one time in my career where my manager had a poor perception of me, and it definitely affected my work. Because I am a flashy dresser, I was perceived by my department head as boisterous and undisciplined. This manager stereotyped me as a trouble-maker and made my life very difficult. This also effected my performance evaluation. Now that I am a manager, one of the things that I would like to change is the subjectivity of the annual performance reviews. I am going to try to give my subordinates concrete goals to shoot for so that it will be easier to measure progress and harder to let their appearance get in the way of an accurate evaluation. Who cares what they look like when you are judging people only on their performance. I am not suggesting to totally get rid of the subjectivity; I am suggesting that it would behoove the whole process to have more tangible goals set for both the employee and the employer that would limit perceptual stereotypes such as this.

Walking the Talk: Select a situation in your life where you made an overgeneralization based on looks. (1) **D**etermine whether you considered appearance in forming your perception of someone or something. (2) **E**valuate the degree to which the way someone or something looked biased your view of them. (3) **A**nalyze where and why appearance was so important to you and how an overemphasis of this factor led you astray. (4) **L**everage these insights to develop a more accurate sense-making approach that is not as dependent on labels related to appearance.

> To avoid making appearance stereotypes in my perception, I will…

3.8   Avoiding Stereotyping Based on Profession

Ask Yourself: Have you ever judged a person simply by the title on their business card or nameplate on their door? Do you feel that someone's job is a good indication about their character? Do you ever group people together by their profession and then made a general assessment of them? Do people who are in the same line of work all think and act alike?

Management Theory: We have already identified stereotyping as the process of perceiving somebody solely on the basis of their attributed "group." In addition to stereotyping by appearance, we also stereotype based on peoples' jobs and professions. When we meet someone new, the first question that tends to be asked is "so what do you do for a living?" This easily leads to categorization based on preformed opinions of that profession. Stereotypes of occupations such as lawyer, police officer, pilot, surgeon, soldier, scientist, accountant, stock broker, computer programmer, and politician abound in our society and are reinforced by the popular media. And if we believe the popular comic strip Dilbert, then all engineers are exactly alike as are all marketers, salespeople, and managers. Of course there is a wide range of personality types in any profession. Yet our ability to make sense of people and their behaviors is obscured because the stereotypes prevent us from considering individual differences. Unfortunately, these professional stereotypes infest organizations and often get in the way of good communication, productive cooperation, sound decision making, and working together on teams to achieve common goals. Some people can readily see how potentially destructive these stereotypes can be whereas others seem destined to learn the hard way. Our story is by a manager who fits into the latter category—they formed negative stereotypes about a potential recruit who was a computer engineer and nearly lost a great worker because of it.

In Action [Case Study]: In my department, there are several people who work the day shift that are trained to be traders and who do all the work in that area. The problem is that the other two people are going to be leaving the department (one person is moving to another department within the firm, and the other person is leaving to raise a family). Obviously the head of the department is looking for replacements. However I came to learn just this past Friday that the managers are thinking about hiring an employee who has a master's in computer engineering from an Ivy League school and worked in IT his whole career. Now I am very impressed with those qualifications but don't feel that he will be a good trader. *I have stereotyped the person to be a computer nerd who thinks he knows everything.* I have already decided in my mind that he will not want to learn from me because he is a technology geek who just understands computers and does not know anything about people. The others who I work with on the trading desk share this opinion. Already I feel that my satisfaction on the job may be hindered. I am going to be put in a position very soon where I will be the senior person carrying additional workload while trying to train this new "technoid." I am concerned that it will have an adverse effect on my performance because of the amount of time it will probably take to get this person up to speed given their probable lack of interpersonal skills and conceited attitude. If the stress I know I am going to be facing begins to take its toll on me physically, and it begins to affect my satisfaction, then I will consider leaving the firm and start looking for another position. [Postscript—It is now about six months since I wrote this and my new hire turned out to be one of the best employees in the department, even though I rode him pretty hard in the beginning. I guess I was wrong to assume things about him just because of his professional background].

Walking the Talk: Select a situation in your life where you made an overgeneralization based on profession. (1) **D**etermine whether you considered someone's job in forming your perception of someone or something. (2) **E**valuate the degree to which preconceptions about their profession biased your view of them. (3) **A**nalyze where and why professional background was so important to you and how an overemphasis of this factor led you astray. (4) **L**everage these insights to develop a more accurate sense-making approach that is not as dependent on labels related to profession.

> To avoid making professional stereotypes in my perception, I will…

3.9   Avoiding Stereotyping Based on Gender

Ask Yourself: Have you ever judged a person based solely on their gender? Do you feel that being a man or a woman is a good indication about someone's character? Has there been an instance where you have grouped people together by their masculinity or femininity and then made a general assessment of them? Do all men (or women) think and act alike?

Management Theory: In the earlier two sections, we have discussed stereotyping as the process of perceiving somebody solely on the basis their attributed "group." In addition to stereotyping by appearance and profession, people also tend to stereotype based on other factors such as gender. Notwithstanding the significant change in the number of women in corporate management and occupying executive positions there still exists workplace stereotypes, both positive and negative, about these individuals simply based on their sexual category. Are women as aggressive as men? More caring and understanding? As good at finance or strategy? Better communicators? More intuitive? Better listeners? Too emotional? Less effective at leading and motivating their followers? Research overwhelmingly points to the fact that there are few if any substantial differences in management performance due to gender differences. Said another way, one cannot reliably predict managerial behavior or success based solely on gender. Yet both male-and female-based stereotypes exist and continue to bias workplace perceptions. For example, studies have found that people sometimes evaluate the effectiveness of others (bosses, coworkers, or direct reports) differently depending on whether the person was a male or female. This type of perceptual bias perpetuates gender-based preconceptions and can on occasion reinforce the proverbial glass ceiling that remains a very real barrier in the advancement of competent female managers. Our story is by a woman reflecting on such challenges including one particularly poignant experience.

In Action [Case Study]: As a female manager in the predominantly male field of engineering, I have been the recipient of much stereotyping over my career. The stereotype that a woman cannot be as good in math or effective at leading people has definitely reared its ugly head in a number of my coworkers and at a number of firms. In my case this is just not true as I have consistently received equal or superior performance evaluations. But this does not stop some people from looking at me negatively just because of my gender. No one, however, was as blatant as one older gentleman in the organization at which I took my first position after graduation. He was the only individual in my department that had a drafting board, which I needed for certain parts of my job, so on one particular project I was stopping by his cubicle for several consecutive days. He badgered me daily with the following comments: "A woman's place is in the home" and "Women should not be engineers." Although I was bothered by his statements, I was new to the job and not anxious to cause waves. Besides, I reasoned, he could just be joking. *So I took it as a challenge to prove to him that I was a good engineer, even if I was in his mind only a "female." Eventually, his perception of me changed and I won his respect.* Oddly enough, he became one of my strongest supporters. Although my story had a happy ending, not everyone is as fortunate. And even though women have become more prominent in the workforce and this industry in particular I (and many of my friends) have still experienced gender bias. Back to my story, the older gentleman's comments could have certainly discouraged me and made me resign my position, and then my company would have lost a valuable employee and my career might have come off track. Or imagine if he was my boss and refused to promote me just because I was a woman. I am now in a better position because my current employer specifically recognizes "gender bashing," even if casual, as sexual harassment and has established policies to deal with situations such as the one I was in so as to provide a more comfortable working environment for all its employees.

Walking the Talk: Select a situation in your life where you made an overgeneralization based on gender. (1) **D**etermine whether you considered someone's gender in forming your perception of someone or something. (2) **E**valuate the degree to which preconceptions about being a man or woman biased your view of them. (3) **A**nalyze where and why gender was so important to you and how an overemphasis of this factor led you astray. (4) **L**everage these insights to develop a more accurate sense-making approach that is not as dependent on labels related to gender.

To avoid making gender stereotypes in my perception, I will…

3.10   Combating the Self-Fulfilling Prophesy

Ask Yourself: Can your perceptions of people influence how you treat them and eventually how they react to you? When you see someone in a good light is it then more likely that they will rise to your high expectations and succeed? Might having poor expectations of someone also cause people to fall down to this low level of performance? Can the act of forming perceptions play a part in making them come true?

Management Theory: The self-fulfilling prophecy occurs when our perceptions actually change peoples' behaviors to make the perception come true. For example, if a manager sees their employees as lazy then these perceptions can actually work to make the employees lazy. Or in a more positive light, if a manager perceives their peoples has having great potential then this could actually impel the employees to reach new heights. How is this possible? In short, our perceptions influence our expectations or what we feel likely to happen. This in turn influences our behavior and the way in which we treat people. When you perceive that an employee has strong potential, you might expect big things from them, which would make you more likely to treat them in a manner that would elicit big things—that is, giving them more responsibility, attention, praise, support, resources, training, and the like. The employees in turn might then develop greater motivation, expend more effort, draw on a wider array of skills and abilities, and actually achieve more than if we treated them in a lesser manner. Thus managers often get precisely what they expect because their perceptions influenced their actions and others' responses. Simply put, if a manager's expectations are high, an employee is more likely to perform at a high level. If their expectations are low, the employee is likely to fulfill that prediction. The same goes for workers, if they perceive their boss to be inflexible and distant then their subsequent actions might make the boss operate in exactly this way. This bias emphasizes the power of perception in shaping ours as well as others beliefs and behaviors in the workplace. It also suggests that you should be careful about how you view people because it could very well influence them to become in line with your image. Our story is by a compliance manager who reasons back on how his low expectations might have affected his employees in a negative way.

In Action [Case Study]: I supervise an organization that is responsible for ensuring that an army base complies with all federal, state, local, and army environmental regulations. Unfortunately, only two of my nine employees had been recruited for their environmental backgrounds. The other seven employees were primarily "problems," transferred into the organization before the environmental regulation explosion. With this onslaught of complex environmental regulations, it was my perception that the employees lacked the technical and administrative backgrounds to perform the major abilities required for their "new" jobs. Those required abilities included reading and interpreting technical and legal information, creating compliance strategies, composing letters, and enforcing regulations. I initially but only half-heartedly encouraged the employees to get more training in their areas of responsibilities but never really supported this. I have realized, however, that I quickly became committed to a perception and expectation that these employees were unable to develop the skills necessary to perform their responsibilities successfully. I think I developed that belief primarily based on my perceptions. I was never really committed to developing their intellectual ability, their training, and their general motivation and effort levels. I am sure I indirectly expressed this to those employees and, true to the self-fulfilling prophecy, they fulfilled my expectations. I expected a low performance and I got it. *I now know that my low expectations ruined any possibility I had of extracting the best possible* *performance from those employees*. It was an utterly lost opportunity. Had I expected more, they may have performed better. If I had seen the best in them and worked with them to, as the army motto says, "be all they can be" then maybe they could have risen to the challenge. Unfortunately, we will never know. My perceptions were not part of the solution and if anything were part of the problem. If I had this all to do over again, then I would have certainly approached it differently.

Walking the Talk: Select a situation in your life where your perceptions might have influenced the people that you were forming impressions about. (1) **D**etermine whether you held preconceptions of these individual(s). (2) **E**valuate the extent to which your perceptions influenced the way in which you treated them and how they in turn reacted to this treatment. (3) **A**nalyze why you formed this picture and if adopting an alternative perception might have changed the outcome of the situation. (4) **L**everage these insights to develop reasonably positive perceptions that might impel you and others to greatness while avoiding unreasonably negative perceptions that unnecessarily pull people downward.

To combat negative effects and promote positive effects of the self-fulfilling prophecy in my perception, I will...

CHAPTER FOUR

Making Better and More Ethical Decisions

Chapter four examines management theories about individual decision making and the management skill of solving problems. Management and decision making are inexorably intertwined; in fact the job of manager is often described as primarily a decision-maker because this is a central if not dominant aspect of how they spend their time and add value. Decision making is particularly important at the very top of the hierarchy with senior management who bear the ultimate responsibility for decisions—that is, the "buck stops there." However individuals need not reach the CEO office to exercise their decision-making skills and meet its challenges. Managers at all levels of the organization make a seemingly countless number of choices each and every day. And they must do so rationally, creatively, and ethically. Rationality suggests taking a systematic and logical approach. Creativity implies incorporating new and useful ideas. Ethically involves determining what actions are "right" and what ends are "good" in a particular setting. Sounds good in theory but, alas, the business press is well stocked with stories about ill-conceived actions, outdated ideas, and "shady" business dealing. Yet on the positive side we also read accounts about managers' shrewd and reasoned deliberations, new and innovative thinking, and awakening to the importance of the environment and social responsibility. Taken together, it can be concluded that making decisions in a logical, creative, and well-intentioned manner are not mutually exclusive goals or irreconcilable characteristics from which we must choose. Managers can be successful, original, and ethical at the same time. In fact they must develop all of these skills if they are to achieve real and lasting performance. Therefore in this fourth chapter we look at how one can manage the problem solving process to make better decisions.

4.1 Appreciating the Importance of Rational Decision Making

Ask Yourself: How many decisions have you made today? This week? This year? Are all of your decisions perfectly rational and mathematically optimal? Do you consistently make the best of all possible choices? Should you? What steps could you take to better maximize your decision effectiveness?

Management Theory: Individuals are perpetual decision makers. Management theory defines this as the act of choosing a course of action to pursue an opportunity or confront a challenge in which there is more than one alternative solution. Essentially it refers to selecting a path when, figuratively speaking, life's roads diverge. Decision making is not a single event but more of a process. Appropriately, management theory contrasts many different approaches to it. A rational or "optimizing" approach is a systematic and comprehensive method for choosing quantitatively superior paths with mathematical rigor. Welcome to the machine. Here the manager defines the problem in unambiguous and certain terms, applies clear goals and indisputably prioritized criteria about what is more and less important, gathers information pertaining to the decision in an unbiased and completely accurate manner, delineates each and every possible alternative courses of action, methodically weighs and objectively evaluates all potential choices, and ultimately computes a course of action that maximizes their objectives. The primary basis of the "optimizing" model is that individuals are able and willing to act in a thorough and orderly manner to maximize their economic payoff. Of course this is not always the case. We are sometimes conflicted in our goals, unsure of our standards, incomplete in our search, biased in our judgment, or lacking in resources or time. However in the Internet age, available tools are enabling more extensive searches and wider access to ideas thus facilitating more informed decisions. All in all, the optimizing model is perhaps best fit for the really big choices in life that merit this degree of rigor and investment. Our story is by a service manager using the model to help solve a major problem related to a strategic issue of his job.

In Action [Case Study]: Recently my department was faced with a big decision of how to minimize our company's cost associated with a license fee for a core service we were offering. This service has been offered to clients for many years, and the cost of this license fee was absorbed by the company. In a major cost cutting effort, we were asked to evaluate the situation and find a way to pass this cost along to the client. The method we used most closely resembles the Optimizing Decision-Making Model. The decision required the systematic analysis of the situation. We first determined our criteria for the decision and then prioritized them, assigning weights to each option: (1) Minimize the financial impact to the client, (2) Remain competitive with other information provider's prices, and (3) Cover all or the majority of the license fee. We then dedicated tons of man-hours researching every source of information about what others have done in this area and their projected impacts. From this research, we then developed a thorough set of alternatives that were boiled down to four primary options: (1) Increase the price of the monthly workstation cost for the service that the customer was already paying, (2) Implement a monthly charge for each office using this service, (3) Charge a one-time installation fee, and (4) Spread a small amount of money each month across every client regardless of whether they were using this service and call it an administrative fee. We then evaluated the options using complex financial metrics and computerized projections. While each alternative would certainly do the job, when we crunched the numbers this led us to choose the first one, increase the price of the monthly workstation cost, as it represented the mathematically best alternative. *Using this method has worked out well for us. Our choice has proven to benefit most of the clients in the maximum possible way, has kept us competitive, and more than covered the license fee.* So far the decision has been very successful and this is due in large part to following the optimizing model.

Walking the Talk: Select a situation in your life where you needed to make a decision. (1) **D**etermine the key stages or steps in this decision-making process. (2) **E**valuate the degree to which they were systematically undertaken and achieved maximum results or were instead suboptimized. (3) **A**nalyze why this happened and how executing the optimizing model could improve the each stage as well as the ultimate decision outcome. (4) **L**everage these insights to enhance your ability to maximize the return on your decisions.

To make better appreciate the role of a rational, systematic approach to decision making, I will…

4.2   Engaging and Moderating the Practice of Satisficing

Ask Yourself: When making decisions, is "good enough" ever good enough? Do you always seek to make the best possible decision or sometimes just choose a solution that is satisfactory? Is every decision important enough to invest the time and resources into optimizing its solution? How do you decide when it is best to make optimal or merely acceptable decisions?

Management Theory: Earlier we spoke about the optimizing approach to decisions. However optimizing requires much effort and time and a simple cost-benefit analysis will reveal that this investment does not befit every decision. Sometimes, as Nobel Lauriat Herbert Simon explains, it is not so important to find the sharpest needle in a haystack but merely one sharp enough to sew with. Instead of behaving like perfectly rational automatons we are, more often than not, well-intended albeit flawed decision makers who do not always make the mathematically best decision but instead one that is simply ok or "good enough." We might not define a problem objectively; our predilections and stereotypes get in the way and lead us to more familiar pictures that have worked in the past. We might do not generate all possible solutions; our habits and search routines lead us to the easy and familiar. We might not comprehensively investigate all relevant information; we forego the supercomputer approach and simply invoke the most easily manageable and readily understood evidence. We might not establish and hold solutions to dream scenarios; instead the bar is set a little lower. This process usually leads us to select the first alternative that meets minimum standards. In other words, we frequently make satisfactory rather than optimal choices—for example, selecting a good enough (versus perfect) meal, outfit, job, commute, candidate, product, strategy. Balancing the time-versus-comprehensiveness trade-off is critical. Sometimes it is simply not worth the resources to optimize. The trick is to know when we should strive for rigorous maximization or settle for the good enough. Our story is by a manager whose company was engaged in such a decision situation.

In Action [Case Study]: Recently my Insurance Company (a big firm) faced a significant problem when one of our very important clients decided not to offer our HMO benefits to their employees in Denver and instead use a local provider. We needed to decide how to respond to this. According to the Satisficing Model, once a problem is identified, the search for criteria and alternatives begins with those that are easiest to find and that once this limited set of alternatives is identified the decision maker will choose the first one that looks good enough to solve the problem. The theory is right on in this situation. The alternative that seemed good enough to us at first review was to go into partnership with the local HMO. This would allow us to stay in Denver while offering its clients the benefits and service they wanted. *This partnership seemed to satisfy the basic goals of the firm: However, since only a simplified picture was looked at, several significant issues were not considered.* (1) Our Insurance Company systems and the local HMO systems are completely incompatible. As a result, special data transfers had to be established between the two systems or else some data will be lost. (2) We cannot completely close down the Denver HMO office if it wants to keep its HMO license. Therefore, although the other HMO will perform all of the local responsibilities, we must go to the expense of keeping a skeletal staff. (3) In the original plan, the local HMO would pay claims and perform member services on their systems. However, several of our important customers have very complex benefit plans that cannot be adjudicated on its systems. As a result, their company's employees may now have to use our systems. This presents learning problems since the two systems are completely different. As I have shown, the Satisficing Model may not be the most efficient when presented with complex problems that could have significant impacts. While the Satisficing Model may be faster than the Optimizing Model, as I am finding out now when it is really important either the time and resources will be spent initially to find the best alternative or they will be spent during the project trying to debug the merely good enough alternative.

Walking the Talk: Select a situation in your life where you settled for "good enough." (1) **D**etermine your minimum criteria for success and how thorough your decision process was. (2) **E**valuate the degree to which you reached or surpassed your baseline criteria. (3) **A**nalyze why the process was simplified, if this level of simplification was appropriate, and how alternative approaches would change the time-versus-comprehensiveness trade-off. (4) **L**everage these insights to develop appropriate levels of rigor to match the nature of the decision.

> To appropriately make use of satisficing in my decision making, I will...

4.3   Tapping into Your Intuition

Ask Yourself: Do you ever make decisions based on your gut? Go with what just feels right? Have you bypassed or even ignored computational analyses and formal procedures in favor of listing to an inner voice that you just could not explain? Is this a good way to make decisions?

Management Theory: Sometimes individuals' experience and expertise help them make decisions that do not follow a rigorous path per se but instead have an "invisible" rationality to them. That is to say, they go with their gut feeling to make decisions intuitively. Although on the surface this method might look haphazard and irrational it may in fact be just the opposite. Intuition is often a distillation of many years and experiences that provide us with insight and communicate a sort of unconscious logic. An intuitive approach to decision making is very different from the optimizing model—it shuns formal routines, detailed analyses, and drawn-out procedures while instead following a more holistic and imaginative approach that allows experts to quickly size up situations and make speedier choices. Witness how the most seasoned and accomplished decision makers, from executives to athletes, can use the same (or even less) information to make faster, more accurate decisions. This capacity is particularly important in the uncertain, ill-structured, and fast-moving situations that characterize the modern business climate. However, we must recognize that the intuitive approach to decision making is extremely reliant on the depth as well as relevance of the decision maker's background as well as their ability to coalesce and apply it to the situation at hand. It is thus more appropriate for individuals whose inner voice is well versed with the situation and who have developed the ability to hear and heed its guidance. Whereas the more comprehensive optimizing process has greater rigor and employs more safeguards, an intuitive approach adds a distinctly human or personal element to the analysis. Our story is by a seasoned securities broker turning to his intuition when needing to make a quick decision at work.

In Action [Case Study]: For many managers like me, we need to make decisions at the spur of the moment quite often. There is often no clear answer and a lack of information to select the best alternative. At the same time three key problems usually arise in the decision-making process. First, I do not always have the luxury of a complete array of choices laid out before me. Second, I do not have the time to look for the best answer and to do complete analyses. Third, the standard solution may not be the best because it goes against my gut feeling about what is right. Too often decisions are influenced by out-of-date policies or other employees when actually a better answer lies within me (and I am not sure why or how it got there). It is very seldom that my job supplies me with a clear road map. *To survive the hectic day, I sometimes make decisions using my gut. I guess this is because with time and experience on the job, I have been able to internalize the decision making and have eliminated the need for a full search, full test, and formal choice of a best alternatives approach.* In one example at work, a problem arose with one particular trade that was extremely large in terms of the traders P&L. The trade had been approved on both sides (buyer and sell) at the wrong price. I had to make a quick decision before the trading day opened, and that particular day was especially important because economic news was going to hit the street. Company norms told me to inform the accountant and simply change the price on the trade. However, I knew from experience that the economic news for that particular day was going to have an extremely important effect on the market. My gut reaction was to call the trader and simultaneously conference the broker in on the conversation to come to a decision fast and give the trader enough time to correctly hedge against his position. All parties were highly satisfied with my decision. Having gathered as much information as I could and arrayed as many alternatives as I had time to, I then had to balance process with my intuitive thinking. In complex problems, few tools exist to complete a thorough examination especially for managers. The competitive advantage often lies in the hands of a manager who can operate quicker with considerate savings in effort and considerable job effectiveness.

Walking the Talk: Select a situation in your life where you made a decision based on a gut feeling. (1) **D**etermine what the situation was and how your decision was made. (2) **E**valuate the role that your inner voice, as opposed to external analysis, played in the decision. (3) **A**nalyze where this feeling came from and if it was appropriate for the decision, as well as how you could have better developed and drawn on your unconscious expertise to increase effectiveness. (4) **L**everage these insights to enhance your ability to intuitively read situations and translate ingrained experience into engaged action.

> To better use intuition in my decision making, I will…

4.4   Avoiding Rationalization

Ask Yourself: Have you ever spent more time justifying a decision than making sure that it was in fact the best choice? Does a solution ever get chosen before you actually engage in the decision-making process? Is it common for people to advance their "pet" project or favorite option and then use the decision-making process simply to make this hidden agenda look good? How frequently do you spend your time rationalizing decisions?

Management Theory: Rationalization can be seen as a sort of "reverse rationality" in making decisions. When individuals rationalize a decision, they are not seeking to make the best choice. For all intents and purposes the choice has already been made. Instead they utilize their time, energy, and resources to simply justify their choice. This is because decision makers often have a preference for a course of action even before they embark on the process. They have a hidden agenda or "implicit favorite" if you will. A solution that they like better than the others for one reason or another—it is familiar, it is personally beneficial, it is easy, it is politically advantageous, and so on. As a result they become more concerned with justifying this decision rather than making sure that it is the best. Rationalization is described as reverse rationality because the decision-making process is essentially undertaken in a backward manner and stages are executed in the opposite order where the decision is made first instead of at the end of the process. Following the de facto choice of an implicit favorite, alternatives are often chosen that are prescreened to fail and make the preferred course of action look better. Comparative solutions are then used only as straw-men to be knocked down instead of being seriously considered as viable alternatives. Evaluation and assessment is then biased and criteria are slanted to favor the favorite. Ultimately managers complete this biased process by arriving at the predetermined solution then celebrating the "winner." Overall, management theory describes the rationalization process as placing a greater emphasis on appearing instead of actually being rational. Our story is by a software manager who is forthright in his admission that he often skews the decision process to convince clients to choose a favored approach even when it might not be in their best interests.

In Action [Case Study]: I manage a department that writes requirements for a software system used by regional operating companies to interface with the telecommunications equipment in their networks. As such, our system communicates with other systems that are manufactured by various companies external to us and the regional operating companies. My work is funded by these other manufacturers since support of their equipment in our system increases their equipment's value to the regional operating companies. Many times there are idiosyncrasies of the equipment that can be supported in our system in various manners, some methods of which are more costly than others, but which may be more beneficial to the operating companies. Typically when this situation arises, I need to speak to the manufacturer since that company will make the final decision as to how the idiosyncrasy will be supported. Although the manufacturer is the decision maker, I perform the steps that lead to the final decision. For better or worse, I believe that I follow the Implicit Favorite Model of decision making. For example, I typically have a standard response of what I want to do when presented with a problem. Then I go on to follow the Implicit Favorite Model of decision making, since I believe that the one solution is the least headache and most opportune from the start. So I give the manufacturer as many reasonable alternatives as possible and try to show him that I determined and evaluated the other alternatives in an objective manner, using ones that I believe are within the manufacturer's cost. After giving him several options, I evaluate these alternatives with various criteria (more or less costly, high or low impact on customers, etc.) but stress the criteria most consistent with my preference. *Then when ranking the options I most likely stop when I get to my "favorite" alternative and make it look like the process supports this decision.* The decision is then made with the manufacturer on how to proceed and, surprise, it is the one I favored from the beginning. This example illustrates to me the importance of looking objective and rigorous when making a decision especially with a client. Even though I did not really make the best decision for the client and in fact just chose the one easiest for me, it looked like I was fair and objective.

Walking the Talk: Select a situation in your life where you "dressed up" your decision to look better. (1) **D**etermine what your implicit favorite was in the situation and if this biased your decision process. (2) **E**valuate the degree to which efforts and resources were spent making the decision look better versus making a better decision. (3) **A**nalyze why looking versus being rational was so important and, if appropriate, how you could bring the decision process back into line. (4) **L**everage these insights to develop a more proactive and less rationalizing decision-making approach.

> To avoid excessive rationalization in my decision making, I will...

4.5   Enhancing Creative Decision Making

Ask Yourself: Are you a creative person? Can you be innovative and break the mold when you need to be? Does creativity typically follow a different pattern than the systematic steps of logical and objective decision making? Who are some of the most creative people that you know and what can you learn about how they make decisions?

Management Theory: Creativity is a critical component of performance across a wide range of jobs. This is because a large number of modern-day decisions address uncertain, complex, nonroutine problems that have no set algorithm or established answer. Therefore a priority is placed on the development of novel and useful ideas that can address these new business challenges. Indeed the capacity for creativity and innovation are consistently identified as central to managerial success. Notwithstanding the creative decision-making model is quite different from the rational model and tends to be underemphasized in formal education and training programs. As a result people tend to be underprepared and often times underrewarded for creativity. A classic model of creative decision making is often portrayed as a series of stages —(1) Preparation by actively researching the issue, (2) Concentration on the essential elements of the problem, (3) Incubation where the mind is freed from traditional constraints and the decision maker is given the opportunity and encouragement to think broadly and divergently about the problem, (4) Illumination when creative insight is recognized and original ideas are captured, and (5) Verification of a solution's fidelity and process of evaluating its practicality for implementation. Several techniques are modeled in management theory for facilitating all or some of these stages. They include but are not limited to the following: brainstorming, or suspending evaluation to generate multiple creative alternatives; synectics, or using analogy to explore alternative understandings of issues and solutions; and Janusean/dialectical thinking, or reversing the definition to simultaneously consider contradictory conceptions and challenge the normal ways that a problem is framed. Our story is by a project manager who uses dialectical techniques to creatively solve a workplace problem.

In Action [Case Study]: I feel that I am not creative enough at work. My plans for developing my creativity in solving problems were based on the method of dialectically "reversing the definition" that is especially effective because both sides of the situation are addressed, making the problem multidimensional. Last month I began to work on a project at work that I used to develop my creativity skills. This project's mission was to develop a straight-through and electronic way of booking anticipated dividends. The process has been extremely manual and increased volume had made managing the accurate booking of dividends a nightmare with high control risk. At the kickoff meeting, I laid out on the table what the issue at hand was. The project team then started to think of ways to improve the process. There were difficulties coming up with ideas because we all were thinking within the current system infrastructure's constraints and abilities. I started to use "reversing the definition" by saying that if our trading system were our books and records, what would it be like? If our custodian's dividend system could be like Bloomberg and Reuters, what could be the outcome? This started to get the team members' creative thoughts flying. The discussion began to turn into an active and productive session that generated three viable alternatives that revolved around: (1) developing an input screen on the existing transaction editor for just dividends and interest thereby having them flow electronically to our books and records, (2) creating a spreadsheet macro that could upload manually prepared dividend and interest journal entries into the books and records system, and (3) incorporating data feeds into our systems thereby using an electronically fed source of validated dividend and interest data. *The team said that it never thought it could have dreamed of such innovative, well-developed decision options in a short one hour discussion.* The earlier example is the only one I have of developing my creative skills. It proved to be extremely fruitful from both a personal and business perspective. I eagerly look for other opportunities to exercise this creative muscle on the job, especially using brainstorming and synectics. The result of definition reversal was positive and the team felt it had achieved an innovative solution. The success in this first meeting did more in establishing the team's healthy creative dynamic than all other teams I worked on ever did.

Walking the Talk: Select a situation in your life where creativity came into play. (1) **D**etermine the role of creativity in making the decision. (2) **E**valuate the degree to which your process mirrored the creativity model and was successful. (3) **A**nalyze why the outcomes were or might not have been as innovative as possible and how different strategies could have provided further direction. (4) **L**everage these insights to better utilize creativity enhancing techniques and develop skills related to creative decision making.

To be more creative in my decision making, I will...

4.6   Enhancing Ethical Decision Making

Ask Yourself: How morally mature are you in your decision making? Do you see something as good or bad depending on how it affects you personally? Or rather on the degree to which it conforms to formal standards and laws? Maybe the extent to which it adheres to a core set of principles? Are there things that you can do to strengthen and develop your personal integrity?

Management Theory: Individual ethics are largely a function of the core values that people use to formulate decisions. To the extent that we act honestly and faithfully in a manner consistent with our values we demonstrate personal integrity. Yet people vary in their degree of moral development when making choices. A widely applied theoretical model posits three general levels of moral maturity. The lowest level is termed "Pre-Conventional" and describes people who judge the ethics of a decision by the way that it affects them personally. If a person believes something is good merely because it helps them avoid punishment or gain a payoff (a "what is in it for me" attitude), then they are said to be self-centered in their values orientation. The middle level is termed "Conventional" and reflects an individual's deference to rules and regulations. If a person believes a decision is good merely because it fits the prevailing norms, complies with the presiding authority, and conforms to current policy (an "obey the rules" attitude), then they are said to be conforming in their values orientation. The highest level is termed "Post-Conventional" and applies to people who base their choices on fundamental ethical principles. If a person believes a decision is good because it advances comprehensive standards of good and bad (a "what is fundamentally right" attitude), then they are said to be principled in their values orientation. The third stage is the hardest to attain, especially given all the pressures that bear on the modern manager, but is best approximated by confronting value-laden issues and from these developing a set of reflective, internalized principles that can guide the individual through moral situations. Our story is by a brokerage manager confronting their company's "if its legal then it is ok" reasoning and attempting to move their decision making to a more principled stage.

In Action [Case Study]: At times I find that my moral values are challenged at my job. The brokerage industry can lead even good people astray with its capacity for big payoffs. Money makes right is the lowest level of values maturity. One case in particular caused me some concern. I noticed that investments in a million-dollar account for an elderly client were depreciating rapidly. The performance coupled with our firm's account fees caused the account to lose more than 10 percent of its value within a month. The client began calling our office and I would speak with her when the salesman in charge of the account was not available. I would tell her to think long-term, realize that she had a diversified portfolio and that she should ride out the current stock market fluctuations. This was of course a canned response I had used before. I began to wonder who was being best served in this decision, the client, or the salesman who is paid whether the account performs well or not. In fairness to the salesman, the client was informed of the short-term risks of the market, and she did sign a discretionary disclaimer for her money to be managed by our company. But my knee-jerk reaction was to tell her to transfer her account to a discount brokerage firm and manage her own money. She really did not need a high-priced asset manager to buy a variety of stocks and hold them long-term when she could do it herself. My thoughts were confirmed when the client placed an order on her own to buy a stock index and it outperformed our expert picks by more than 12 percent. I tried to rationalize that if she were not at our firm, another salesman at another firm could be treating her a lot worse. It just seemed that the business was tilted in favor of the salesman. *This situation made me consider whether my level of moral development was compatible with the decisions I was forced to make in my work. Just because what we were doing was legal did not make it right.* This would be just the middle level values maturity. The idea of confronting the salesman and asking him to lower the fees occurred to me, but that would be illegal because you cannot compensate a client for poor performance. I also thought of using another money manager for this client, but the new manager might create deeper loses. I made the choice that I would move to the analytical side of the business. That way, I can help clients and remain true to my principles by trying to ensure that the money managers pick better stocks and help them make decisions based on the best interests of all parties in the transaction. I start next Monday.

Walking the Talk: Select a situation in your life where your moral development was tested. (1) **D**etermine what type of ethical reasoning you applied to resolve the situation. (2) **E**valuate the degree to which your maturity was at an advanced (i.e., principled) stage of moral development. (3) **A**nalyze precisely where your actions diverged from your values and the reasons why this was the case. (4) **L**everage these insights to develop a plan for becoming more morally mature in your decision making and enhance your ability to act with integrity.

> To be more morally mature in my decision making and act with integrity, I will…

4.7   Reconciling Your Ethics with Industrial Standards

Ask Yourself: Do industries have different ethical standards? Are the dominant ways of thinking about ethics dependant on the field in which you are employed? Are these standards always appropriate and useful? How might you improve your professional ethics?

Management Theory: It can be said that industries, because of their different task and role demands, tend to enforce different professional standards and guidelines for behavior. Although ethical principles have been debated for millennia by many of the greatest philosophic minds of history, management theory has derived from them several themes that more or less apply to modern-day business practices. For example, a utilitarian perspective reinforces a results-oriented belief that the right way to behave is in whatever manner delivers the greatest amount of good to the greatest quantity of people. Its message to professionals is to make decisions that help the largest number of people in the biggest way—for instance "Maximize shareholder wealth." Alternatively a rights perspective promotes value-oriented beliefs that good behavior is that which respects peoples' basic endowments and privileges. Its message to professionals is to honor people's inalienable rights such as freedom and privacy—for instance "Protect the powerless." Finally a justice perspective encourages process-oriented thinking and defines good behavior as that which is fair and objective. Its message to professionals is to undertake reasonable and equitable decision processes—for instance "Do due diligence." Insofar as industry standards vary, they would seem to attract and develop different types of people whose personal values fit with their standards. A person whose personal ethics better match his or her industry ethics would be more likely to achieve higher levels of job satisfaction and, from a career management perspective, greater success. Yet if there are excessive professional pressures on managers to ignore personal ethics, say by encouraging people to take shortcuts and do whatever it takes to make a buck, then it could create the conditions for widespread ethical lapses. Our story is by a senior accountant whose observations explain some of the rampant ethical problems that plague the accounting industry.

In Action [Case Study]: Ethics has become an important issue in contemporary business world and as an executive in the accounting industry my field is no exception. Corporate scandals and economical downturn have induced trends toward creating rules, standards, and codes of ethics. Over the past several years, the accounting industry faced scathing criticism for failing to uncover massive accounting blunders. The scandals cost investors billions and led critics to contend that auditors are too afraid to confront management for fear of losing multimillion dollar consulting contracts. For the most part, conflict of interest is the major arena for dealing with ethical issues in decision making. *It is important to see that the out-of-control utilitarianism climate that we operate in the accounting industry can lead to less than ethical behavior and in some sense could possibly validate an auditor's decision to avoid going public with negative conclusions regarding a client's dishonorable procedures!* Typically once questionable practice becomes public, investor's stockholdings diminish significantly. Therefore, revealing of unethical practice is not beneficial for investors at all. Moreover, this unethical practice is meant to create artificial value for the investor, which of course could be realized as monetary profit for company's executives and larger fees for the auditing firm. On the other hand, unethical practice grants unfair advantage to this company over others in their competition for capital resources. In other words, auditor's decision to let such practice go vigorously violates principles of individual rights and social justice. To create ethical guidance, The American Institute of Certified Public Accountants sets U.S. auditing and professional ethics standards with the Financial Accounting Standards Board. This policy is targeted to help auditors root out dishonorable practice, reduce the climate of purely utilitarianism that has led people to do bad things, and restore integrity in the accounting industry following the slew of corporate scandals. I could not agree more with these changes in professional standards because it is hard for people to do the right thing on their own with so much money at stake. I also feel that the better laws and stricter enforcement will work only if they are continuously updated so it is difficult for dishonorable people to find creative ways around them.

Walking the Talk: Select a situation in your life where professional ethics were important. (1) **D**etermine what the professional ethics were. (2) **E**valuate the degree to which they helped you to appropriately and successfully make decisions. (3) **A**nalyze why the professional ethics evolved in this manner and how they might be enhanced. (4) **L**everage these insights to better match your and your profession's ethical standards and/or act to proactively improve them.

To make decisions that reinforce or improve my professional ethics, I will…

4.8   Reconciling Your Ethics with Organizational Standards

Ask Yourself: Do organizations have different ethical standards, even those that operate in the same industry? Are the dominant ways of thinking about ethics dependant on the firm in which you are employed? Are these standards always appropriate and optimal? How might you contribute to improving your organizational ethics?

Management Theory: It can similarly be said that organizations, because of their different histories and business models, have different standards and value-sets. These are referred to as organizational ethics. Even in the same industry, two corporations might apply different codes of conduct to what should otherwise be similar types of jobs and practices. Thus management theory suggests that organizations will vary in terms of their moral codes, value systems, and in the types of decisions that they tolerate and reward. Employees operating within this environment both effect and are affected by it. Certainly individuals will pick up cues about what is right and wrong from the prevailing organizational climate and their bosses who perpetuate it. Thus a firm's dominant ethics are strong influence on individuals' decisions. However employees also bring their own ethics, values, and standards of behavior into the firm. These personal standards can affect others who can choose to abide or challenge the firm's prevailing ethics. Thus ethical climates can be managed and even changed. The result of all of these different codes operating under one proverbial roof is an intermingling of approaches that can facilitate or undermine moral decision making. Of particular importance are managers who, in addition to their influence on formal rules and informal understandings, serve as role-models for others in the organization. Of course this does not mean that other individuals have no responsibility to stand up against unethical practices and, as per the "whistle-blower" who risks their job to report ethical transgressions, act as a check on organizational activities. Our story is by a marketing manager who was faced with an executive's apparently sanctioned unethical behavior at their firm.

In Action [Case Study]: Good people can be encouraged to do bad things when their organization's reward system positively reinforces wrong behaviors. My last position was as the creative resources manager at a major direct marketing advertising agency. I reported to chief creative officer of the agency. My responsibilities included finding candidates for open positions and obtaining their portfolio of work for review by the four creative directors. If I liked the portfolio, I showed it to the chief creative officer. For one of the positions open in the agency, I received a portfolio of a woman who worked for one of our major competitors. As the chief creative officer reviewed this portfolio, he noticed an advertising campaign that was going to air for one of our client's competitors. He took the TV spot, copied it, and sent it around to several other people in the agency. He attached a note saying do not ask where he got it but here is the next TV spot for one of our major competitors, what can we do to counter it. I believe this action was unethical. Although this woman included the TV spot in her portfolio, it was proprietary information and should not have been copied and used by the agency. The management theory states that when an organization praises and offers other desirable rewards to employees who lie, cheat, and misrepresent, its employees learn that unethical behaviors payoff. When the other people in the agency received the TV Spot, they were very impressed that the chief creative officer obtained a copy of the spot. He was given significant praise because his actions put the agency and our client a step ahead of our competitors. His thought process might have been—by stealing the TV spot, we would gain a competitive advantage so the actions are validated. *This situation presented special difficulties for me to address the unethical behavior since the chief creative officer, one of our top manager, committed the act. This is very important since their actions actually help shape the behaviors of others in the agency.* I decided to recommend that the agency take several steps to correct this situation and promote ethical decision making: (1) investigated where the chief creative officer obtained the TV Spot, (2) immediately demanded that all copies of the TV Spot be returned and destroyed, (3) inform the other agency that employees are including proprietary information in their portfolios, and (4) taken action against the chief creative officer so he and others in the agency would learn that unethical behaviors will not be tolerated. Regardless of how this situation works out, you can be sure that I will carry this experience with me when I am someday running my own advertising company.

Walking the Talk: Select a situation in your life where organizational ethics were important. (1) **D**etermine what the organization's ethics were. (2) **E**valuate the degree to which they helped to you appropriately and successfully make decisions. (3) **A**nalyze why the organizational ethics evolved in this manner and how they might be enhanced. (4) **L**everage these insights to better match your and your organization's ethical standards and/or act to proactively improve them.

> To make decisions that reinforce or improve my organizational ethics, I will…

4.9   Promoting Social Responsibility

Ask Yourself: Do managers have a responsibility to the larger community in which they work? Should their abilities and energy be used beyond the boundaries of their organization to help outside stakeholders, communities, or the environment in general? Is this type of behavior something that managers should also encourage among their employees? If so then how might a manager best support social engagement?

Management Theory: An large and growing stream of management theory argues that employees and their organizations have a responsibility that goes beyond profit-generation and maximizing shareholder wealth. At least this is the thesis as put forth in theories relating to (corporate) social responsibility. It is derived from the idea that business and society are unavoidably interdependent. People need organizations for the jobs that they provide and the goods and service that they produce, and organizations in turn need people and the larger society from which they come for the resources and structure that they provide. Therefore there is an ethical obligation for managers, as the agents of business and residents of society, to bring them into harmony. Specifically, there exists a social responsibility by managers to behave ethically and contribute to economic development while improving the quality of life of the workforce and their families as well as of the local and larger community. This relates to the ethical issue of "sustainability"—the pursuit of higher standards of living in a manner that does not compromise the well being of future generations. The principle is also crystallized in the business framework of a "Triple Bottom Line" where managers are encouraged to make decisions that simultaneously enhance outcomes along economic, social, and human dimensions. In addition managers can facilitate social responsibility through programs or initiatives that promote philanthropic endeavors that are consistent with the mission and scope of their organization. Not only are socially responsible decisions supportive of an enlightened ethical framework, but they have also been found to be good business by increasing individuals' satisfaction, strengthening their identity with and potential within the organization, and enhancing the organization's and employees' reputation. Our story is by a manager involved in her company's outreach efforts but not completely satisfied with its level of support.

In Action [Case Study]: All competitive firms advertise some level of community engagement and social responsibility. The level of interest does seem to depend on what the expectations and ethics are of its top managers which made this theory particularly interesting to me. My firm appears to be very socially responsible on paper, we even financed a children's hospital (and by we I mean the employees personally donated most of the money raised), but it is my belief that it is truly the individual managers who create the socially responsible environment. The children's hospital recently had an event that I had the opportunity to participate. I was disappointed with the lack of funding and concern that the firm had but saw that the managers' involvement in donating their time and promoting the cause were the primary reasons for a successful event. It pains me to say this, but I have found that many firms, including mine, tend to participate in socially responsible events more for the appearance than truly good intentions. *This is why it is so important for the managers to take the initiative and bring a real attitude of social responsibility into the firm.* Another example is the scheduling for employees to volunteer. My firm publishes volunteer opportunities but does not want to loose you for the day to volunteer; you are expected to do it on your own time. Many people in my department volunteer on their own and keep asking for more opportunities to do this company-wide. I decided to approach top management and mentioned that if the firm was truly interested in the cause then they should be more flexible with time and allowing employees to participate. They seemed to agree but we will see if this translates into any action. People are more likely to be loyal to a firm that they see encouraging them and allowing them to act in a socially responsible way, allowing employees to participate in community events to give them a sense of accomplishment and self-worth. This in turn can decrease attrition and even increase productivity. I know that I would be more likely to stay with a firm and work harder if I felt that it was genuinely concerned not only with their bottom line or meeting budgets but also with other stakeholders such as their local community and larger causes such as the environment.

Walking the Talk: Select a situation in your life where as a manager or employee you had the opportunity to contribute to the larger community. (1) **D**etermine whether you in fact engaged in these types of behaviors. (2) **E**valuate the degree to which your decisions would be deemed socially responsible. (3) **A**nalyze why you did or did not act in a socially responsible manner and how you could have better facilitated this in yourself or your employees. (4) **L**everage these insights to develop an enhanced approach to social responsibility and the skills to execute and promote it.

To make decisions that better promote social responsibility, I will...

SECTION II

Meso Management (+Them): The Interpersonal

For Engaging in More Effective Interactions

You **+ Them** = Us

CHAPTER FIVE

Communicating Effectively with Others

Chapter five examines management theories about interpersonal communication and applying the management skill of communicating accurately and supportively. Communication is the process whereby people transfer their thoughts into symbolic form (encoding), interact with others to convey this message (channel), and then listen to and interpret others' feedback (decoding). As such it is the bridge that unites us, the bond that links us, the conduit that brings us together— for without it people would simply coexist without the potential to cooperate or collaborate. In the business world, it is how people share information and convey ideas to one another. Think about it—Are we communicating right now? Perhaps. This would depend if I was successful in articulating the ideas from my head onto this paper, if this book is the proper medium for expressing its meaning, and if you are relating to and internalizing its message. Across all of our face-to-face, written, and electronic communications we have, the above three-step model provides a common platform for understanding and managing their processes. Management theories provide a set of essential principles for conducting the communication process that, if applied well, can enhance the success of our interactions. Therefore in this fifth chapter we begin our examination of interpersonal management by looking at how one can better communicate more effectively with people.

5.1 Appreciating the Importance of Communication

Ask Yourself: To be a good manager do I need to be a good communicator? How much of my time is spent communicating in one form or another? How much of what goes wrong in my interactions with others is because of poor communication? To what extent does communication determine personal, team, and business success?

Management Theory: Communication is the process where two or more people construct, transfer, and receive meaning. Research shows that nearly three-quarters of a manager's time is spent engaged in some form of communicative activity and, due to advances in technology and information systems, this is now being done through an increasingly diverse and complex set of tools. Managers communicate when they craft a policy report or post a blog, send an e-mail or deliver a speech, and read memoranda or listen to others at meetings. And it is through this inter-personal dynamic that people connect with each other to accomplish tasks and achieve results. Thus communication is the proverbial glue that binds people together and gets them on the "same page." Communication skills permeate all facets of managerial life and facilitate the individual-level topics discussed in section one (e.g., getting feedback on self, making sense of the world, motivating others effectively) as well as underlie the organi-zational-level processes in section three (e.g., building a positive culture, harnessing the power of diversity, leading people successfully). As such the quality of communication contributes to whether positive or negative synergy is attained. Thus it makes sense that good communication is the subject of so many popular books and self-help manuals, numerous college majors and academic studies, and entire corporate departments and pro-fessional careers. Yet notwithstanding this attention, interpersonal activity is rife with miscommunication, and research suggests that poor commu-nication skills are one of the most frequent sources of managers' problems. Upshot—good communication can create a harmonious and focused entity, but poor communication can unravel and alienate even the best intended manager. Our story is by a manager describing some problems caused by dysfunctional communication processes in her organization.

In Action [Case Study]: Communication is a skill that I feel most man-agers have yet to master. At my old company this was particularly true. Communication there was mean spirited, inefficient, and created a neg-ative work climate. I remember one incident when an attorney wrote a long flowery letter to our department head describing a problem. I hap-pened to be in the head office when the letter arrived. She immediately told the attorney to come to her office, and she ripped up the document right in front of him and berated him like a child. The attorney from that point lost all loyalty to the company and never really gave their best effort to support the manager. The downward communication between execu-tive management and the rest of the company was also terrible. We were merging with another company and all of our employees were on edge. Management was not sharing any details about this merger. When I and some colleagues worked up the guts to ask our boss directly about this, he just made some excuse for leaving and did not say anything. As a result, we turned to the "grapevine" to gather information about the pending merger. Was the gossip right? If you listened to the grapevine, we were all laid off about five times and there was a new CEO about three times. I felt that this lack of communication affected my decision to leave the company. I did not really want to quit my job but felt that I had no choice. If management had made an official announcement about the pending merger, the whole situation could have changed. Department heads could have met with their team members and had open and honest dialog about the company's future. *I learned from this that without good communication from senior management no one really knew where he or she stood with the company and that without this they would never earn our loyalty.* Even if you were not laid off, no one knew what the future of the company was going to be and no one knew what their role in the merged company was going to be. If management had been more honest, I wouldn't have been so distrustful and apt to look for other employment. When I left the company, I did not even do an exit interview! At this interview maybe I would have suggested that the company need to improve its internal communication.

Walking the Talk: Select a situation in your life where good communication was critical. (1) **D**etermine whether communication was a factor in the outcome of the situation. (2) **E**valuate the degree to which the quality of communication helped or hurt the situation. (3) **A**nalyze where and why communication went awry and might have been improved. (4) **L**everage these insights to develop a healthier appreciation for the importance of communication in personal as well as professional success.

> To better appreciate the importance of good communication, I will...

5.2   Encoding: Using Language Well

Ask Yourself: How important is it to select the "right words" when communicating? Do words have only one meaning or can this change depending on the way people use and hear them? Is it helpful to use acronyms and highly technical terms when communicating? What are the advantages and potential problems to jargon-laced communication?

Management Theory: The communication process can be understood as a series of three types of activities that happen in a recurring loop. The first is "encoding," or when a speaker translates his or her thoughts into a symbolic form such as words, pictures, or expressions. How well someone encodes his or her thoughts into words sets the stage for the entire communication process. This can be done more or less ably depending on the skills of the writer or speaker. As there are many different languages in the world, the global manager must first take care in matching the encoded language to that of the listeners. It is also important to note that even in the same formal language, there are different dialects, styles, and subsets of languages—for example, U.K. versus U.S. English, academic versus street English, New York versus California English, and baby-boomer versus Gen-Y English. We can further identify systematic language differences between industries, companies, departments, and occupations (e.g., IT versus manufacturing languages). Thus it behooves us to encode our thoughts into the appropriate form. One of the potential barriers to this is in the misuse of jargon, or specialized terminology. Jargon can be useful because it allows that members of a group use to express complex thoughts quickly and accurately among themselves with simple, standardized symbols and acronyms. However, jargon can impede communication between people from different groups because it has little to no meaning to those outside its user group. When thoughts are conveyed using foreign difficult-to-understand terminologies, communication begins to break down from the get-go. Therefore management theory suggests that jargon should be used only when it leads to in-group efficiencies but should be limited when communicating with those outside the specialized group. In general a simple, clear encoding strategy that is customized to the listener avoids the trappings of overly technical language. Our story is by a manager reflecting on the pros and cons of encoding with jargon-laden terms.

In Action [Case Study]: One of the biggest barriers to effective communication is "language." Within an organization, the grouping of employees into departments, functionally, geographically, and so on can lead to the development of jargon or technical language. According to management theory, this can lead to misinterpretation and misunderstanding when there is communication between groups that have modified language in their own ways. During this past summer when visiting our Midwest division, I was exposed to a group that had developed a language entirely of its own. *The use of jargon is so extensive in this group that I was given a list of acronyms and definitions my very first day, just so that I could understand the daily conversation.* It was like I was visiting a foreign country and did not speak the language. Not only did the division as a whole speak in code, each team had its own dialect. In other words, there was a full set of acronyms or buzzwords that were understood throughout the branch, and then there was another list that would specifically apply to a particular discipline or customer group. To confuse matters even more, there were many overlaps. For example, depending on the topic of conversation and the person to whom you were speaking, I found out that B.I. could mean bodily injury or business income. It was not unheard of for managers who had been with the company for years to sometimes stop a speaker in the middle of a meeting and ask for clarification. The heavy use of jargon had very different effects on performance depending on who you were. Within this group the use of this verbal and written shorthand proved to be very efficient. I believe that the level of satisfaction may have been higher than otherwise as a result of this use of language. It was almost like playing a game or being in a special club. However when communicating with people from other departments and people outside the company, they simply could not understand what we were talking about half the time and on more than one occasion assumed we meant one thing when we actually meant something else. Language can definitely strengthen the connection between employees and their group. However we really need to be careful not to get so lost in our own language that we harm our ability to coordinate with the rest of the company and connect with customers.

Walking the Talk: Select a situation in your life when you or someone else encoded in a technical manner. (1) **D**etermine whether jargon was applied to the interaction and to what extent it was used. (2) **E**valuate the degree to which the jargon helped or hindered communication. (3) **A**nalyze where and why jargon impacted encoding effectiveness and how it could have been better used (or not used). (4) **L**everage these insights to enhance your ability to use technical language appropriately.

> To better encode my thoughts into words and effectively utilize technical language, I will...

5.3   Encoding: Avoiding Excess Filtering

Ask Yourself: Do people always tell the truth, the whole truth, and nothing but the truth? Or is it more common to communicate (or hear about) only a small part of the picture? Should you always strive to give a complete account of issues or instead might it sometimes be better to finesse them to help you look good? What are the potential interpersonal problems which arise from excessively filtering information?

Management Theory: A second type of encoding barrier to communication is excessive "filtering." Just as an air filter traps some particles while letting others through, people filter communications to selectively convey pieces of information while holding back others. Filtering happens for a variety of reasons. It can be a natural outcome of the many mouths and minds that are involved in the communication process. Thus it acts to prevent us from being overwhelmed by too much information. Furthermore people unconsciously interpret and repackage messages according to their preferences and perceptions. This is why you typically see more filtering in large groups or organizations—there are just more layers and people (i.e., filters) that a communication needs to pass through. Filtering can also be purposeful. It is not fun to be the "bearers of bad news" so people often subtlety spin a message to appear rosier and avoid being victimized by a "kill the messenger" mentality. There might also be blatant manipulators who have few qualms about actively distorting messages to serve their career interests. Thus filtering can serve political rather than logical interests when information is intentionally manipulated just to make the speaker look better—sharing good news and hiding the bad news, citing the supportive evidence while omitting the contrary data, emphasizing your successes while having selective amnesia about your failures, and sending what you think the listener wants to hear while withholding the parts of a message that you feel they do not need to know. Notwithstanding the motive, filtering is a potential barrier to good communication because it can distort information given to managers and other decision makers and hide problems that could be better addressed with the proper input. Our story is by a manager who encountered filtering problems with an overly ambitious colleague.

In Action [Case Study]: Debbie, the General Manager of my record label, was very public about her career ambitions. The information Debbie filtered to upper management often did not reflect the true level of performance of her division, but rather was designed to show her managerial strengths in the best possible light to further her own career ambitions. A few months ago, the organization was restructured. One of Debbie's key managers, Kim, was offered a lateral position within the company, with more opportunities for career growth. Kim enjoyed a wonderful reputation within the industry and was highly effective in her job. Debbie did not want to lose her. When Kim came to Debbie and told her of the job offer, Debbie responded by saying that it was impossible for her to leave her current situation because she must honor the terms of her employment contract that was another two years. This was partly true but what Debbie conveniently left out (filtered) was that there were several instances in the past where employees were allowed to leave their contract early. Debbie reported the incident to her boss Sam and told him that she was successful in keeping Kim with her contract but did not say how this was done (more filtering). Shortly thereafter, the manager who made the job offer to Kim phoned Sam and asked why Debbie's division would not be flexible and release Kim from her employment contract. He pointed out that it was a bad idea and against the general organizational culture for the company to hold back the careers of promising employees. He also asked why others were let out of their contracts early and not Kim. When Sam learned the truth about how Debbie filtered this information to him, he was understandably furious. *Upper management would not be able to make effective decisions about the division with the incomplete information that Debbie provided. Debbie's propensity to filter and spin information also reinforced her reputation as a shameless self-promoter.* None of her direct reports trusted that she would represent their individual accomplishments to upper management, but rather would try to take all the credit for herself. As a result, morale by her staff was very low. Debbie's direct reports were united in their mistrust of Debbie. These factors led to even lower satisfaction and more turnovers within the division.

Walking the Talk: Select a situation in your life where you or someone else filtered communication. (1) **D**etermine whether a complete or selective accounting of the situation was given. (2) **E**valuate the degree to which this filtering was excessive and whether it helped or hurt the communication. (3) **A**nalyze where and why filtering occurred and how it might be used more appropriately. (4) **L**everage these insights to better manage your use of filtering and develop mechanisms for adjusting its use in your and others communications.

> To avoid excessive filtering in my and others' communications, I will…

5.4   Channel: Matching the Media to the Message

Ask Yourself: Is it usually best to communicate with others in person? By e-mail or text? Perhaps in a letter or memo? Can you bias the communication process by using channels that provide too little or too much information? How do high-performing managers match the communication media to best suit their message?

Management Theory: We now consider the second stage of the communication process and the managerial challenge of selecting the appropriate medium to best connect the speaker and listener. Management theory points to the concept of "richness" as a key determinant in deciding which channel is best for which message. What is richness? It refers to the information carrying capacity, speed, direction, and personable nature of a communication channel. The more information that can be transmitted faster and with multiple cues makes for a richer communication media. For example, face-to-face communication is the richest channel available with maximum information potential, verbal as well as nonverbal cues such as gestures and expressions, high interactivity via rapid response and instant feedback, and within a generally closer, more intimate setting. By contrast a memo is less rich because it neither conveys the same amount of information, nor does it as fast or personably. Telephone and e-mail would be somewhere in the middle as would texting and video conferencing. When do you use richer channels? Theory directs managers to select channels that fit the relative complexity and ambiguity of what is to be communicated. In other words, managers should match the media to the message. On the one hand, less critical and routine messages can be handled through relatively poor media. If media is overly rich for the message, then it introduces too much extraneous information and overcomplicates the communication. It also uses too much time and resources; consider the seemingly endless meetings that go on and on about issues that could more efficiently be addressed through less-rich media. On the other hand, important and nonroutine issues should be discussed through richer media. If media is too poor for the message, then it restricts the exchange of vital information and oversimplifies the communication. Bottom line—high performing managers are more media sensitive. Our story is by an employee who witnessed a violation of the richness principle in his workplace.

In Action [Case Study]: Many work environments, such as my own, have multiple channels of communication. The channels can vary from simple face-to-face feelings or gestures to e-mail or telephone. Sometimes poor media choices cause a mixed message to develop a misunderstanding. One example of this recently occurred with a product that I was working on, a short-term money market derivative that auctions daily and settles next day. The manager on the financial desk had sent a quick note asking me to change the date on the trades so not to reflect the next days settlement because it was considered a holiday. Unfortunately, I misunderstood his casual e-mail request to simply mean changing the date on the hard copy trade that the input staff entered into the system. What in turn happened was a complicated problem that caused the auctions to be wrong in the customers view, and consequently the problem took three days of time to fix instead of ten seconds. *The information-poor one way communication approach that my manager used led to an unnecessary misunderstanding that disrupted operations and wasted both of our time.* What happened that day is a perfect example of a poor choice of information medium. When not enough of a message is sent to indicate the presence of urgency or priority, miscommunication will occur. I realize now that communication is a two way street, if you are not sure of the message you should ask more questions, and if important it is critical to use a richer communication medium. I was not able to "feel" the importance of the message, and I was not able to "hear" the tone of the language he was trying to convey. I thought I knew what my manager wanted me to do but as it turned out the request involved a complicated manipulation of the computer system that I did not fully understand. The choice of medium that you use to communicate at work is a critical decision that must include consideration for the receiver of your message and the level of importance of the message.

Walking the Talk: Select a situation in your life where the selection of a communication channel was important. (1) **D**etermine what media channel was utilized and its level of richness. (2) **E**valuate the degree to which the choice of media helped or hurt the communication. (3) **A**nalyze why the channel was chosen and how a better match might have been selected. (4) **L**everage these insights to enhance your use of communication media and develop a more sophisticated approach to channel selection.

To more effectively match the media to my message, I will...

5.5   Channel: Facilitating Upward Communication

Ask Yourself: Do employees always communicate openly and honestly with their boss? Do you with your boss? Do your people with you? Why not? How can you get workers to engage more freely in upward communication?

Management Theory: Communication within an organization can flow in many different directions: downward from a manager to a subordinate, horizontal between two people at the same level of the hierarchy, or upward from an employee to a manager. Each of these has its own peculiarities but none perhaps is as challenging than getting their employees to communicate openly and honestly up the chain of command. Upward communication is necessary for managers due to a host of reasons—it keeps them informed about what their employees are working on and their progress, accesses worker knowledge and ideas to make improvements, enables them to involve others in the decision-making process, improves the morale of their people, and completes the communication cycle by gathering feedback about how well their own downward communications have been received and understood. Yet upward communication is continuously reported in management theory as being among the most difficult and least frequently executed forms of communication. This is because of several barriers to communicating in an upward direction. Status differences between an employee and manager can interfere with open dialog by limiting the number and quality of interactions, intimidating employees, or distancing managers. The fear of giving bad news can prevent employees from sharing complete information. The desire to be liked can motivate employees to become a sycophant and only agree with the manager instead of providing honest information and good judgments. The need for rewards and favorable reviews can promote the covering up of issues that might prove damaging to the organization. Ultimately managers need to hear about bad news, different opinions, and potential problems if they are to solve problems and do their jobs properly. This often requires special efforts to keep the upward flow alive, such as suggestion boxes, open-door policies, no-risk feedback sessions, and other interventions that promote trust and openness. Our story is by a manager who successfully implemented several such methods for promoting upward communication.

In Action [Case Study]: As a manager at a multinational corporation I have found that encouraging upward communication is one of the best ways to get feedback, monitor progress toward goals, and get a sense of current problems that would normally not be detected until it is too late. Upward communication keeps me aware of how employees feel about their jobs, coworkers, me, and the organization in general. It reduces uncertainty and helps me adjust my style in dealing with some of my subordinates. I also rely on upward communication for ideas on how things can be improved. One of the methods I started using more was one-to-one discussion with my subordinates through the scheduling of "gripe" sessions. *I found that through these sessions the upward communication raised many issues and concerns that I was unaware of.* Just last week at one of our meetings, a subordinate told me that their team was going to be late on a deadline. The gripe session gave them the freedom to open up to me about their frustration with out-of-date tools, territory battles, and personality clashes without worrying about being disciplined for their honesty. This is something that I normally would never hear if I was pent up in my office, too busy with other business to talk informally with the staff, or too closed-minded to want to hear the truth. As they were given the opportunity to speak freely about these things and as I genuinely listened and helped out where possible, the upward communication has definitely increased job satisfaction among my subordinates. By clarifying distortions and ambiguities, and straightening out who should be doing what, uncertainty was reduced and this had a positive effect on job satisfaction. I can relate to this because I have also begun to use upward communication better in dealing with my boss, where I am the one communicating upward, and found it to be very satisfying. Job performance was also improved through upward communication. This was mainly due to questions that were asked by subordinates about clarification of certain tasks and the overall goals of the department. I believe that the opportunities that were given to the staff for upward communication helped to motivate them and build trust and this has resulted in a low-turnover rate as well as a low-absenteeism rate.

Walking the Talk: Select a situation in your life where upward communication was critical. (1) **D**etermine whether upward communication took place and in what form. (2) **E**valuate the degree to which these upward flows were adequate in amount and quality. (3) **A**nalyze why the levels of upward communication persisted and how they might be increased or improved. (4) **L**everage these insights to enhance your ability to promote and initiate effective upward communication.

To facilitate upward communication, I will...

5.6   Channel: Managing the Grapevine

Ask Yourself: Do you ever engage in office gossip? Listen to rumors or even help spread them? How can managers reduce the negative effects of the grapevine? Alternatively how might they strategically use it to become better communicators?

Management Theory: Managers communicate through both formal and informal channels. Formal communication typically follows the official reporting hierarchy as specified in the organizational chart. Alternatively, informal communication is more spontaneous, free-forming, and unpredictable in a manner that resembles a grapevine as it winds its way around the office skipping levels, bypassing divisional or hierarchical barriers, and circumventing authorities. This grapevine exists in response to an information gap—the difference between what employees want to know versus what they are told by management—and fuels rumors that can diffuse rapidly throughout an organization. The grapevine thus supplements more formal channels and can help people make sense of their surroundings, reduce stress caused by lack of information, and provide a check on managements' message. Management theory suggests that grapevine communication tends to be quite fast and for the most part accurate, but it can also do much harm by magnifying half-truths and misinforming employees. Indeed it is its very speed and lack of formal direction that makes the grapevine so open to inaccuracies. If allowed to grow too strong, it can even overwhelm formal channels and reduce management's ability to control information flows. Thus managers can take the starch out of the grapevine through more accurate and complete formal communications that reduce the need for rumors and gossip. And because grapevines can rarely be eliminated entirely, managers are advised to be sensitive to the informal network, monitor its accuracy, and address any potential contradictions in its message. Managers can also harness the power of the grapevine to further formal agendas since they too have the potential to plant messages (employees typically regard informal communication as more believable) or to listen for information and rumors circulating among their employees. Our story is about a manager learning about how to use the grapevine in their firm.

In Action [Case Study]: Just like it says in management theory, my company grapevine is filled with gossip and rumors that flow vertically and laterally, skips authority levels, serves the self-interests of those within it, and is perceived as being more believable and reliable than formal communications. It is also frequently false. In my organization this was definitely true especially for a worker named Laura. Laura's desk was located near the conference room. We later found out that she could overhear most of what was discussed in our triweekly managers' meetings or any other meeting for that matter. The power of "letting others in" on the fragmented or pieced-together information became a meaningful part of Laura's "job." *To the majority of the workers, the rumors and gossip supplied by Laura and others was an important way to acquire information not supplied by the managers.* Truth be told, we did not always level completely with the employees in our weekly briefings so people relied on her to fill them in on what was really happening in the company. The information back road was a remarkable piece of work. It was rather amusing to test the grapevine one day by walking by Laura and saying something completely false to my colleague, loud enough for Laura to overhear. The speed at which the rumor went around the company was astounding. This showed me how powerful the grapevine was and how important it was for managers to control it. It also made me skeptical of any information that came out of it, knowing how easy it was to plant and spread false rumors. Overall the need for and power of the grapevine, as a conduit of information for the rank and file, was immense. The secrecy between management and our production employees created an environment that encouraged and sustained it. If we were more honest and open about things, its power would go away but this was not the case. The informal network had a roller coaster effect on the satisfaction of the workers. Their mood would go up and down before I or other managers would find out about and formally discount, reinforce, or clarify false gossip. The production of the workers was also negatively affected, as too much time was spent conversing with coworkers discussing rumors. Although we cannot completely control the informal network, I learned that more effective feedback in my formal communications would reduce its consequences. In the future I also intend to get even more plugged into the grapevine to find out about rumors before they spread too far.

Walking the Talk: Select a situation in your life where you witnessed the grapevine in action. (1) **D**etermine whether informal networks coexisted, supplemented, or substituted for formal channels. (2) **E**valuate the degree to which the grapevine helped or hurt communication. (3) **A**nalyze why people engaged in gossip and how this process could have been better managed. (4) **L**everage these insights to develop the ability to reduce or more effectively utilize the grapevine.

To better manage the grapevine, I will…

5.7   Decoding: Engaging in Active Listening

Ask Yourself: Are you a good listener? (Most people say "yes," but…) Would other people agree with your answer to this question? Do effective managers spend more of their time talking or listening? Should listening be a passive or active process? How important are listening skills to ensuring effective interpersonal communication?

Management Theory: Managers are generally a social bunch and like to talk. In fact people in general tend to think that what they have to say is more important than other peoples' messages, and many gain much more pleasure, status, and a sense of power when they are the ones doing the speaking. However the most effective communicators spend a larger portion of their time and energy listening to others. This presents a significant communication challenge. Whereas in this chapter we have discussed encoding and channel skills we must therefore pay due attention to decoding skills—that is, interpreting a communication. The central challenge here is to truly grasp the information that was sent instead of processing a partial, distorted, or mistaken message. One of the most effective tools for improving decoding is through active listening. This happens when the manager avoids unnecessary distractions to fully embed themselves in the listening process by engaging in such behaviors as questioning, probing, and reflecting to ensure that they have received the message. Active listening involves not just passively hearing (using your ears) but giving full attention to the speaker to really understanding what is said (using your brain). For example, listening is active when a manager asks a coworker questions to make sure that they fully understood their daily task, briefing, instructions, or report. One of the most effective tools for active listening is also ironically one of the simplest—"paraphrasing," or restating the sender's ideas in your own words so that you can check to ensure that your perceptions match that of the speaker. Paraphrasing is not parroting or simply repeating the very same words that were spoken to you, it is reflecting back what you understood as the meaning of the message to assure that all parties are on the same page. Our story is by a manager who discovers the power of a more active style of listening.

In Action [Case Study]: I found that most successful business individuals I encountered are active listeners. Unfortunately, I probably spend more time hearing people than I do listening to them. This became apparent to me last month when shadowing Harvey, the president of my division. I noticed that he is always patient to listen attentively when somebody is speaking to him. During this day I was surprised when I watched Harvey talking to the cutter in the sample room. Normally the cutters are regarded as unimportant people and most of the time they just take orders. Harvey was listening to the cutters' complaint about one of the sample fabrics that frays constantly. The cutter did not think it was a good idea to run the program. *Harvey listened and asked the cutter to explain which direction the fabric frayed. If it was not for Harvey's conversation with the cutter, who gave him the idea to have the textiles mill add different finish to the fabric, we would have lost a lot of money in the program.* He later interpreted to me that the cutter did not really directly say the fabric was fraying. He was just complaining to the production manager that the fabric kept ended up being smaller than the pattern and it ruffles a lot. Harvey happened to be there when the conversation occurred. He then intervened between the manager and the cutter.

He asked the cutter to show him the before and after fabric. He then asked the cutter to demonstrate the shifting of the fabric. By paraphrasing the cutter speech, he was able to understand that the fabric was actually fraying. This had an effect on the bottom line. Harvey's performance was complimented by all of his subordinates. On the other hand, had Harvey not been there, the manager who does not have good listening skill would have yelled at the cutter for cutting the fabric poorly and missed the opportunity to improve the process. The cutter was very satisfied that his complaint was being heard and understood. He went on to try and do a better job because he felt that he was appreciated. At the same time Harvey was happy that his subordinates are doing their job well. If Harvey did not know about this problem until it got to production level, the production manager would probably be fired. This has definitely shown me the error in my ways and motivated me to become a better listener.

Walking the Talk: Select a situation in your life where being able to listen was critical. (1) **D**etermine whether the parties genuinely listened to each other. (2) **E**valuate the degree to which listening was engaged and active or merely passive. (3) **A**nalyze why this level of listening occurred and how it might be improved. (4) **L**everage these insights to develop better decoding skills and become more active in your listening.

To become a more active listener, I will...

5.8   Mastering Nonverbal Communication

Ask Yourself: Can you communicate without using words? In what ways do people exchange messages even when they are not "speaking" per se? Are things like eye contact, tone of voice, gestures, and facial expression important in conveying ideas and information? How many ways can people give and receive meaning "nonverbally"?

Management Theory: Usually when one thinks of communication, the image that comes to mind is of someone speaking or writing. However this picture misses much of the important information exchanges that occur nonverbally. Nonverbal communication includes all of the ways that we express ourselves without the use of words. In fact research suggests that more than half of our messages are nonverbal. One way managers communicate nonverbally is through kinesics, or their "body language" of movements and gestures. A folding of the arms, wink of the eye, glance at the watch, shrug of the shoulders, raised eyebrow, subtle grin, or solid handshake can communicate volumes. In addition we communicate with our tone of voice. Adding overt emphasis or even the use of silence and subtle pauses can change the meaning of our words. We communicate through our proxemics, or use of space. The ways we design our office, arrange seating at a meeting, manipulate physical layouts, or move closer or farther away from another person, can all speak volumes about our intentions and preferences. We communicate by the way that we dress. Our appearances signal much about our status, goals, motivations, and priorities. We communicate through the use of time. The order in which we select and prioritize tasks, length that we ask people to wait, and speed in which we move and act are cues to a person's method and message. All of these nonverbal sources can serve the function of reinforcing (adding emphasis to drive a point home), substituting for (speaking in silent language across a room), or even contradicting (revealing deeper meanings and hidden motives) our verbally conveyed ideas. This is especially important because people usually believe nonverbal communication even more than the words themselves—hence the expression "actions speak louder than words." Our story is about a manager's efforts to hone his nonverbal communication skills.

In Action [Case Study]: Nonverbal communications when taken out of context or run contrary to verbal communications can create mixed messages. I remember years ago at a prior employer my vice president held a budget meeting and, while telling us everything was ok, revealed through his facial expressions and uneasy disposition that in fact there was deep trouble in the company. Because of this none of us felt we could trust him and started looking for other employment, which coincidentally led me to my current position. I carry this experience with me and try to link nonverbal with verbal communications to actually add meaning to what is being conveyed and help people understand me better. I try to utilize nonverbal communications in my work especially if I feel it will enhance the message I am trying to convey. I will often use body language or facial expressions during a staff meeting in which I am explaining decisions made by senior management. For example, recently, some terminations of key employees occurred in the company I work for. Many employees began to feel threatened by these terminations and were wondering whether they were going to be next. I immediately called my staff together when the memos announcing the changes were released. I was able to assure them that this was an organizational necessity and not part of some hidden plan to downsize the staff. During this meeting, it was very important for me to utilize some nonverbal communications to reassure everyone. I needed to show them I was compassionate about their feelings, and I also needed them to believe what I was telling them. Needless to say, there was some skepticism, but I think they felt somewhat reassured. *I believe I gained their trust and confidence not only by telling them I was compassionate, but also by showing them through direct eye contact and genuine facial expressions.* It was also important that the meeting was held in my office with the door wide open and we were all in close proximity to one another. I think that also helped them to feel that I was telling them the truth. The effect of nonverbal communications on performance can be positive if done correctly. It can also be detrimental if done poorly, particularly if the recipient of the communication misinterprets the message being conveyed.

Walking the Talk: Select a situation in your life where nonverbal communication occurred. (1) **D**etermine whether critical parts of the message were transmitted outside of the actual words used. (2) **E**valuate the degree to which the nonverbal communication helped or hurt the process. (3) **A**nalyze why this occurred and if its use and interpretation could have been done more effectively. (4) **L**everage these insights to enhance your ability to detect and utilize nonverbal cues.

> To master nonverbal communication, I will...

5.9   Developing Supportive Communication

Ask Yourself: Can communication build or destroy relationships between people? Do you ever communicate in a way that makes people defensive or feel bad about themselves? Can you send the same message in a way that creates stronger versus weaker bonds between others? Is there more to good communication than just exchanging information?

Management Theory: Communication is not only a means of transferring meaning; it is also a mechanism for enriching or impeding interpersonal connections. Communication is supportive when it builds relationships and creates positive feelings between the encoder and decoder; it is non-supportive when it diminishes people and makes them feel put down or distracts people and makes them feel threatened. In this sense managers can use communication not only to convey a message but do it in a manner that also builds bonds, establishes trust, and strengthens interactions with their coworkers and employees. We focus on several best practices proposed by management theory and that emerge in the following case. First, managers communicate supportively when they take ownership of and not hide from their message. They invest in relationships when they use first-person language and assume responsibility for their ideas or decisions, rather than weakly attribute them to "higher-ups," company policy, or some other third party. This shows a willingness to put themselves on the line and expresses the idea that the other person is worth their time, energy, and explanation. Second, managers communicate supportively when they focus on the problem at hand and not engage in personal attacks or play the "blame game". This shows a willingness to get things done together and expresses the idea that shared actions and results matter more than fault finding or harping on personality differences. Third, managers communicate supportively when they emphasize specific, changeable issues or behaviors and not general tendencies or cookie-cutter comments that gloss over the particulars of the situation. This shows a willingness to help the other person understand a message or improve their performance and expresses the idea that they are someone worthy of developing rather than merely a target for your empty palliatives and frustrations. Our story is by a manager who has worked hard to master these skills and become more supportive in her communication.

In Action [Case Study]: I have learned that supportive communication seeks to preserve a positive relationship between the communicators while still addressing the problem at hand. As I felt extremely uncomfortable giving negative feedback, there were three communication areas that I wanted to correct: First, I used to give negative feedback using disowned statements such as "we think" or "they say." Now I realized that this habit made me seem aloof, uncaring, or that I was not confident enough in my ideas to take responsibility for them. Now after keeping my statements in the first person, *I began to see that it is possible to give negative/constructive feedback in the first person without destroying the relationship.* In fact, in two cases in particular, I found that my subordinates took me more seriously when I used the "I" versus "they" method. Perhaps this person now felt that it was me, rather than some unknown entity, who cared about the issue. If what I am saying is true, then I should have no reason to feel uncomfortable in taking responsibility for my words. The second communication error I improved on was keeping my communication specific, rather than global. In the past, I would make general "safe" statements about problems that I felt my subordinates were having with their work. This is critical because without having a clear listing of actual items they could not know what they need to improve. For example, I would have said in the past

"You have to improve your customer service skills," but now I say "You have to improve your turn around of customer requests from twenty minutes to fifteen minutes" and I give specific examples of ways that I think this improvement could happen. I found that making a list before speaking with my subordinate helped me to avoid global statements. Third, I wanted to become more problem- instead of person-oriented. I am in the process of cross training a new employee, and we have been clashing frequently. I decided to describe behavior that she needs to modify while avoiding accusations. I presented her data and evidence that can be mutually confirmed. For example, last month she completed her work late. I focused on the behavior, not on her attributes. I described the objective consequences that have resulted or will result. I used sentences such as "I am concerned about this month payment because of the year end. In order to avoid late fees, we should ready our invoices by the 15th so vendor will receive the check before the 31st." As a result of this communication her performance increased dramatically. I feel such a huge satisfaction when I realize that our relationship became a lot better than it was a month ago and has led to higher productivity, faster problem solving, and fewer conflicts. With these three steps, I have made the commitment that I must be able to communicate in a professional and supportive way. These changes seem to be working.

Walking the Talk: Select a situation in your life where the supportiveness of communication was important. (1) **D**etermine whether supportive communication was or was not used. (2) **E**valuate the degree to which this helped or harmed the relationship between parties. (3) **A**nalyze why more or less supportive approaches were taken and specifically how they might be improved. (4) **L**everage these insights to increase the supportiveness of your communication and develop a strong set of supportive communication skills.

To communicate more supportively, I will...

CHAPTER SIX

Motivating and Inspiring Others

Chapter six examines management theories about interpersonal motivation and the management skill of inspiring people. Motivation is a widely used but poorly understood term. Some estimate the number of scholarly definitions for the concept in the hundreds. To complicate things further, it can be viewed both as a thing/noun (such as a set of forces, personal characteristics, or internal state) as well as a process/verb (such as a set of stages, collection of actions, or method of getting someone from one place to another). Shining through this fog is the simple yet practically relevant question: What is the best way to motivate someone? The seeds to an answer begin with the insight that motivation exists to fill a "gap"—the different between where one is and one wants to be. Thus managers can motivate their employees by either highlighting threats to avoid (negative gaps) or opportunities to pursue (positive gaps). How to best do this? Major theories of motivation can be usefully divided into four categories that correspond to a common type of recommendation: (1) Diagnosing Needs—Figure out what people want, (2) Designing Jobs—Enhance what positions offer, (3) Actions—Guide behaviors through goals and expectancies, and (4) Outcomes—Reinforce efforts both appropriately and fairly. Managers do not have to choose between one theory and another; instead, they can use them in a complementary manner as part of an overall motivation program. Therefore in this sixth chapter we look at these methods for better motivating people.

6.1   Appreciating the Importance of Motivation

Ask Yourself: Is motivation important? When an employee fails do you usually attribute it to their lack of ability or lack of motivation? Can a manager increase someone's level of motivation? What is the best way of doing this?

Management Theory: Notwithstanding the dizzying diversity of motivation frameworks competing for managers' attention, we can identify several basic principles that can be mastered. What is most fundamental about the theories of motivation is that it involves (1) the arousal of energy, (2) directing it toward a particular objective, and (3) inspiring a commitment or persistence of activity toward this end. Therefore managers can motivate better by helping people exert more effort, focusing it better, and maintaining it longer especially when they face obstacles. On the other hand, managers' failure to motivate someone might result in a poorly motivated, even lazy person with less drive, direction, and determination. In a hypercompetitive business climate where technology and other resources have diffused rapidly to create a relatively flat playing field in terms of capacity and potential performance (i.e., what people "can-do"), a firm's competitive edge often depends on the inner drive and motivation of its employees (i.e., what they "will-do"). Indeed when two individuals, teams, or organizations are equally matched, it stands to reason that the more motivated usually wins. Motivation tends to be a key difference maker that sets apart successful managers from the also-rans. Furthermore, as employees get stressed out and hop from job to job, motivation becomes even more essential in maintaining performance and satisfaction levels while reducing unnecessary absenteeism and turnover. Our story is by a manager who learned a lesson or two about the power of motivation and the important of knowing precisely how to motivate their employees (hint—it is not always money).

In Action [Case Study]: I was guilty of the fallacy that money motivates everybody. Now, after studying management theory realized that I made the mistake of thinking that what motivates me must motivate everyone else as well! This could not be farther from the truth. Since making a conscious effort to really find out what motivates people, I have found that my managerial effectiveness has definitely improved. *I have discovered that if you know what motivates people you can get them to do their job better and in turn, you can do your job better.* For example, I had a clerk working for me who was very unmotivated. Whenever he received a project, he would take up to a week to complete it instead of the two days it normally took to do the job. I had a conversation with him, and it turned out that he was disheartened with his workstation and it was causing his work to suffer. When the company realigned some of the workstations, they placed him very close to the freight delivery entrance, and it was very noisy. We switched his workstation to the other side of the factory floor and within that week we noticed a remarkable improvement in his work. This just illustrates the point that not everyone is motivated by money. This gentleman just needed his workstation to be moved. All I had to do was talk to him for a few minutes to see what the problem was. Since I have taken the time to see what motivates people, I have made other observations within my department. Other employees might be motivated by flexible hours or recognition of a job well done. These are all things that can be done that won't cost the firm any extra money! In fact, it might save the company money by making employees more productive in their efforts. I guess the main thing I realized is that I have to take the skills I learned from management theory and to do some serious thinking. Before the end of the summer, I will suggest a "cafeteria" style of benefits for employees to the HR VP. If I stress the fact that we need to think of new and creative ways to motivate people, then this plan will go over well. I also have to be cognizant that I always have to be flexible in dealing with people and the way that they are motivated. Because what motivates someone today might not motivate them tomorrow or next year.

Walking the Talk: Select a situation in your life where getting others motivated was important. (1) **D**etermine the role of motivation in succeeding in this situation. (2) **E**valuate your employees' level of motivation. (3) **A**nalyze why this was the case and how changing your approach to motivation could have altered the outcome of situation. (4) **L**everage these insights to increase your awareness of how motivation affects managerial and organizational success.

To better appreciate the importance of motivating others, I will...

6.2   Diagnosing Peoples' Motivational Needs

Ask Yourself: What do people want? Is everyone motivated by the same things and in the same ways? Are employees motivated by identical things throughout their careers or does what motivate them tend to change? How does a manager target the right need when motivating someone?

Management Theory: Figuring out what people want is no easy task for many reasons. First people are not always sure about their own needs let alone what lights the fire of others. Plus the things that people desire often change—think about it, do you actually want the same things now that you did five or ten years ago? When you were a teenager? Plus what one person needs may be different than their colleagues and coworkers.

Therefore answering the seemingly simple question is tricky because the target is unclear, moving, and varies widely from person to person. This is particularly true with an increasingly diverse workforce. Management theory offers several frameworks to aid in better diagnosing needs. One of the oldest and most widely known is Maslow's Hierarchy that posits that people share a universal ordering of needs and are motivated by their lowest unsatisfied gap. Unfortunately the buzz for this model was greater than the evidence supporting it and thus Alderfer's ERG model followed with streamlined categories and more complex dynamics. David McClelland further extended our understanding with his "three needs theory." Using a variation of an ink-blot test, he developed a framework for making sense of three central needs that motivated individuals: (1) Need for achievement (nAch), or motivation through the drive to accomplish tasks, meet standards, and strive to solve problems, (2) Need for affiliation (nAff), or motivation through the drive for friendly and close relationships with others, and (3) Need for power (nPower), or motivation through the drive to control, influence, or be responsible for others. Since different people are moved by different levels of these three needs, it is important for managers to match their motivational approach to the specific state of the person. Our story is by a real estate manager using the theory to better understand their high level of motivation by looking at how their needs are satisfied at work.

In Action [Case Study]: The three needs in McClelland's theory really shed light on what motivates me in everyday business situations and how these needs shape my job performance and satisfaction. As a real estate vice president engaged in lending and sales, I strive for personal achievement and the need to succeed in any task that I am asked to perform or any assignment that I am presented with. In the business environment, I am always looking to other ways of performing daily tasks more efficiently and excel past my own expectations. As an example, my firm provides a specialized rentbill printing service for its client base. I have a great relationship with my customers and over the past year they have been asking me where the firm is going with reference to technology. Currently, we utilize an outdated technology for this and so I decided that it was time to waive the flag and discuss this issue with senior management because that firm could possibly lose business to third-party providers if our system is not enhanced soon. After a couple of meetings, the firm decided to make the necessary changes to accommodate the customer base. *I felt a level of high achievement after these changes were made. I also felt personally responsible, and I received commendation from my customers and senior management.* I also have the need for power and use it most of the time. I believe gaining power is part of the reason that I wanted to climb the company ladder. I enjoy using my position to get my employees to do what I ask of them so that they serve the company interests. I feel that my need for affiliation is limited to a certain group of firm people (senior management and selected others). My need for affiliation with customers is not limited, I want them to like me and I want to be accepted by them. I feel that this closeness is great for overall firm relationships and helps motivate me to do an outstanding job. Not everyone will be motivated equally by all three factors in McClelland's theory. I tend to need all of them but mostly achievement so it is most essential that this need is satisfied. If it was not I would probably look for another position.

Walking the Talk: Select a situation in your life where your employees' needs either were or were not met. (1) **D**etermine the extent to which your employees had different needs on the job. (2) **E**valuate specifically their achievement, power, and affiliation needs and the degree to which you were able to satisfy them. (3) **A**nalyze how specific managerial actions by you could have better addressed these needs. (4) **L**everage these insights to develop action plans for diagnosing and meeting employees needs.

> To more accurately diagnose people's motivational needs, I will...

6.3   Designing Motivating Jobs

Ask Yourself: What do jobs offer? Have you had some positions that were just inherently more motivating than others? Why? Are there key factors that make the difference between more and less motivating jobs? How does a manager use these factors to design jobs that better motivate their employees?

Management Theory: It is a basic truth of management theory that different jobs are inherently more motivating than others. Surely you have had some jobs that "did it" for you more than others. Something about them was just better. But the reasons why jobs' motivations differ are not always clear. The way your boss acts, the colleagues you work with, the nature of the work itself, the context and location where the work is done, and so many other factors can make jobs more or less motivating. In management theory, the Job Characteristic Model (JCM) is perhaps the best-supported and most illuminating frameworks understanding, predicting, and influencing a job's level of motivation. The framework proposes five core job dimensions that managers can focus on to influence a job's motivating potential: (1) Skill Variety: The degree to which a job includes a range of activities and requires different skills and talents of the employee. Broader is usually more motivating than narrower. (2) Task Identity: The degree to which the job entails completing a whole and identifiable piece of work from beginning to end. Having a visible outcome is usually more motivating than being just another cog in the machine. (3) Task Significance: The degree to which the job has a real effect on people and contributes to the organization or society. Meaningful is usually more motivating than trivial. (4) Autonomy: The degree to which the job involves significant freedom and discretion in making decisions and determining courses of action. Freedom is usually more motivating than scripted. (5) Job Feedback: The degree to which information is given regarding how well the job has been done and the objectives obtained. Seeing actual results is usually more motivating than being kept in the dark. Together these dimensions provide a means for assessing and affecting the degree to which a job is potentially more motivating to an employee. Our story is by a services manager using the JCM to identify and remedy a motivational problem at work.

In Action [Case Study]: *I have learned from the job characteristics model that a lack of any of its five dimensions will decrease motivation.* My group is service-oriented. We do research and write white papers on problems and their solutions to support our Navy customer. Our main task is to "integrate" Engineering Change Proposals (ECPs). On a monthly basis, we take one piece of paper with a concept on it and develop the concept into sixty plus pages of design details. This task is very repetitive with little room to personalize the proposal (low autonomy). The customer has set guidelines as to what, and in what order, details are to be provided. Everything I need to know for this task, I jokingly say, I learned in Kindergarten: cutting, pasting, and counting the pages. Skill variety is definitely low. The proposals go through a customer review board where sometimes we would not hear back until a year to eighteen months later (low feedback). Often times the engineer who produced revision one is on another project when revision four gets in house and a new engineer is assigned to the proposal. The ability to actually complete a piece of work (task identity) is certainly low. The proposals are given to the shipbuilders so that on one level they are important. But the importance often loses its luster when it gets bogged down in the navy's bureaucratic requirements. To move one piece of equipment 6 inches can take up to 20 pages. Sometimes we put together proposals that get rejected because the organization does not want to spend the money on it. So our efforts seem useless. Task significance is low. Whether one adds skill variety, task identity, and task significance, divides by three and multiplies by autonomy and feedback, a low score will and has produced low motivation. Engineers in the group dread to go to the weekly meeting to discuss proposals. Often that day has a higher rate of absenteeism. At least three engineers have transferred out of the group this year. Job satisfaction is extremely low. And productivity is definitely lower on this task than on others which our group performs. If ever asked, I would definitely look to change the job's characteristics as a good way to fix this.

Walking the Talk: Select a situation in your life where the nature of your employees' jobs influenced their motivation. (1) **D**etermine the essential nature of the job(s). (2) **E**valuate the jobs on each of the five dimensions of the JCM theory and the degree to which each was more or less motivating. (3) **A**nalyze how you could adjust one or more of these dimensions to improve levels of motivation. (4) **L**everage these insights to design more motivating jobs with greater motivation potential.

To design more inherently motivating jobs, I will...

6.4   Setting Motivational Goals

Ask Yourself: How do goals inspire people? Do you set goals and, if so, do you do this using best practices? Will a general or specific goal tend to motivate someone more? What about a relatively easier or more challenging goal? How can a manager effectively use goal setting to better motivate their employees?

Management Theory: Goal setting is the process of developing objectives and implementing targets for these objectives that a person will be held responsible for accomplishing. Management theory tells us that goals are among the most important factors in determining someone's motivation. When people are given an objective for which to strive it can focus their attention, inspire them to make plans and commitment, and increase their persistence on the task. Perhaps you have noticed that when you have had a clear goal, versus simply a free-floating and ill-defined hope, it was easier to energize, focus, and sustain effort. In short, it makes sense for managers to use theory to set goals correctly. Here are the top three things we know about properly setting goals: (1) Goals are more motivational when they are challenging—to help people reach farther and strive to greater levels of performance. A high standard is better than a lower one in bringing out superior performance. Even if you miss the lofty target, your results are often better than when you hit a lower number. (2) Goals are more motivating when they are specific—to help people aim properly and more accurately direct their efforts in the desired direction. A clear target is better than a vague amorphous one. Attaching numbers to goals is often better than a vague "do your best." (3) Goals are more motivational when they are accepted and involve feedback—to help people share them and actually use them as an active intention. An interactively set and managed objective is better than a dictated one. Getting people involved in goal setting will often result in greater levels of goal commitment. Our story is by a manager using goals setting theory to learn how to set motivating goals for their staff personnel.

In Action [Case Study]: I recognize that increasing motivation and performance among employees is essential for creating a successful and productive work environment. This task was not easy because there are many components that have to be evaluated to understand each employee's specific situation. *My work experience has shown me that goal setting is necessary to accomplish a high level of motivation, productivity, and effort among employees.* As the chief examiner and quality control manager in charge of my department, my responsibilities included giving each staff member his or her assignments and timetables, as well as guide other examiners and help them find and utilize the resources they need to complete their assignments. To do this I did a couple of things. First, I established expectations and set goals for the team. I made it clear to each individual what their assignments involved and what was expected from each of them. For example, what steps should be completed first in order for the audit to run smoothly and a general timetable of when each step should be given in for review. By setting specific goals, examiners could execute their assignments efficiently. I gave them goals as to when they should be completed and how long each step should take. Overall, developing specific goals for each staff member and making timetables is quite effective, the audits run quite smoothly and are completed on time. In addition to selecting the right type of goal, an effective goal program must also include feedback. Feedback provides opportunities for clarifying expectations, adjusting goal difficulty and gaining recognition. I also provide each staff member with timely performance feedback as the audit progressed with suggestions on how I thought they were progressing. I think they really appreciate that I take the time to tell them how they are doing. All in all, motivating others was not an easy job. You have to provide the right goals and make sure that they have the resources and abilities they need to accomplish the task at hand. I think I have become effective at managing a team and setting goals for them to accomplish. I have seen first hand the negative effects that managers who lack these skills can have on a work unit. I plan on continuing to improve these motivational skills in my next position.

Walking the Talk: Select a situation in your life where your employees' goals influenced their motivation. (1) **D**etermine the extent to which you set or assisted in setting goals for your employees. (2) **E**valuate the goals on the above aspect of goal setting theory to deduce their stronger and weaker aspects. (3) **A**nalyze why these goals influenced their motivation and how they might be improved. (4) **L**everage these insights to set more motivating goals for your employees.

To set more motivating goals, I will...

6.5   Establishing Motivational Expectancies

Ask Yourself: How do expectations inspire people? Are employees more motivated when they believe in their ability to do a good job? What about when they feel that superior performance will get them more rewards? What about when they feel that they will really benefit from the things you offer? How can a manager affect these three types of expectancies to motivate their employees?

Management Theory: In general most people try to act rationally in choosing the course of action they feel most likely to be productive and best fulfill their needs. The Expectancy Theory of motivation lays out the three key links that determine this belief and hence act to drive or inhibit employees' from exerting, properly directing, and sustaining their effort: Expectancy, instrumentality, and valence. In determining motivation for a particular task, a person first assesses the likelihood that they are able to perform the needed actions. This is their effort-to-performance expectancy (E→P). If they feel that they can do something, then they will be more motivated than if it seems impossible. Managers who build confidence, place employees properly, better train people for their jobs, and objectively assess their performance increase their employees' expectancies. Second, a person assesses the likelihood that acting in a particular way will be rewarded. This is their performance-to-outcome instrumentality (P→O). Managers who reinforce superior performance give their employees a reason to work harder and hence build up instrumentality, as opposed to those who merely pay people a straight salary that does not go up or down depending on how well they perform. Third, a person assesses the likelihood that what they get in return for high performance will help satisfy their personal objectives. This is their outcome-to-goals valence (O→G). Managers who reward employees in a way that both helps them attain personal satisfaction and aligns this outcome with overall strategic objectives will be more effective at motivating people than say a manager who gives promotions or more responsibility to people who do not really want these things. Our story is by a trader using Expectancy Theory to discover why their job is not as motivating as it could be—yes, it comes down to weak E-P-O-G links.

In Action [Case Study]: Analyzing the level of motivation at my prior job with Expectancy Theory, I now realize that most of my effort and determination to achieve a goal was overlooked, unacknowledged, and eventually submersed. I was able to identify three reasons that, I believe, contributed to my diminished motivation and eventual contempt for my job and company. First, my aspiration to become a trader initially produced high levels of effort and exceptional performance that was above that of other recruits. However, the company has never presented me with or prepared a formal written evaluation and the job was so vague that I did not know if I was doing the right things. As a result, a year into my employment I wondered whether my immediate manager or anyone in upper management was aware or keeping-track of my performance and if so what they really thought about it. Subsequent inquiries into the matter surfaced no conclusive confirmation. This E-P link became weak for me. Second, because no one was tracking my performance, I was not rewarded or praised for my achievements or level of motivation. There were no salary raises. At this time, I questioned my motivation since it was rather obvious that my extra work would not be compensated. Therefore this P-O link was also broken. My satisfaction, as I questioned the work situation increasingly, went plummeting down. Third, as the end of the program approached, I noticed that my position with the company did not help me in my overall aspiration to become a trader. The job was a dead end. Therefore my O-G link was broken as well. Subsequently, I felt discouraged and "used." I eventually quit my job. In conclusion, *my experience has helped me recognize how broken expectancy links led to a lowered performance and satisfaction. In my situation all three links were weak, yet I see that even one broken link can reduce motivation.* Now I know what NOT to do as a manager and how not to treat my employees.

Walking the Talk: Select a situation in your life where your employees' expectancies influenced their motivation. (1) **D**etermine the extent to which you influenced the expectations of your employees. (2) **E**valuate the degree to which these expectations effected their motivation. (3) **A**nalyze why one or all of the three primary links of expectancy theory were weak and how you could target your efforts to strengthen them. (4) **L**everage these insights to more effectively influence the expectancy, valence, and instrumentality of your employees to better motivate them.

To strengthen the links of motivational expectancies, I will...

6.6   Motivating People through Participation and Involvement

Ask Yourself: How does participation inspire people? Can involving people in the management process motivate them at a higher level than if they were excluded from these types of decisions? Could giving people a say in what happens in the workplace increase their commitment and drive? How can a manager effectively use job involvement to better motivate their employees?

Management Theory: Participative management focuses on actively seeking the input of employees, consulting with them on decisions, and actually taking their suggestions into account before determining and implementing policies. It views management as an inherently interpersonal process and, as such, shares information and power with subordinates thus motivating them to become more involved with and engaged in the decisions that affect their jobs. This process lies at the core of the perennially vogue but frequently mischaracterized concept of empowerment. A participative and empowering management approach is often effective at increasing employees' job involvement, which is the degree to which people relate to their work and consider the jobs to be personally important to them. This is because participative management aims to utilize more of people's skills to enhance their identification with and loyalty to the company. For instance, if an employee is given real input into a task that has a tangible effect on the bottom line then they may take more interest in their job and increase their level of effort in supporting the well-being of the organization. Overall, participation and subsequent feelings of empowerment and involvement affect motivation by bearing on peoples' willingness to work hard, align with organizational objectives, and sustain this focus beyond normal job expectations. Our story is by a downtown New York City worker in the aftermath of September 11, 2001, reflecting on the motivational power of involvement and the distinct negative consequences of a lack of participation.

In Action [Case Study]: The theory of Participative Management indicates that subordinates feel motivated by sharing in a significant degree of decision-making authority with their superiors or company. My office surely has a negative example of what happens when this theory is violated. After 9/11 my office, which used to be locate at 6 World Trade Center, had to start from scratch to return to the regular working agenda. Every staff member was eager to contribute to the rebuilding project and my team called my home almost everyday to express their loyalty. I, as the Administrative VP, talked to the regional manager and represented all staff members' willingness to contribute to the rebuilding project. The manager, however, decided everything by himself and did not even allow anyone, including me, to participate on temporary/new office designing and new workplace setting projects. In his opinion, everything would be better if he was the only one involved in the process. He did not involve the public affair specialist in any press release; he did not ask any recruiters when to cancel or reschedule recruitment events; and he did not inquire of the contracting authority about any procurements. Staff members showed their concerns during meetings and other events. Still, the regional manager kept his own ways. *Everyone was offended by the "unshared decision making" and refused to participate in the process or fully commit to the organization since then.* To a person we were all once very loyal to the organization. I even wore the company logo on my t-shirts and baseball caps. But now since we were dealt out of the major decisions and treated like little children we do not identify with the firm as much. Basically, since they stopped caring about our feelings and ideas, we stopped caring about them. I seriously cannot remember even one time when anyone in senior management asked about what the employees needed or thought would be best. The performance of everyone on my team has lowered significantly. People started to call in sick and planned longer annual leave days even in peak months. The turnover rose relatively faster than normal: one specialist submitted her resignation letter exactly two weeks before her decided last day and she intentionally left all her work unsolved. All three internal applicants for the recruitment coordinator position declined the offer one and everyone in the office is searching for new jobs. As for me, my company t-shirt has found its way to the bottom of the drawer and never sees the light of day. We say that the "career center" is open 24 hours and 7 days within the office—everyone is on the Internet looking for jobs during working hours.

Walking the Talk: Select a situation in your life where participation (or lack thereof) effected motivation. (1) **D**etermine the extent to which you shared power, information, and choices with your employees. (2) **E**valuate whether the degree of participation influenced their motivation. (3) **A**nalyze why the level of participation was or was not appropriate for the situation and how different strategies might have increased their feelings of involvement. (4) **L**everage these insights to more effectively utilize participation to motivate your employees.

> To better use participation and involvement in motivating others, I will...

6.7   Using Rewards to Motivate People

Ask Yourself: How do rewards determine people's actions? Are individuals more likely to repeat behaviors if they are reinforced for doing them? Less likely to repeat them if they are punished when they act in this undesirable way? To what extent are your behaviors at work shaped by the promise of rewards and the fear of punishers? How can managers effectively use rewards and punishment to motivate their employees?

Management Theory: It is axiomatic to management theory that people behave in a manner that increases rewards and limits punishment. This is derivative of psychological principle advanced long ago by psychology researchers who motivated rats to push a bar by providing food and to stop pushing it by delivering electric shocks. In the modern "rat race" things are not much different—employees tend to do what is reinforced, what gets them their proverbial cheese (bonuses, recognition, pay, promotion, etc.) if you will. On the flip side, people are usually motivated to avoid acting in ways that get them yelled at or fired. Thus managers motivate people to perform desired behaviors by reinforcing them while discouraging undesirable behaviors by punishing them. Sounds simple, but this commonsense lesson is too often not common practice. Steve Kerr, a former academic who studied the use of reinforcement and, later in his career, moved to executive positions where he instituted effective reward-based programs, noticed that contrary to this basic principle poorly performing organizations did the exact opposite. All too often managers fail to motivate people in a desired direction because they hope for one behavior—say putting the company first, good teamwork, or being creative—but actually reward contrary actions—such as watching out for oneself, pursuing individual achievement at the expense of others, or playing it safe and not making mistakes. This is management folly because it works against the goals of the organization. People focus on what is inspected, not expected.

People do what is compensated, not desired. Our story is by a worker reconciling two companies stock ownership plans with how managers want their employees to behave.

In Action [Case Study]: Employee Stock Ownership Plans have become increasingly popular for corporations to motivate their employees. When employees own stock (or options to buy stock) in the company, and can therefore benefit directly from the company's success, those employees will be motivated to work harder and will be more dedicated to the company. Basically it rewards employees for promoting the success of the organization. In my career, I have now been involved with two companies offering stock option plans to its employees and interestingly have seen it produce different results. The first company offered only a small batch of options, and they were easily rolled over or redeemed based on the short-term fluctuations of the market. Right from the start, the options were seen as token rewards with limited value and ultimately acted as a drain on company morale. Worse yet, they encouraged people to look only at the short-term performance and quarterly returns so that they can cash out at higher rates while ignoring longer-term initiatives that would take some time to develop. However, the second firm offered a generous quantity of options, with a gradual vesting schedule and a very attractive employee stock purchase program tied to long run performance. The result has been a highly motivated and excited workforce, with employee participation in the stock purchase program at nearly 100 percent and almost all participants electing to dedicate the maximum allowable percentage of their salaries to the program and keep them there. Managers want us to work hard and be dedicated, so they are linking our financial rewards to these behaviors and we are responding. *It is one thing for managers to ask us to work hard and put the company first, but it is an entirely different one to actually put their money where their words are.* I think that by offering the long-term stock options in combination with a strong incentive for employees to invest a significant portion of their own salaries in company stock, the firm has hit upon a winning combination that both motivates employees to perform and strengthens their commitment to the long-term health of the company. We work harder because the company's success is our success. Likewise, I will most certainly remain at the company for a while.

Walking the Talk: Select a situation in your life where rewards were a factor in motivation. (1) **D**etermine the rewards and punishments that you administered in response to employee behaviors. (2) **E**valuate the degree to which these reinforcements influenced their motivation. (3) **A**nalyze why rewards increased desired behaviors and punishments decreased undesired behaviors to deduce if and how you could have approached these differently to better achieve results. (4) **L**everage these insights to more effectively utilize rewards and punishment to motivate your employees.

To more effectively use rewards in motivating others, I will...

6.8   Motivating Equitably

Ask Yourself: Do people ever compare their salary with what other people get? How important is it that compensation procedures and amounts are seen as fair? Might employees who are otherwise happy at work suddenly become demotivated if they believe that they are being underpaid? How can managers effectively manage workers' equity beliefs to better motivate their employees?

Management Theory: It is not enough for managers to motivate their employees simply by giving out more and better rewards—the rewards must also be seen as fair. Fair in the way that rewards are determined (procedural justice) and paid out (distributive justice). This is because people are social animals—they talk, look around, and compare themselves with others both within their companies and industries. To emphasize, the central motivational issue here is perceived fairness. People do not necessarily want to be given the same exact rewards as everyone else—after all, it is called "equity" and not equality theory—but instead want these rewards to be distributed reasonably and based on just principles. More specifically to the theory, employees look at the ratio of their outcomes (what they get from work) relative to their inputs (what they give at work) and compare this to the relative outcomes and inputs of others. If they give more to their company then equity-sensitive employees will feel that they should get more from it. For example, greater inputs of experience, education, effort, or ability should warrant better outcomes in terms of pay, responsibilities, experiences, and perks. The trouble begins when employees feel that people's inputs and outcomes are not in balance. Witness the professional athlete who rejects a multimillion dollar contract because a teammate with similar statistics is getting a little bit more, or the high performing office worker who suddenly thinks their large bonus is unfair because they heard that everyone got the same amount, including those who did not work as hard. For most people the belief that they are being underpaid (i.e., feelings of inequity) is deeply demotivating. Our story is by a manager utilizing equity theory to understand the role of fairness in motivating people at their workplace.

In Action [Case Study]: In our department the biggest source to stay motivated is the relation of what we get for our performance compared to others. We are constantly comparing ourselves to either fellow coworker with similar experience or skills, a person occupying the same position in different division or organization, a friend or relative of the similar age who we are measuring up to, or a manager who we want to become. When doing these comparisons I look at all the components of compensation, including money, bonuses, fringe benefits, vacation time, profit share plan, and compensation days, as a whole package rather than each one separately. And, we want to know the reason behind it as well. *For as long as we get equitable package for our performance in relation to the referent we choose, we stay motivated.* There are several potential implications that I see with equity theory. The first one has to do with identification of the referent. It is usually determined by us—employees—and not by the company. But, in order to reflect our performance appropriately, the organization needs to know who we choose as our referent. It is impossible to know this for each employee. Thus, the solution could be for the company to benchmark to ensure that we receive equitable distribution in comparison to employees in our group, other divisions, similar companies, and on the market in general. My organization did not do this, and many people in my department became unsatisfied when they found out that their peers at other firms made more money so they left to work for the competitors who paid better. A second concern has to do with effort. Even though some of us put in extra hours and always met out deadlines, last year everyone got the same amount of bonus. The main issue is that if my hard work was not getting me more pay than coworkers who did not put in as much effort then I would lose my motivation. If some people put in more effort and everyone gets paid the same then it is not fair, so why bother. To solve this problem our managers should give us some type of extra compensation for our inputs like extra days off or special perks. Otherwise I will not work so hard in the future. So, in my mind, the equity theory explains perfectly the motives of the people in my department.

Walking the Talk: Select a situation in your life where fairness was a factor in individual motivation. (1) **D**etermine whether people developed feelings of inequity. (2) **E**valuate the degree to which these misaligned ratios translated into higher or lower performance. (3) **A**nalyze why peoples' outcomes did or did not match inputs and how you could adjust any of these dimensions to make things seem more just. (4) **L**everage these insights to better insure individuals' perceived fairness in the way that you motivate your employees.

To ensure perceived fairness and equity when motivating others I will…

6.9   Increasing Intrinsic Motivation

Ask Yourself: Have you ever been passionate about doing a job? Ever seen highly motivated employees work harder not because of the money but because it just made them feel good inside? Is firing up someone internally different from getting a person to do their job because they are paid to do it or otherwise forced to do it? How can a manager effectively focus on peoples' intrinsic drive to better motivate their employees?

Management Theory: Motivation is not just about rewarding and punishing. It is also about lighting the fire from within. It is one thing to do something because you are told to do it by someone or given external inducements (e.g., salary, bonuses, praise) or threats to do it. It is another thing entirely to act because you are driven from inside, believe in what you are doing, and can really buy into the cause. In the latter case you are "intrinsically" motivated. Intrinsically motivated employees often work harder, are more committed and satisfied, and perform better that extrinsically motivated ones because they truly like the work and performing it well becomes inherently enjoyable. The behavior is performed for its own sake, doing the work is its own reward, and succeeding at it is inherently gratifying. These people neither dread coming to work nor putting in the extra effort to do it at a high level of quality. In fact many of these internally motivated employees would probably keep doing their jobs even after winning the lottery. Money is not their primary motivator. Managers can enhance intrinsic motivation by making jobs more interesting, enjoyable, or even challenging. In turn higher levels of intrinsic motivation have been shown to increase employees' feelings of importance and achievement, that they are making a difference, accomplishing something tangible, and advancing an issue or value that they really care about. Our story is by a manager who utilizes intrinsic motivation theory to develop plans for better motivating themselves and others.

In Action [Case Study]: I would like to discuss the importance of intrinsic outcomes when management is trying to enhance motivation. I concluded that, in my job, I receive many external rewards by management but these do not guarantee my satisfaction and productivity in the long run. *What I really want is to be educated, entrusted with real* *responsibilities, assigned to challenging tasks, and involved in something that I care about.* I use my experience at this job as a clear example of how, even though our team was showered with raises, promotions, and such, many of them still thought of either transferring to another department or leaving for another job as soon as opportunity arises. To the extent that our management was not very concerned with our long-term motivation and skill improvement, I planned to take an initiative and try to make some changes toward getting more intrinsic satisfaction out of our job: First, I requested from our management that they permit representatives from different departments to visit our group for an hour and share their experiences. The "round table" was very productive as we were able to learn about the big picture of how our daily work effects the entire organization and also address some of our concerns we have and ideas for making the process more efficient. Second, I asked our management to be signed up for at least one of the ongoing training session related to our job skills. I gained much needed knowledge in understanding not only what each of the corporate actions does, but also, what is more important, what reasoning underlies our jobs. This has generated genuine excitement among the team about doing our work better. Third, as we get more experienced working on our new system, we feel the need to enrich our everyday activities and responsibilities. After long discussion we now get to send e-mails and call our system support people directly when there are issues. This improves our ability to help others in the process and better serve clients. As a result it makes the job more enjoyable and interesting. Finally, at my annual review a month and a half ago I brought up a concern that I do not have a say in the decision-making process. I used to participate on the meetings, conference calls, and informal get together while on another project. That activity made me feel important, valuable, needed, and a respected member of the inner circle. To my surprise, my manager acknowledged my request and just the other day I was assigned to do a special project with our client in London. I talked to some of my coworkers and know for a fact that the improvements in our job functions are translating into greater internal satisfaction, higher morale and, as a result, increased performance and reduced turnover intentions.

Walking the Talk: Select a situation in your life where a lack of intrinsic motivation was a factor in employee motivation. (1) **D**etermine the methods that you used to motivate them. (2) **E**valuate the degree to which these approaches influenced their internal as well as external motivation. (3) **A**nalyze why this happened and how you could have better focused on internal factors in your approach. (4) **L**everage these insights to more effectively increase the intrinsic motivation of your employees.

To increase peoples' intrinsic motivation, I will…

6.10   Applying Stretch Targets

Ask Yourself: Have you ever been challenged to achieve something so big or important that it could not be accomplished through your normal methods or everyday patterns of behaviors? Might these types of visions inspire employees to move outside their comfort zones and fundamentally improve their approach to work? Could these big ideas inspire them to achieve things that were seemingly unimaginable under the old system of doing things? How can managers effectively use stretch targets to motivate their employees?

Management Theory: Stretch targets, which are extremely ambitious but not implausible objectives, are motivational tools that change the way people work and thus push them to higher levels of performance. By setting aspirations that are seemingly unreachable with present processes and methods, these audacious challenges make employees think about their jobs differently. If managed well a stretch target can get people to perform in ways they never imagined possible. Of course when setting stretch targets managers must provide their people with the knowledge, tools, and means to meet such ambitious goals. If not the effects of setting stretch targets can be disastrous in terms of eroding their self-confidence and motivation. In the public arena we see stretch targets in such motivational calls to put a man on the moon (along with an allocation of the necessary resources to enable it) or in modern times to achieve energy independence (future unclear). At work we also see them in motivational methodologies calling for divisions to be first or second in market share or for a large portion of yearly revenues to come from newly developed products. Stretching requires that employees do things differently, and it is this "double-loop" learning that requires them to question their assumptions, break their habits, push their limitations, and reengineer their processes. Indeed this motivational approach is a driving force behind many of the world's most innovative accomplishments and successful organizations. Our story is by an insurance manager who developed and began implementing a plan to employ super-challenging "stretch-targets" but, to their chagrin, has found that it is not as easy as one would hope.

In Action [Case Study]: The purpose of stretch targets is not only to allow employees to stretch their abilities to new levels, but also to change the organization's competitive position by dynamically altering its thinking and business processes. This was a timely skill for me to focus on as I work for an international insurance company undergoing reorganization. My division currently underwrites Domestic (U.S.) health plans, as does our office in Dublin, Ireland. The parent company decided to merge the two operations. Obviously our cultures are very different. Our ambitious goal was to mesh the operations and develop best practices without losing the momentum and motivation of the staff on both teams. We also wanted to minimize turnover and increase employee satisfaction. *The only way we could do this was to radically redesign the way we did things, the way we set targets, and how we measured success.* My task in attempting to apply "stretch targets" was to first find out from the group how they felt about their job and its motivating potential for them, how we could foster a highly motivating and rewarding work environment, and how we could use this environment to work seamlessly together. It was at this time that I felt "stretch targets" should be applied. The theory motivated me to develop the following plan: (1) Establish a ten-point plan of aggressive objectives that would make us change the way we do business and integrate global markets, (2) Structure the team with enough autonomy and empowerment to achieve them, (3) Modify the environment to support the team's effort by reducing structural and bureaucratic barriers, and (4) Develop a culture of continuous support and encouragement. To date my implementation plan has been moderately successful. We are currently in the process of combining the teams and meeting to discuss the assumptions that are holding us back from achieving our ambitious targets. The process has been slow, however, as it has taken a while for certain key decision makers to break old habits and get on board. I now realize that implementation will take a bit longer because not everyone wants to be "stretched." Some want to play it safe and keep doing the same things in the same way. Moving forward I will need to address this resistance to change in order to "get it right" and make the stretch targets stick. We really have no choice if we want to compete globally.

Walking the Talk: Select a situation in your life when you needed to motivate employees to achieve ambitious results. (1) **D**etermine what had to be accomplished and the current methods in which employees did their jobs. (2) **E**valuate the degree to which these results could have been achieved by normal methods. (3) **A**nalyze why people did or did not buy into your approach and how you could have overcome obstacles to this. (4) **L**everage these insights to more effectively utilize stretch targets to motivate your employees.

To apply stretch targets, I will...

Gaining Power and Influencing Others

Chapter seven examines management theories about interpersonal power and the management skill of influencing others. There are few, if any, places that both involve people and are apolitical. For all practical purposes, we pursue our careers in a workplace that is characterized by unequal distributions of power, different agendas, and efforts by people to get their way. The interpersonal concept of power describes one's relative potential to influence another, or in other words, the capacity to get them to do what you want them to do. Power comes from many different places and can be used to a greater or lesser degree. When used in accordance with official channels and formal organizational rules it is called authority. When used informally to supplement or bypass these arrangements then it is called politics. For better or worse, Machiavelli's ancient aphorisms about the importance of power continue to play out today from Main Street to Wall Street. Put simply, it is hard to get anything done without the necessary clout and the skills to use it well. A stark fact of the business world is that managers who get ahead are not necessarily the most knowledgeable but instead are often those most adept at leveraging their power bases and playing the political game. Therefore in this seventh chapter we look at how one can better use power and influence people.

7.1   Appreciating the Importance of Power and Influence

Ask Yourself: Is it important to have power? How does it feel to be powerless? Do you always use all of your potential power in the most effective way to maximize your influence? What happens to performance if the wrong people get too much power? To what lengths might people go to gain and keep their power?

Management Theory: Power is the potential to influence someone, or get them to do what you want. People in organizations ideally aspire toward a shared goal, the company's, but in reality they come at things with different personal agendas and interests. It is for this reason that a proper understanding of power is so important. Let us make some things perfectly clear about power. First, it is a noun, not a verb. It represents a potential so, as such, might be realized to a greater or lesser degree. Indeed most people systematically underappreciate and underutilize their power. Second, power often has a negative connotation. This is misleading. Power is a tool that can be used to benefit a company or misused for personal gain. It can be amassed or drained. It can be applied or wasted. It can be uplifting or corrupting. Third, power is found not only at the top of organizations but instead can reside anywhere. Seasoned veterans, connected secretaries, clever technicians, popular rank-and-file employees, well-placed gatekeepers, hardworking subordinates, intimidating bosses, smart colleagues, appointed office-holders, engaging coworkers, and resourceful clerks all wield different forms of power and thus the potential to influence others. Fourth, power is not a side-issue or distraction but instead a natural and essential element in any social or interpersonal setting. It is simply a reality of managerial life. And people will go to great lengths to acquire and keep it. High-performing managers cannot ignore the dynamics of power because being powerless is seldom a useful or enjoyable position. The trick of course is to distribute and use power in a way that promotes versus inhibits organizational objectives. Our story is by a manager observing the promises and pitfalls of power in her small company.

In Action [Case Study]: It is important for a company not to let a single group or persons have too much power. I work in a small family business that has been around for over a hundred years. Recently I experienced what power can do in the wrong hands. The problem is with the bookkeeper who has been here for more than forty years and all financial aspects of the company go through her. She is at retirement age but she refuses to train anybody. The owner wants to make sure someone else knows how to do her job because a lot is dependent on it. When a person was brought in to assist she refused to teach her anything and did not give her any responsibility. Eventually the new person left. Then the bookkeeper complained about being overly busy but still did not allow anyone to help her. Another problem is that the bookkeeper did not want to change anything about her job and only do things her way. This is a problem because we are in the process of installing a new computer system but she refused to conform by playing dumb and stalling. She has power over the owner and she knows this. Without her cooperation the company cannot switch over. By doing this she figures no one can take her place. Needless to say her actions are hurting productivity. The turnover rate is high in the office because her coworkers cannot deal with her. The owner cannot find a person to assist her. What to do? Well come January the bookkeeper is finally going to retire (I will believe it when I see it) and the person who eventually replaces her has a lot of work to do. In the short run things are going to be tough. In the long run the company will bene-fit from this change. Productivity should improve, absenteeism should be lower, and job satisfaction should be higher. From watching this unfold I realized that power is very important in business today. *Everyone wants it and once they have it they will do anything to keep it. If a person has power and misuses it for his or her advantage, it could seriously damage a company.* It will be best for our company to allow more than one person to have control over our important tasks. The owner should oversee this or the same abuse of power could happen again.

Walking the Talk: Select a situation in your life where power was impor-tant. (1) **D**etermine whether the interpersonal dynamics were affected by unequal power distributions. (2) **E**valuate the degree to which people were effective in gaining and keeping power. (3) **A**nalyze why they were able to turn their power potential into influence and how it could have been better employed to further versus harm company objectives. (4) **L**everage these insights to enhance your appreciation of the role of power and influence.

> To better appreciate the importance of power and influence, I will…

7.2   Increasing Others' Dependency

Ask Yourself: What happens to your power when you become impor-tant, unique, and indispensable to your boss or organization—that is, they really need you? Alternatively what happens to your power when you must rely on someone else to do your job and accomplish your objectives? How can you increase others dependency on you? Minimize your depen-dency on others?

Management Theory: Power is a function of dependency. A manager has power to the extent that he or she control something that other people desire. The more that someone else needs you the greater your power is over them. Alternatively, a manager is subject to power to the extent that somebody else controls the things that they require. The more you need them the greater their power is over you. Thus dependency is a two-way street insofar as it is reciprocal and relative. There are three tenets managers must understand about dependency. (1) Dependency is higher when the asset you manage is perceived as important. Controlling the flow of valuable resources such as blood, oil, cash, promotions, or information provides power. (2) Dependency is higher when the resource you manage is perceived as scarce. When the above items are plentiful people can get them anywhere but when supply is restricted they have fewer options and will "pay" a higher price for them. (3) Dependency is higher when the resource you manage is perceived as nonsubstitutable. When nothing else will do then you are in the proverbial driver's seat. The same rules that form the bedrock of separation of power in governments also apply in the workplace where, for example, alternative career tracks and emerging industries are shifting influence away from traditional power brokers by making their resources less important, scarce, and unique. Of particular relevance to the modern workplace is in the power of information, where the three dimensions of dependency combine to suggest a clear strategy for managers to increase dependency and maximize their influence: Learn something that is of critical importance to the organization, not widely understood by others, and address an indispensable aspect of its strategy or operations. Our story is about a worker discovering the way dependency relationships work at her organization.

In Action [Case Study]: At the local newspaper where I work, there is no elaborate formal hierarchical structure. The publisher is the chief executive of the company whom everybody on staff reports to. Yet, one could argue that some employees have a substantial amount of power because of their particular division of duties and others dependency on them. For these positions there is no surplus of labor on staff; it is a lean work force where the specific employee is responsible for their domain and no one could "fill in" because other employees' skills do not overlap. From the very beginning of my employment here, I have made it a point to take on as many new and important responsibilities as possible to establish my domain and increase my value as an employee. For example, one day when I was out of the office my boss needed pertinent information regarding a project I had worked on but was not able to ask anyone else because no one else was familiar with this project or technically trained in my position. *Therefore, this gives me considerable power within the company because they are dependent on me.* If I was to suddenly leave, and there are many papers who would hire me in a minute, then there would be no one ready or able to perform the duties of my position. This is the case with a number of key positions at this publication that are important, scarce, and nonsubstitutable giving those select employees a certain amount of power as well as job security. For example, the circulation/distribution manager has a considerable amount of power through her long tenure here and her personal relationship with hotel concierges throughout the city, which no one here can replicate, and who are vital to the success of our publication. This type of leverage leads to a high sense of satisfaction among myself and the other key employees because we are all, in a sense, masters of our domain and work with people and for a boss that need us more than we need them.

Walking the Talk: Select a situation in your life where someone was dependent on another. (1) **D**etermine whether dependency relationships determined the power of the parties involved. (2) **E**valuate the degree to which importance, scarcity, and substitutability influenced the relative dependency of one person on another. (3) **A**nalyze why this dependency dynamic occurred and specifically how your influence position could be improved. (4) **L**everage these insights to increase others relative dependency on you and better develop your power.

> To increase others dependency on me and not become too dependant on others, I will...

7.3   Growing and Using Reward / Coercive Power

Ask Yourself: Can you influence someone by handing out benefits and bonuses? How about by making threats and using intimidation? Is one approach usually more effective for you than the other? How can you acquire, and how should you use, rewards and punishers to best influence people?

Management Theory: Power is derived and dependency generated from a variety of sources. Classic models posit several fundamental bases of power. The first two that we will discuss are complementary and involve the ability to help and to harm others. If a manager can help others then they have reward power. They can provide attractive resources and deliver positive results such as promotions, raises and bonuses, praise and recognition, nice offices and assignments, personal acceptance and friendliness, or enhanced learning opportunities. Reward power operates on the basis of desire and is fueled by the provision of assets. Bosses, parents, and other resource holders have it, but anyone who can control and provide something of value can achieve this type of power. The flip side of reward power is coercive power. If a manager can harm others, then they can influence people by threatening to impose undesirable sanctions and deliver negative outcomes. These include dismissal, demotion, discipline, poor work space and assignments, personal coldness and ostracism, and the specter of future retribution. Coercive power operates on the basis of fear and is fueled by the application of punishment. Bullies, tyrants, and terrorists strive for this, although anyone who can strike fear into another can achieve coercive power. Although they are mirrors of each other, these bases of power have different consequences and potential side effects. A system based entirely on rewards places a high priority on payoff and can pull people to achieve objectives but also lead to an ethic of greed and consumption. A system based entirely on coercion places a high priority on intimidation and can push people to abide with requests but may lead to an ethic of reluctant minimum-level compliance and cause interpersonal animosity. Our story is by a salesperson who experienced both the use as well as abuse of reward and coercive power.

In Action [Case Study]: I witnessed the application of reward and coercive power while I worked as a sales manager at my past company. I got along with my first divisional supervisor. He was generous with complements and gave out bonuses when things went well. He even found out what each manager liked and adapted his rewards for them. One manager got opera tickets, another got tickets to the basketball game, and once when I worked all weekend on a project to meet an important deadline, I was rewarded with concert tickets. We all would do practically anything to help him out as long as he had the ability to deliver the goods. But when he was promoted and my new boss came on board things changed. The first week of his tenure when I made a small mistake on an estimate, he used profanity to berate me in front of the entire department. In one instance, he threatened to "throw me out of the bleeping window" if I made any further mistakes. When a transfer of funds was delayed I was called into his office and told that "heads would roll" if the transaction was not completed by the next morning. On another occasion he simply said that I would "be gone" if a statement error was not corrected immediately. *The threat of dismissal was enough to make me do whatever was required to remedy a problem in the assigned time frame. However my primary concern was surviving until the next paycheck rather than excelling at or enjoying my work.* Needless to say, I felt very little satisfaction with my job and found that most of the threats I endured were unnecessary. I rarely put in any extra effort and worked at the bare minimum level that would not get me fired. One time when I broke my chair the boss said aloud, "it would be cheaper to fire you than to replace the chair." I knew right then and there that I wanted out. As soon as the economy improved, I left for another job to my current company.

Walking the Talk: Select a situation in your life where you influenced or were influenced by someone based on rewards or coercion. (1) **D**etermine whether the power potential was more a function of resources and/or threats. (2) **E**valuate the degree to which desire or fear determined the relative influence of the parties involved. (3) **A**nalyze why or why not these strategies were effective at translating power into influence and how you could have more effectively applied or neutralized these types of power. (4) **L**everage these insights to enhance your ability to grow and appropriately wield reward and coercive power as well as develop methods for reducing your vulnerability to it.

To grow and effectively use reward and coercive power, I will...

7.4   Growing and Using Expert Power

Ask Yourself: Do you rely on experts for important information which affects your life or work? Can you influence someone by virtue of your superior knowledge, education, or insight? How does one get to be seen as an expert? How might you use information to gain power and become more influential?

Management Theory: In addition to providing rewards and applying coercion, power is also sourced through real or perceived expertise. This type of power is derived from a person's superior capability to perform a task as well as the ability to provide information, knowledge, or insight to others in its pursuit. We listen to doctors and lawyers, teachers and scientists, computer-fluent coworkers, life-savvy elders, and high-powered consultants based largely on the degree to which we feel they possess a level of specialized know-how. We also go back to school to earn a degree, take training modules, subscribe to journals, travel to conferences, and read the newspaper to buff up our own expert power. Indeed expertise is a valuable currency in this age of rapidly advancing technology, increasingly sophisticated business systems, and burgeoning service economy where a premium is placed on how much you know about your craft. This type of power is not constrained by ones position in an organization. Depth and breadth of expertise can be acquired by any person in any area of a business. In fact it is not uncommon for lower-level employees to possess superior technical expertise than their supervisors. And as per the dependency postulates, the more a person's expertise is central, unique, and critical to a team's or organization's endeavors the greater their expert power becomes. Expert power can therefore be enhanced by the development of cutting-edge competencies related to important and urgent matters deemed critical to ones profession. On the flip side, it is limited by the scope, relevance, and usefulness of the particular domain of expertise. A person would gain little expert power by possessing trivial, peripheral, or outdated knowledge. Bottom line—People listen to and are swayed by others who they think are in the know about important and current matters. Our story is by a bank manager who has learned how to systematically build his expert power over a twenty-year career.

In Action [Case Study]: I am a corporate officer with a large Fortune 500 institution. I was able to attain this position by continuously and relentlessly building my knowledge of the core issues effecting my organization. I have become one of the foremost authorities for our cash management systems and services. I manage these functions for the firm and sell different packages of these products to our most important clients. I can discuss with our clients what products and services they should utilize to be most effective and profitable in both the short and the long term. I can discuss with our board of directors (they call me the "money guru") how to use our financial resources in support of corporate objectives. I am also very technologically literate and have integrated these two areas to carve out a unique niche for myself in high technology sectors, and I am (pat on the back) one of the only people in the company that can handle this specialized client base. Whenever another officer has this type of customer to call upon, they will ask me to sit in the meeting. I am always being asked questions in the office for my opinion or knowledge. *Now you may ask "what about my boss, does not she have the same expertise?" She does not have the depth or up-to-date expertise that I have developed to give advice, set a customer's systems up, or "get techy."* That is why she relies on me so much. How did I get this power? I worked my way up the corporate ladder learning the ropes and devouring all the information I could find on how things really worked and where they were going. I met with as many customers as I could and took as many continuing education classes as the company would allow. I went to as many seminars and conferences as I could to learn about trends and best practices in the industry. I was not afraid to learn the technical end of the business and did not rely on others to set up my computer applications and systems for me. It would be very hard to find a person with my combination of skills and expertise (another pat on the back). Overall, an individual who strives for the expert power that I have can gain considerable power and influence in their organization and feel the satisfaction that comes with it. The company must treat them well or that individual might decide to leave the job and the company will be faced with a significant loss.

Walking the Talk: Select a situation in your life where you influenced or were influenced by someone based on perceived expertise. (1) **D**etermine whether the power potential was a function of superior know-how. (2) **E**valuate the degree to which peoples' inequities of information and knowledge determined the relative influence of the parties involved. (3) **A**nalyze why or why not these strategies were effective at translating power into influence and, if not, how you could have more effectively applied or neutralized this type of power. (4) **L**everage these insights to enhance your ability to grow and appropriately wield expert power as well as develop methods for reducing your vulnerability to it.

To grow and effectively use expert power, I will...

7.5   Growing and Using Referent Power

Ask Yourself: Are you ever swayed by the aura or mystique of someone's persona? Moved to do something for a person because you like, admire, enjoy being around, or are attracted to them? Influenced by them because of their magnetic or dynamic qualities? Do you have this influence with others? Can you acquire and increase your referent power?

Management Theory: Managers can also gain power via the sheer force of their personality. We are often influenced by people because we admire them, enjoy their company, or hold them in high regard. Referent power refers to this type of appeal that enables one to be influenced by famous celebrities, larger-than-life executives, and likeable or even "magnetic" coworkers. It is present when you identify with an individual, respect them, want to be liked by them, or see them as a role model to emulate.

Referent power is fueled by interpersonal attraction and admiration. It is that intangible but simply irresistible quality that draws others and makes them actually want to be influenced by you. And because it lies within the person anybody can gain and wield referent power, not just those in high offices. So how might one develop his or her referent power? Management theory suggest several methods: acting likable and friendly, improving ones appearance and exuding a pleasant demeanor, trusting and being trustworthy, treating people with respect and earning it from others, thinking big and acting boldly, achieving successes and high stature, and developing overall prestige and a good reputation. Ultimately these qualities give you the potential to influence others because of who you are and not per se what resources or forces you control. Referent power is perhaps the broadest base of power because it is not dependent on specific contingencies, bound by specific positions, or constrained by the reach of specific expertise. It is more about developing a general image or persona and thus is holistic in its influence on others. Our story is by a worker discovering and modeling this type of power from his highly admired boss.

In Action [Case Study]: Once I had an incredible boss who just oozed referent power. He was a sharp dressed man who was liked and admired by pretty much all of the employees. Their identification with the boss influenced employees to do their jobs to the best of their abilities because they wanted his approval. My boss was so inspiring and so influential because he treated everyone like a beloved family member or close friend. He fostered two-way communication; he did not only concern himself with what you did but also how you felt. Everyone trusted and respected him. Employees were open and comfortable to share their criticism and problems with him. And most importantly, he would keep this confidential and not use such information against them. On many occasions employees had financial need and he lent the money to them without hesitation. Or sometimes, when an employee was ill, he would go and personally get the medicine for them. *He had such influence to make one believe he or she was important and was being respected so we would do just about anything for him.* Simply speaking, he exerted his referent power to influence employees to do a good job and be loyal. There is no wonder that the employees, including myself, were high in job satisfaction and performance and tended to stay at the company, which is low in turnover. And in order not to disappoint our boss or make ourselves look badly in his eyes, we would not be absent or arrive late if it was not necessary. He was and continues to be one of my role models for how to treat others and succeed in business. I have never worked harder for anyone than him. As for my colleagues, they could receive the same amount of salary and benefits somewhere else but there is no other employer who would treat them and respect them like the way he did. Even though we have gone our separate ways in our careers,

I carry his image in my mind when I deal with my employees and I think this has made me a better and more influential manager.

Walking the Talk: Select a situation in your life where you influenced or were influenced by someone based on the power of personality. (1) **D**etermine whether the power potential was a function of interpersonal admiration and attraction. (2) **E**valuate the degree to which their inspirational and magnetic qualities determined the relative influence of the parties involved. (3) **A**nalyze why or why not these strategies were effective at translating power into influence and how you could have more effectively applied or neutralized this type of power. (4) **L**everage these insights to enhance your ability to grow and appropriately wield referent power as well as develop methods for reducing your vulnerability to it.

> To grow and effectively use referent power, I will...

7.6 Growing and Using Position Power

Ask Yourself: Are some people more powerful simply by virtue of their legitimate office or location in an organizational hierarchy? What about some positions make them more powerful than others? Can one position afford more influence than another even when they are technically on the same level? How can you increase the power of your position by managing its centrality or visibility?

Management Theory: A person's interpersonal power is partly a function of the formal position that they occupy in their organization. This refers to a legitimate source of power, or the influence potential that is grounded in an appointed role vis-à-vis the official organizational structure and rules. By virtue of their location in the hierarchy of authority some people (e.g., bosses) clearly have the right to influence others (subordinates and direct reports). Thus legitimate power is enhanced by rising up the corporate ladder. However place on the organizational chart is not the only important aspect of a position. For instance, people can become more powerful if their job has certain sets of characteristics. One is that it is located within an important workflow or provides access to key information; say like an executive secretary or key project liaison. Lesson—You become more powerful if you can implant your role in the middle of the action. This is because influence potential is greater when important matters go through or are reliant on you; it increases your resources and connections. Another aspect of a position that determines its power is its visibility. That is to say, power is greater when a position is seen as prominent and easily noticed by others; say like a division head or team spokesperson. Lesson—You become more powerful if you can locate yourself in a position with high exposure and recognition. This is because influence potential is greater when people can attach your face to a project, performance, or idea; it increases your identification, notoriety, and perceived standing. It is for these reasons that power-savvy people often act to enhance their centrality and visibility. Our story is by a worker who learned how to be successful in this type of pursuit.

In Action [Case Study]: In my company, people are very competitive and always looking for a way to get ahead. The key formula for promotion is excellent performance multiplied by visibility. Unfortunately many times my boss received the credit for work that I prepared. I realized that I was lacking visibility as an important determinant of position power. Therefore it was critical that I changed this. Since my boss began traveling more I have offered to take on more responsibility and "pitch in." She agreed and I have begun taking her place in more and more meetings and am now actually having direct contact and face-to-face communication with senior management. Another opportunity for gaining visibility was participation in multigroup projects. I recently contributed to a project such as this and it has proven to be very beneficial in terms of new relationships. In addition, there is currently a new project that is extremely visible to high-level management so I have asked to be part of this and it was approved. Since I started taking on more responsibility, people outside my group have actually begun to contact me directly with their questions, including top management. *Since I have become involved in more meetings and projects, I have increased my name recognition tremendously.* I am very pleased that I have been able to make myself more visible at work. I feel that not only am I being challenged more, but that my power has also increased. To continue improvement in this area, I will continue to strive to meet new people in the organization through meetings, phone calls, and projects and make them aware that I am a hard worker who they will be able to rely on. I have also started to go out with people from different groups for drinks after work. Through this I have been increasing my contacts within the firm. Also now I usually try to arrive early at meetings to "work the room" and make impressions with the right people. By becoming more visible, I am finally being recognized for my accomplishments and this has already helped me advance in my career.

Walking the Talk: Select a situation in your life where you influenced or were influenced by someone based on their location or office. (1) Determine whether the power potential was a function of ones position. (2) Evaluate the degree to which peoples' centrality or visibility determined the relative influence of the parties involved. (3) Analyze why or why not these strategies were effective at translating power into influence and how you could have more effectively applied or neutralized this type of power. (4) Leverage these insights to enhance your ability to grow and appropriately wield position power as well as develop methods for reducing your vulnerability to it.

To grow and effectively use position power, I will...

7.7   Playing Proactive Politics: Being on the Offensive

Ask Yourself: Is your workplace (or any for that matter) political? Why are some places more political than others? Is it more important what you know or sometimes who you know? Do people ever play politics to try and get ahead? What are some of the ways in which they do this?

Management Theory: Whereas politics is frowned upon by many, by others it is a common and potentially legitimate means to get things done. Quite simply politics is often a fact of organizational life and to ignore it is to put oneself and ones interests at a distinct disadvantage. Formally defined, politics is the use of one's power bases outside of specified job descriptions. It supplements formal means and authority mechanisms for achieving objectives. At its extreme, it might also substitute or sublimate the prescribed order where bending the rules becomes a sort of rule into itself. We know from management theory that interpersonal dynamics are more political under many circumstances: when resources are scarce and political behavior seeks an edge in obtaining them, when standards are unclear and political behavior seeks to proactively customize them, when expectations or pressures are high and political behavior seeks an artificial boost in meeting them, when trust is low or rules are oppressive and political behavior seeks to circumvent them, when higher-ups act in this manner and political behavior seeks to model them, and when facts are open to interpretation and political behavior seeks to define them. Managers and employees will often engage in "politicking" to obtain a desired goal or career opportunity. From proactive networking to subtle manipulations and blatant "brown-nosing" the astute political animal will be able to exploit opportunities that exist in the organization before the next person even notices them. Among the many political tools at a manager's disposal are making connections and building alliances, controlling and accessing information, acclaiming and advertising ones successes, and shaping ones image and managing others' impressions. Indeed these types of political skills have been linked to increased influence and promotions on the job. Our story is about a manager who has learned some of these ways to "work the system."

In Action [Case Study]: Managers like me have to learn how to get resources and cooperation from people. Many companies are extremely high in "politicking" due to the extremely competitive corporate environment. In particular at my company if you do not look out for yourself you will fall behind the masses. It is up to the individual to control his or her own destiny. This is something I recently took into my own hands in regards to a future job opportunity. I knew that I want a different job but had a limited interaction with this department. Using the theory as a guide I developed working and recreational relations with members of this department like going out to lunch or drinks. I also began sending out e-mails to key people in the department with information about their clients that could help them. Last month even took a few workers there out to the ballgame. At the same time I made sure that they knew about my accomplishments at work and would "go to bat for me" when needed. I also became involved with a project that will directly benefit this department's future and made myself available at all times to help in any way if needed. When a job opened recently I found out before anyone else. The normal procedure for a job-change is to go through HRM. However, I approached the head of their department at a recent social outing and inquired about the position. He already knew my name and much about me because of the contact I have had with his department. We sat down over a beer (which I bought) and talked about working in the department and I expressed my eagerness for the job. *I knew that I had to go over and above the normal channels of applying for the position because of the extremely high competition coming from within the organization and from outside applicants. If I did not then one of my coworkers would gain an edge over me.* The fact that I received the promotion mostly on my own inner drive has increased my performance and satisfaction on the job. However, the pressure at times from knowing that your career can be made or broken through political maneuvering can have a negative effect. Politics can also cause someone stress when they do not win at the game.

Walking the Talk: Select a situation in your life where someone played offensive politics. (1) **D**etermine whether the behavior was both proactive and political in nature. (2) **E**valuate the degree to which the behavior was effective in achieving its desired goals. (3) **A**nalyze the reason why the parties involved played politics and how you could have more effectively engaged them. (4) **L**everage these insights to enhance your ability to detect as well as proactively practice politics and develop skills for better playing the game.

To more effectively politic and play offensive, I will...

7.8   Playing Reactive Politics: Being on the Defensive

Ask Yourself: Do people ever attempt to play politics to escape blame for a mistake? Get out of a doing job or task? Avoid responsibility for a failed assignment? Defend their area or turf from others? Pass the buck on a tough decision or dilemma? Is this behavior part of an effective manager's repertoire? How can you best utilize or defend yourself against this behavior by others?

Management Theory: Sometimes politics is also needed to protect oneself. That is to say, one can also play defensive politics. These behaviors are defensive in nature because their aim is not to obtaining resources or seize opportunities but instead to simply get out of a jam. Yet these techniques can actually be quite sophisticated and involve complex maneuvers. They can also be outright manipulative through such actions as boldface lies or subtle deceit. Management theory has identified several types of political defensive behavior strategies—(1) Attempts to avoid work, say by feigning incompetence, playing dumb, clinging to set routines, or through stretching and stalling techniques to make oneself look busy; (2) Attempts to avoid blame, for instance by passing the buck and scapegoating others, rationalizing and reinterpreting events to obscure responsibility, meticulously documenting actions and creating paper trails to build alibis; demonstrating selective memory by advantageously forgetting mistakes, misrepresenting facts to alter storylines, and concealing evidence (as with the good old shredder) to hide misdeeds; and (3) Attempts to avoid incursions, for example, by defending ones "turf" from others meddling, resisting changes in policy or procedures, or rigidly interpreting formal guidelines and historical boundaries to maintain existing power bases. Whereas politics can be useful in getting things done it can also be a mechanism for escaping penalties or putting ones own well being ahead of that of the larger whole. Managers must therefore guard against those who would abuse these techniques. They might also verse themselves in such strategies to sniff our and counter them. Our story is by a manager who has done just this, using her knowledge of defensive politics to overcome another's deceptive defensive efforts.

In Action [Case Study]: Unfortunately I was recently affected by someone's defensive behavior and attempts to avoid blame through the misrepresentation of information. I had a colleague who tried to advance up the corporate ladder no matter what it took. Last Wednesday, he went a bit too far. During a meeting, he was asked about an old document on which we had both served as reviewers. The document contained some information that our supervisor was searching for but could not locate in the proper files. The content of the document was my colleague's primary responsibility so it was his error in not filing it correctly. Afterward he requested a backup copy from our auditors and, instead of coming clean about the error, circulated a doctored-up copy at the meeting with only my initials appearing on it! After the meeting I asked our auditors for a copy of what was faxed to my colleague and found that he had whited-out his initials to make it appear like I was solely responsible for the document. The original document not only had his initials on it, but also some additional information that was pertinent to the document in his handwriting at the bottom of the page. The entire bottom section had completely disappeared from the copy circulated at the meeting. My colleague was trying to pass the blame to me for misfiling this document. He made sure nothing on the document had either his initials or any of his handwriting on it. This is an unethical example of avoiding blame through misrepresentation. *Fortunately I was able to counter this through my own defensive behavior of rigorous documentation.* Management theory tells us that in the long-run defensive behavior usually catches up to an individual. In my colleague's case this has happened. I went to my boss to clarify what had happened and "clear my name." Apparently, my colleague had done similar things before and no action had been taken. However, what he did to me was the most serious and my employer was now forced to fire him. The impact of defensive behavior on performance in the long run is usually negative. It tends to reduce effectiveness by distracting energy from solving the task at hand. A person who consistently engages in defensive behavior eventually loses the trust of his bosses and peers, which is exactly what happened to my colleague. However defensive politics can also save you from unethical attacks, which is what happened to me.

Walking the Talk: Select a situation in your life where someone played defensive politics. (1) **D**etermine whether the behavior was both reactive and political in nature. (2) **E**valuate the degree to which the behavior was effective in achieving its desired goals. (3) **A**nalyze the reason why the parties involved played politics and how you could have more effectively engaged them. (4) **L**everage these insights to enhance your ability to detect as well as reactively practice politics and develop skills for better playing the game.

To more effectively politic and play defense, I will...

7.9 Playing Group Politics: Forming a Coalition

Ask Yourself: Is their strength in numbers? Can you become more powerful by aligning yourself with more powerful or like-minded others? Does it help to gain the support of other people when pursuing a common cause? Does your ability to influence someone ever depend on who and how many people back you up?

Management Theory: Even when one does not have very much personal influence, politics can still be played on the group level. One way is by aligning individuals around a specific issue to integrate their power and increase your combined influence. This is known as a political coalition tactic. The essence of coalitions is that there is strength in numbers. Where an individual lacks the needed power or political clout to get a job done, or if it is too difficult or risky to act on their own, then they can form a coalition to expand their combined level of influence to achieve the desired objective. One way to look at coalitions is that they are in a sense the formation of a larger, and theoretically more powerful, "individual" comprised of the many smaller individuals. In addition to pure numbers, quality as well as quantity counts in a coalition. Therefore coalitions might also seek to gain the support of an upper-level ally or powerful other who can legitimize or even lend their considerable influence to support the collective effort. In this sense coalitions can increase ones power by tapping into the significantly larger power base of a higher-up. All together, coalitions often are aimed at countering more powerful or senior parties that cannot be confronted on ones own—for example, a boss or a bully. They are also often formed as a response to others' opposing coalitions—for example, labor versus management, allies versus axis, and jets versus sharks. Our story is by a manager who was able to achieve their objectives and counter a more powerful other by using a group-level political coalition tactic.

In Action [Case Study]: Two weeks ago we received our yearly bonuses, and they did not meet our expectations. For myself, the bonus was approximately one-third of what I had expected based on previous bonuses and the fact that I was more than 150 percent billable in that quarter that is the primary determinant of one's percentage of the bonus pool. However, when presented with the bonus figures for his approval, the Division VP felt that they were too large and so decided to reduce the overall bonus pool by some 40 percent and then recalculate the individual bonuses. To compound the problem, he did nothing to communicate this to the affected employees but instead chose to simply implement the revised bonus structure and let the chips fall where they may. In my view, this represented a considerable violation of trust and presented the potential to drive a significant wedge between the employees and management. I therefore felt that the situation was worthy of bringing it to the attention of the decision maker, but at the same time I was concerned that I lacked the power and political clout to get my point across as an individual. *It was at this point that I put into practice what we had learned from management theory about playing politics. I sought to form a coalition to build my power base and gain some additional clout.* I began by securing the support of two higher-level senior vice presidents above me and then enlisted the assistance of several managers at my level to begin an e-mail campaign to the Division VP voicing our concerns on this issue. I believed I was successful in forming an effective coalition and that it was the right thing to do under the circumstances. Judging from the immediate impact, the formation of an effective coalition, being one which actually increases the power of the individuals within the coalition, had a positive effect as the individuals felt more in control of their work environment. It has also had a positive effect on our wallets as the coalition was successful in reinstating the bonus pool to its prior amount. We received adjustments for our bonus checks that were in line with the most optimistic of expectations. Applying management theory pays, literally.

Walking the Talk: Select a situation in your life where you suspect someone purposefully formed a coalition to improve their influence. (1) **D**etermine whether the behavior was indeed both collective and political in nature. (2) **E**valuate the degree to which the behavior was effective in achieving its desired goals. (3) **A**nalyze the reason why the parties involved played group-level politics and how it could have been done even more effectively. (4) **L**everage these insights to enhance your ability to display as well as detect group politics and develop skills for better playing the game.

To more effectively play group politics and form coalitions, I will…

CHAPTER EIGHT

Resolving Conflicts with Others

Chapter eight examines management theories about interpersonal conflict and the management skill of resolving conflicts with others. It is striking to consider just how many conflicts big and small that we experience with others in the course of a typical workday, week, month, or year. Yet in some sense it should not be all that surprising when one also realizes just how much potential for conflict there is in the interpersonal workplace arena. We might even think it inevitable that social beings who come from such diverse backgrounds and experiences, who possess varying needs and proclivities, whose tastes and preferences are so different, whose goals and objectives are so distinct, and yet whose jobs are increasingly intertwined and outcomes interdependent, will eventually come to some degree of disagreement. Interpersonal conflict occurs where there is the real or perceived clash of interests or subsequent influence attempts. That is to say, conflict happens when one person thinks that another might intentionally or even indirectly negatively affect something that they care about. Despite widespread notions that conflict is a bad thing that should be avoided whenever possible, it can be quite functional and actually serve to enhance the quality of an interaction—if managed to the right form, amount, and direction. In fact, management theory supports the idea that there are better or worse ways to deal with conflict that then produce positive or negative results. Therefore in this eighth chapter we look at how one can better navigate the conflict process and achieve positive conflict outcomes with people.

8.1 Appreciating the Importance of Conflict Management

Ask Yourself: Is conflict a good or bad thing? Do the best performing projects experience zero conflict? If not how do they handle it? When should managers suppress or encourage conflict among their workers? Can interpersonal conflict, if managed well, actually boost the production and satisfaction of its participants?

Management Theory: Although it might appear counterintuitive and contrary to common ways of thinking, the highest performing ongoing interactions tend not to be conflict-free. That is to say, it is rarely in the best interests of managers to completely snuff out interpersonal conflict. Instead there is a sweet spot where there is neither an overabundance nor paucity of conflict. Too much conflict can lead to discontent and disharmony, where people seem to be at each others throats and spending more time fighting then working, and this situation is seldom productive or enjoyable. However the absence of conflict can similarly harm interactions by promoting apathy, complacency, stagnation, and a false sense of security and confidence. Conflict-free is typically not the best place to be in order to stir people to action, motivate their strongest efforts, and inspire their best ideas, or push a group to its maximum potential. A team of rivals has much richer potential than a homogonous horde or complacent collective. Thus a good starting point for appreciating the value of conflict is to accept that it is probably inevitable in interpersonal engagements of any significant direction or duration. This is especially the case in our era of globalization where historically unprecedented levels of diversity and interdependence in the workforce have increased both the probability and promise of conflict. Managers thus must build the conceptual understanding and practical skills to tap the divergent yet potentially complementary insights and interactions of their employees. Our story is by a manager who redirected conflict in her firm to turn around a bad situation and achieve positive results.

In Action [Case Study]: As a manager I deal with potential conflict every day. For example, because of orders placed incorrectly, missing approvals, or requests not placed on time, my employees encounter difficulties in our ongoing operations. Every month we have found several discrepancies between billing and monthly recoveries and this was an ongoing issue. For the longest time I suppressed conflict with the belief that it was better not to make waves. However after familiarizing myself with the theory it made me initiate a conflict to solve the situation. First, I went to the supervising manager of the problem division and described the issue by explaining why his actions cause our projects to be delayed and require more work and man-hours. Second, I outlined the specific observable consequences of these behaviors. It had to do with mistakes made by his group. Third, I described the feelings I experienced as a result of this problem. My human resources are diverted and I get very frustrated and angry making it even more difficult to meet deadlines. *Our conflict* *was very helpful because the other manager worked with me to fix the problem, and we have actually become more productive and better friends as a result of this.* To solve the problem together, I worked closely with his group to establish a positive climate by inviting other workers to express their opinions and ask questions about the process. Because all parties should be committed to the solution and satisfied that they have been treated fairly, my posture was "I am committed to finding the best possible solution." I gave them specific examples such as situations when orders were incorrectly placed and duplicate billing took place. In our discussions I did not let frustration sour my tone. I strongly believe that my approach was very effective because changes were made and seen in their group. They were willing to be more conscientious in the process and help us with any issues or acquire backup documentation. Overall, this group started to improve their performance and our employees interacted on a much higher level to produce better results for the organization. I will follow the same steps when dealing with future conflict situations and not shy away from issues just because it is easier or less confrontational. I used to be terrified of conflict but have learned that it is nothing to fear and can actually solve problems and strengthen relationships if managed correctly.

Walking the Talk: Select a situation in your life where you experienced a conflict situation. (1) **D**etermine whether the conflict was created by a real or perceived clash of interests. (2) **E**valuate the degree to which you were willing to engage in the conflict. (3) **A**nalyze in what ways the conflict influenced your performance and/or morale and if it could have been better managed. (4) **L**everage these insights to enhance your appreciation for the importance of good conflict management.

To better appreciate the importance of conflict management, I will...

8.2   Identifying the Sources of Conflict

Ask Yourself: Where does conflict come from? From what conditions or factors does it tend to arise? How can managers identify the actual source(s) of conflict? How can they use this knowledge to better manage the conflict?

Management Theory: The extent to which we can pinpoint the source of a conflict increases our ability to successfully manage it. Management theory shows us that there are a myriad of reasons why we might experience interpersonal conflict at the workplace. First, aspects of the general climate in which interactions take place can feed the potential for conflict. These include recessionary economies or scarce resources that create conditions of overly stressed and on-edge employees, unclear policies or shifting standards that create conditions of excessive ambiguity and multiple interpretations, and new technologies or changing competitive or institutional/political platforms that create conditions of uncertainty and opposing positions. Second, conflict can arise from the organizational roles and responsibilities that people are charged with executing as they work together. These include interdependent jobs that cause problems sorting out divergent objectives, opposing time tables that cause problems blending different priorities, hierarchical and status differences that cause problems ranking varying performance criteria, ill-defined responsibilities that cause problems harmonizing overlapping lines of authority, narrow functional specializations that cause problems reconciling contrary mindsets, poor working conditions that cause problems overcoming physical discomforts, insufficient communication systems that cause problems connecting ideas and agendas, and inconsistent reward systems that cause problems meeting dissimilar targets. Third, conflict can stem from personal variables such as those factors discussed in the initial section of the book, for example due to clashes of personalities, value systems, or motivations. As these lists illustrate, there are a multitude of potential sources that can seed conflict so managers need to diagnose and identify where the actual conflict is coming from if they are to avoid missing the target and have any realistic chance of successfully addressing it. Our story is by an entrepreneurial manager uncovering the various sources of conflict in the venture and learning valuable lessons on how to manage them productively.

In Action [Case Study]: Conflict is the lifeblood of vibrant, progressive, stimulating organizations. Yet conflicts often become highly emotional and if not managed properly can destroy a group and sink a company. Our new business venture was in danger of this about six months ago when constant conflict threatened our ability to work together and be productive. *By analyzing the feedback given by my partners and executive team we have isolated where the conflict was coming from and this made it possible to manage.* I figured out that one of the sources was personal, that I was too much of a perfectionist. I liked to have control over everything and wanted things to work as a Swiss Watch. I have since learned along the way to be more flexible and understanding by asking for feedback from my business partners and coworkers and placing elements on the table to get as many points of view as possible. Another source was structural, that we had different areas of expertise and simply came at problems from different points of view. We eventually agreed upon customer satisfaction as the central metric that would let us arrive at a consensus. Realistic action plans were adopted to get past our different perspectives and agree on the tasks to be prioritized to further this shared goal. I really learned a valuable lesson: that my way is not always going to be right. Differences are an important tool to provide better solutions to the way the business is managed. I used to feel frustrated when we saw the same issue in different ways but now we keep the lines of communication open to get ideas together and get the whole group involved to solve problems together. Even though we do not agree on everything, we get useful input from each other. My executive team members actually said in the last board meeting that I was being much more flexible and better able to see that there are other sides to issues. I have begun to take things less personally and look at things from a broader perspective then just my own job responsibilities. I will continue to work on this and remember an important lesson, to listen to valuable and honest feedbacks so that I could identify where conflict is coming from, be it the roles in the organization or the people in them including myself, and address it in the proper manner.

Walking the Talk: Select a situation in your life where you found cause to enter into conflict. (1) **D**etermine whether the conflict was the result of single or multiple factors and where it was coming from. (2) **E**valuate the degree to which you could successfully identify and appropriately address the source of conflict. (3) **A**nalyze why you were or were not able to pinpoint the source of conflict and how this affected your ability to deal with it. (4) **L**everage these insights to enhance your ability to isolate and remedy different sources of conflict.

To more accurately identify the source(s) of conflict, I will...

8.3   Managing the Stages of Conflict

Ask Yourself: How does conflict happen? Does it hit people all at once or are there fairly predictable patterns in which a conflict unfolds? Are there different challenges at each point of a conflict? Are there better and worse ways to manage these various stages of the conflict process?

Management Theory: Conflict tends to build through a series of phases or predictable patterns of activity. In each of these stages there are better and worse ways to manage the interpersonal interaction. The first stage of the conflict process is the creation of the seeds, antecedents, or incompatibilities that give rise to a potential clash of interests. Pinpointing and managing these sources is essential. The next stage occurs when this latent conflict becomes personal. People become aware of these divergences and experience tensions that affect their relationship. Often time parties begin to get emotional and focus on the conflict in a negative way. Alternatively managers can frame conflict as an opportunity to positively effect change. A third type of dynamic occurs is when the conflict escalates into full-fledged opposition. Here conflicting parties stake out positions regarding the conflict and form different strategies for dealing with it which can be more or less competitive and cooperative in nature (see section 8.6). The next phase happens when people actually interact with the other person or persons to try and resolve the manifest conflict. These actions can also be guided in more or less positive directions. Finally the outcomes of the conflict can be steered to either facilitate or impede the goals of the participants as well as those of the larger group or organization. It is the astute manager who can understand how a conflict process is moving forward so that they can identify its stage of progress and manage it appropriately. Whereas conflicts sometime need to be simply shepherded along their path other times they might be better served by restarting, regressing, or redefining particular stages in the process that have gone awry. Our story is by a manager doing the latter, essentially reshaping multiple phases of the conflict process that were going in the wrong direction thereby turning the situation around to a positive resolution.

In Action [Case Study]: A little more than a month ago, I went through the stages of conflict with my current employer over year-end rewards. In the first stage of potential opposition, it was anticipated through rumors that compensation benefits would be slashed. This conflict was not felt until the second stage of the conflict process where employees, including me, got the actual numbers and were shocked at the frugalness of the firm. My emotions got involved and I felt that this was something that was real and personal. It was a confused moment filled with frustration. This led me to question the intent of the firm, which is the third stage of conflict. However, before I could form a strategy for dealing with the conflict, I felt like we were in the fourth stage of the process, which is behavior. We started to openly challenge the motives and actions of the firm. I was infuriated with the firm and accused my director because all the hard work done the previous year was overlooked and the yearly assessments, which gave me the top tier rating, did not reap any rewards. This led to the fifth and last stage, which was a dysfunctional outcome for everyone involved. There was hostility and a reduction in employees' cohesiveness and performance with echoes of loud complaints heard throughout the department. This led to me using management theory to better improve the process. We cycled back to previous stages and adjusted our perspectives to make the conflict less personal and try to see the situation from upper management's point of view. Then we changed our strategies and behaviors to collaboratively voice our opinions and justify different monetary as well as nonmonetary ways of compensating us. *By reshaping the stages of the conflict the end result of the new process became much more positive. We received a promise of year-end adjustments and until then we could work on flexible time schedules.* This was very lucrative to me personally as I could now come in a half hour early and leave work early allowing me to make it to graduate school on time, something I was unable to accomplish in the past. In return there were less complaints throughout the department, less absenteeism, fewer people jumping ship, and productivity got back to usual in hope of the midyear adjustment. Both sides of the party were happy and better off.

Walking the Talk: Select a situation in your life where you found yourself in a conflict process. (1) **D**etermine whether the conflict unfolded in a series of different phases. (2) **E**valuate the degree to which the stages were managed well. (3) **A**nalyze why the conflict unfolded in this manner and how the process could have been improved, redirected, or redefined. (4) **L**everage these insights to enhance your ability and develop requisite skills to manage the conflict process.

To better manage the conflict process, I will…

8.4   Achieving Functional Conflict

Ask Yourself: Are some types of conflict inherently better than others? Why do these particular forms of conflict tend to energize versus drain a group? Impel rather than subvert it? Focus rather than destroy it? How can managers facilitate this positive or functional conflict?

Management Theory: The right type of conflict can impel people to higher levels of efficiency and effectiveness. Conflict is functional when it focuses squarely on solving the central issues that bear on achieving the group's objective without care or concern for unnecessary tangents or peripheral agendas. Functional conflict is that which establishes the best objectives for the interpersonal interaction and the best methods for realizing them. It takes up the big issues and tasks that determine the success of the collective and its membership. It constructively promotes problem solving, creates a dynamic environment of positive exchanges, capitalizes on opportunities to learn and grow, and improves processes and progress related to the parties' central objectives and concerns. It stays on tasks and does not degenerate into personal squabbles or petty arguments. It recognizes the legitimacy and value of differences and works to reconcile them with respect and an eye to the larger ends. It encourages and supports minority views and dissenting opinions rather than suppressing potential insights. It lessens rather than magnifies negative tensions, unleashes creative energy, and allows for the integration of perspectives to develop better solutions. It builds a common identity and interpersonal bonds rather than segmenting and dividing its parties into irreconcilable factions. It launches innovative solutions and promotes positive change. Thus managers are well advised to promote this type of functional conflict by facilitating the above characteristics. Our story is by a manager who succeeded in creating functional conflict in the organization.

In Action [Case Study]: Is it possible to control the conflict in such way that it does not harm the well being of the employees and employer, and even improves it? Based on my experience at work, the answer is "Yes." *I have learned that it is possible, with some effort on the management part, to stream the conflict in the positive current.* It starts with selecting "right" people for the job who would contribute new dimensions to the discussion. It could be such factors as an unusual background, different culture, rich experience, or unique personality. Looking with naked eye, such mix of people would never produce desired results. I held similar opinion when I became part of a major project a few years ago. When we got together for a meeting these people started to propose and debate various, untraditional ideas on how to handle the situation. Eventually, the best alternative evolved. I doubt we could have found the solution if we came at this from a single perspective. The second ingredient in a functional conflict is the "right" setting. We had people participate from different departments. Thus, there was implicit conflict between our operations department and other managers. We cared about quality and focused on the deadline. The reporting group looked for accuracy of reports. Programmers emphasized performance and fixing bugs in the system. The initial intent of the representatives of these departments was to compete with each other but our manager made them all realize that, no matter how important their departments' objectives, the bottom line was to maximize performance and profits as one unit. Soon enough the individuals made arguments in terms of "us" instead of "me." Members of the meeting really worked together. There is another aspect to functional conflict that is good communication. At one extreme the argument can become too aggressive and personal. Another side of communication is passive when issues are postponed and parties avoid communicating on conflicting matters. At first we were quiet and disinterested. When things warmed up tempers flew high quickly transforming into personal accusations. Our managers calmed the storm by refocusing the conflict and asking us: "What can be done?," "When it will be done?," "Who is going to be doing it?" instead of "Who's fault is it?," "Why is it not done yet?" Soon we shifted back from personal to business matters. It is hard to control the conflict but since it exists naturally in organizations and our lives we should be using it to our advantage. If proper conflict management is put together the outcome can be very positive.

Walking the Talk: Select a situation in your life where you had a good experience with conflict. (1) **D**etermine whether the conflict helped or hindered the interpersonal interaction. (2) **E**valuate the degree to which the dynamic resembled functional conflict and resulted in correspondingly positive outcomes. (3) **A**nalyze why the conflict produced these results and how the characteristics of functional conflict could be facilitated. (4) **L**everage these insights to enhance your ability and develop the skills to promote functional conflict.

To more effectively achieve functional conflict, I will...

8.5   Minimizing Dysfunctional Conflict

Ask Yourself: Are some types of conflict inherently worse than others? Why do these particular types of conflict tend to drain versus energize a group? Subvert rather than impel it? Destroy rather than focus it? How can managers reduce this negative or dysfunctional conflict?

Management Theory: The flip-side of the previous discussion about promoting functional conflicts is the desire to reduce poorly formed conflicts that can eat away at performance and morale. These types of conflicts are NOT opposite ends of a continuum; rather they represent fundamentally different types of interpersonal dynamics and hence are conceptually as well as practically distinct. One needs to be increased, the other reduced. Conflict is dysfunctional when it is centered on tangents and personal variables that neither promote the collective good nor facilitate the achievement of important tasks and objectives. This type of conflict is like a disease that diverts the attention, saps the spirit, drains the resources, and hinders the progress of its participants. When conflict gets the group off track and forces it to spend time and energy on unessential, nonactionable, lower-level, or unrelated issues then it is more likely to harm the interaction. When conflict focuses on personal variables, affective predilections or idiosyncrasies, and personality differences then it is more likely to harm the interaction. When conflict promotes excessive politicking, personal agendas, and myopic views that may work against formal goals and strategies then it is more likely to harm the interaction. When conflict creates more problems and tasks than it solves then it is more likely to harm the interaction. In each of these cases conflict weakens rather than strengthens the parties involved and inhibits their effectiveness. Our story is by a manager who experienced a dysfunctional workplace conflict that could have been better managed but, because it was not reduced, caused significant negative fallout in his company.

In Action [Case Study]: Dysfunctional conflict arises when differences in opinion, personality and/or background sidetrack a group's activity and hinder a group's performance. A dysfunctional situation involving a line producer and the production staff at my company began with what was thought to be a reconcilable situation but ultimately resulted in a horrible working environment and an eventual loss in productivity and human resources. As a line manager my major responsibility was to oversee the media production of a show. One of our new producers experienced problems with her people, but initially the difficulties were viewed as personal adjustments to the company. Unfortunately, the producer turned out to be a poor communicator who was abusive with her command. The entire staff realized that the difficulties hindered productivity. They took an optimistic approach when they came to the producer with the problem. Unfortunately, the producer took personal offense at this and from then on, she intentionally mistreated her workers. At the time, reasons for her reactions were not clear, but in retrospect, it was obvious that she was only concerned about her well-being and to compete for recognition and personal promotion. She was eventually confronted by me and other senior people but still there were no positive results as the ill-will and out-of-control bickering destroyed teamwork and torpedoed the entire project. Predictably the loyalty of her subordinates deteriorated, and people no longer wanted to work for my company just because they did not want to end up working for this producer. As you can see from this example, dysfunctional conflicts are detrimental not only to group goals but also to emotions of individuals and the business environment. *The conflict was never about matters essential to the job but only minor issues and personal disagreements.* In my company's situation, performance suffered from the poor working relationships. The production staff was unsatisfied due to the petty and adversarial climate. No one was willing to accommodate or tolerate the producer. They called in sick often and pawned responsibilities off. Literally her entire staff eventually left the company within a year. The sad irony is that this whole situation could have been prevented by addressing the dysfunctional conflict. It was stupid and completely unnecessary. Unfortunately it was allowed to spiral out of control and take a big chuck out of our talent pool and bottom line.

Walking the Talk: Select a situation in your life where you had a bad experience with conflict. (1) **D**etermine whether the conflict ultimately helped or hindered the interpersonal interaction. (2) **E**valuate the degree to which the dynamic resembled that of dysfunctional conflict and resulted in correspondingly negative outcomes. (3) **A**nalyze why the conflict produced these results and how it might be redirected. (4) **L**everage these insights to enhance your ability and develop the skills to minimize dysfunctional conflict.

To avoid dysfunctional conflict, I will…

8.6   Promoting "Win-Win" Integrative Thinking

Ask Yourself: Is conflict management just about getting what you want at the expense of the other party? Is it simply a zero-sum game of winners and losers? Or can the interpersonal interaction be managed, even in the face of apparently irreconcilable incompatibilities, to produce win-win solutions where everyone is happy? What are the techniques you can use to facilitate this type of integrative thinking?

Management Theory: There are better and worse ways to handle a conflict situation. Whereas there are a variety of potentially appropriate strategies for doing this management theory posits that, all things being equal, it is generally best to work toward an integrative solution. The key to this type of approach is to reconceptualize the situation in a manner that makes it possible to fully satisfy the interests of all involved parties. An integrative conflict handling style is uniquely collaborative insofar as it expresses a high concern for both (1) your own interests and (2) the interests of the other party. It simultaneously seeks an outcome where everyone gets what they want. There are no adversaries or opponents, only interdependent partners with a long-term interest in each others well being. This makes it possible for everyone to get what they want through a mutually beneficial and satisfying process. Integration is thus the only approach to conflict that embodies true "win-win" thinking. To be sure we hear this term thrown around often yet moving beyond the cliché is not easy. More so than cutting a compromise deal where each participant gives up one thing to get another, an integrative approach to conflict transcends myopic perspectives and moves past transient positions to creatively address deep-seeded interests so both parties can fully satisfy their needs. It does so by asking the magical question "why"—Why do these people want these outcomes? Asking why cuts through the bluster to reveal fundamental objectives that might be solved synergistically. This allows participants to get beyond infighting over the distribution of slices within a "fixed pie" but instead grow the pie to accommodate all concerns. Integrative interactions promote open discussions and innovative solutions, create empathetic camaraderie and big-picture thinking, and inspire high levels of interpersonal trust and mutual commitment. Our story is by a manager who has learned from his team leader how to successfully approach conflict in an integrative manner.

In Action [Case Study]: I work on a team where win-win thinking is encouraged. The purpose of the team is to provide ongoing re-engineering of a major R&D function through design and implement of automation initiatives. *Our team has gained recognition from senior management as being innovative, creative, and working well together. The primary reason can be attributed to the collaborative attitude we structure into our team meetings.* The key to our success is a process we call "threshing." The term comes from the farming tool used to harvest crops, and we use this time in a similar way but to harvest ideas. My senior manager would tell you the purpose of the sessions is to challenge, as fully as possible, and to improve, as best as possible, the presenter's ideas. She insists on it. In fact, she wants ideas to be threshed even if everyone is in agreement, in an attempt to look at the ideas from as many viewpoints as possible—even if she herself is doing the presentation. It is not an easy process, but it is a necessary one. One that I have come to appreciate and would not have any other way. Why? Because it makes me do the best work I have ever done and give the best presentations I have ever given. Although one person is initially generating the ideas, the process forces seven other people to challenge and generate ideas for making it better. The criteria for making a decision are always the best interest of the team and not any particular individual. Since we spend so much time working together to build off each others ideas the final decisions are always win-win. Our sessions are very dynamic and exciting and fun. Sometimes people think from all the noise and activity that we are arguing and we are going to kill each other. In fact what we are doing is pushing each other to come up with solutions that everyone can really buy into. The results are recommendations that are seldom challenged by senior management and have gained widespread recognition. If it passes our team sessions, it usually goes all the way. Affective conflict simply does not exist. It is not allowed. Our manager only need to say it once—"it's never personal." If you cannot see that you do not belong to the team, then it is the end of story. Our collaborative team structure is one of the major reasons why I enjoy my work. Getting out of bed is not a chore. My performance is high, I am happy and I have yet to miss a single day of work.

Walking the Talk: Select a situation in your life where you actively managed conflict. (1) **D**etermine whether you approached the conflict from a truly integrative perspective. (2) **E**valuate the degree to which you were able to achieve a win-win solution. (3) **A**nalyze why you were able or failed to collaborate and what characteristics of the integrative process you could use to better facilitate this approach. (4) **L**everage these insights to enhance your ability to think and act win-win when managing conflicts.

To promote win-win thinking when managing conflicts, I will...

8.7   Reducing Excessive Avoiding Behavior

Ask Yourself: Do people sometimes avoid conflict even when it is better to address the situation head-on? Why? What are the disadvantages and long-term costs of ignoring important albeit contentious or controversial issues? What can managers do to better address tough situations instead of habitually sidestepping them?

Management Theory: Notwithstanding the advantage of increasing ones response range, managers (even upper-level and senior ones) often regress into their comfort zones and apply default preferences to handling conflict even if they are suboptimal. In this section and the next we will address two of these common problems. First, conflict avoidance tends to be overpracticed and inappropriately applied. That is to say, too often we simply sidestep conflict with the hopes that if we wait long enough it will go away. We ignore it and pretend that it is not there. This ostrich like bury-your-head-in-the-sand approach rarely makes things better and in fact can allow otherwise addressable conflicts to fester and grow, infecting other interactions and derailing the achievement of other goals. Just as ignoring a disease will seldom cure it, avoiding a problem will rarely fix it. Instead failure to engage a conflict implicitly favors a faulty status quo over the potential advantages of addressing the situation. Avoidance is neither assertive, promoting ones own interests, or cooperative, addressing others' interests, so in this sense can be seen as lose-lose. To be fair, there are some situations where avoidance is called for (such as when the issue is too controversial, peripheral to core objectives, or when building the relationship is more important than willing the point) but the reality is that all too frequently people avoid conflict more as a matter of convenience rather than a conscious strategic choice. Inappropriate avoidance could happen for a number of other reasons: An excessive aversion to disagreements and reticence to engage another in a potentially adversarial manner; misreading of the importance of conflict; or lacking sufficient commitment and energy to address the issue at hand. The result of overavoidance is often that important issues, difficult problems, and contentious matters do not get resolved. Our story is by a manager's plans to rectify this in the professional endeavors.

In Action [Case Study]: I dislike confrontations. I know now that avoidance is not usually the best way to handle conflicts. It reflects to the other individual involved that the issue is not very important and there is no open communication to resolve the problems. This causes the problem to persist and cause work performance to breakdown, extreme dissatisfaction to develop, and eventually people to leave. I used management theory to overcome my avoidance by acting on something that has long bothered me. I decided to address a conflict with other members in my Parish, specifically on one of my church's worship teams. Because I tend to avoid confrontation, I ended up neglecting the expression of my dissatisfaction to the group about our way of setting a vision, goals, and plans for further development. This just created more dissatisfaction for me and made me want to withdraw from the group without fully expressing the reasons why I was dissatisfied or not giving the members a chance to become aware of my concerns. In this situation, *I realized that the avoiding strategy was definitely not the appropriate way to handle this conflict because the members would never know that I had this concern if I never voiced it.* Therefore, I decided I needed to approach the group to talk about my concerns and suggest a collaborative method to resolving this conflict. I worked up the courage to bring this up at our last meeting. The membership was very supportive to acknowledge my concern and consequently we have set the next team meeting to discuss implementing a plan for better defining our vision and goals. Communication was opened up so that at the future meeting we would be able to discuss the concerns openly and possible solutions to improve our direction. Although the avoiding method was easy to use because there was no confrontation, it was definitely not the most productive or satisfying approach. Since we are all striving toward the same goal, I have suggested that quality time be spent for all the members to meet and openly discuss the possible development plans for growth. Since our team has meetings once every other month, I will be able to continue to keep track of the progress of this conflict resolution process.

Walking the Talk: Select a situation in your life where you failed to successfully manage conflict. (1) **D**etermine whether you actively addressed the conflict or essentially avoided it. (2) **E**valuate the degree to which you were able to initiate, rather than sidestep, the conflict management process. (3) **A**nalyze why you might have avoided the conflict and, if inappropriate, how you could apply strategies to overcome this tendency. (4) **L**everage these insights to enhance your ability to reduce excessive avoidance behavior when managing conflicts.

> To reduce excessive conflict avoiding behavior, I will...

8.8   Reducing Excessive Accommodating Behavior

Ask Yourself: Do people sometimes fold and simply give in to the other party when a conflict arises? Is it ever better to stand ones ground? Why? What are the disadvantages and long-term costs of acquiescing to others, especially when considering important issues? What can managers do to proactively address controversial situations instead of habitually appeasing others?

Management Theory: Here we consider the misuse of another frequently overused conflict management approach—accommodating. An accommodating conflict management strategy describes the tendency of giving-in to another person whenever conflict arises. It is in a sense an appeasement to the other party by acquiescing to their demands at the expense of ones own interests. It seeks to keeps the peace through self-sacrifice of ones personal welfare and, at its most extreme, perhaps even submission to others' transgressions against it. As per previous discussion, accommodating can be on some occasions the best path and might be effective in certain circumstances such as when one realized that they are wrong, too weak to win, or want to accumulate goodwill. It is not the intention of this section to blanketly discourage accommodating altogether. However adopting a habitual, reflexive, or perennial giving-in approach to conflict is not generally advisable for a number of reasons. It is unlikely to lead to a long-term sustainable and productive relationship. It effectively ignores the contributions, perspectives, and inputs of the accommodating party and allows bad blood to develop. It can harm the interests, agents, and clients whose welfare is entrusted to the accommodating party. It allows the underlying causes of the conflict to remain unaddressed and even fester and grow. It prioritizes short-term harmony over engaged collaboration and long-term effectiveness. In this sense it can actually result in a suboptimal scenario if all facets of the situation are not considered and important issues are not solved in the best possible manner. Thus managers must remain on guard to accommodate only when it is strategically advisable to do so and not because of expediency, comfort, or otherwise lesser objectives. Our story is by a manager who sought to overcome the overly accommodating tendency.

In Action [Case Study]: I challenged myself to become less of a pushover. Accommodating has gotten to be so ingrained in me that I think it takes quite an effort to just increase my awareness that I am so timid so often. The plan was to become less accommodating in small ways to develop the habits for doing so in big ways. I noticed the fruits of my efforts immediately when I told my new boss that I would not be able to meet her unreasonable deadline of completing hundred contracts in a week. I told her that either I need assistance or another week or two. It actually worked—she gave me two new people! I did not want to accommodate her for the sake of being accommodating. I just did not see the benefit of speeding through all these documents only to keep the same pace in the batch the coming week. It simply did not serve my or the organization's best interests. I thought to myself that I have to stand up now. *My reaction was one of surprise. I overcame my timidity and stood strong and actually got what I wanted.* I thought it might hurt productivity or our relationship, but she acknowledged my position and was willing to talk to me about spotting two other colleagues. I think that experience is the highlight of my initial efforts on being less accommodating. I also noticed that I have become less accommodating with my feelings and vocalization on other things at work. I am standing professionally strong when addressing my more aggressive coworkers—not just give in to their bullying. I even successfully stood my ground on getting my company to financially support me in an important training class. I drove home the benefits to both of us that could derive from this course. I was proud that I pushed for it. I found myself even saying things like "I expect to be educated for this job." I sometimes found myself in these situations to have such gusto that I wondered who this person was. Overall, I learned to take ownership of my future and realize that I deserve to be treated in a fair way. I am thrilled that I am no longer so timid at work and plan to stick to this development plan, without going overboard and creating a monster, because know that sometimes it is necessary to stand ones ground and as my career progresses I will only have more challenges to come.

Walking the Talk: Select a situation in your life where you failed to successfully managed conflict. (1) **D**etermine whether you actively addressed the conflict or essentially gave-in to the other party. (2) **E**valuate the degree to which you were able to stand up for rather than discount or ignore your interests. (3) **A**nalyze why you might have acquiesced during the conflict and, if inappropriate, how you could apply strategies to overcome this tendency. (4) **L**everage these insights to enhance your ability to reduce excessive accommodating behavior when managing conflicts.

> To reduce excessive conflict accommodating behavior, I will…

8.9   Negotiating Effectively

Ask Yourself: Are there better and worse ways to negotiate a conflict? Should negotiators always be "tough guys" and take the "hard line" in order to succeed? What factors can help managers negotiate in an integrative versus distributive manner? Are there certain methods or strategies that promote effective bargaining?

Management Theory: Negotiation can be a useful conflict management strategy if conducted appropriately. Drawing from previous discussion, a central principle to successful negotiation is to view the process as win-win, creatively attempting to benefit each partner rather than engaging in excessive positioning or aggressive posturing while trying to defeat ones "opponent." Management theory offers several methods to help people improve their interpersonal negotiation. Some of the most effective strategies include the following: Depersonalize the negotiation by untangling the issues from their proponents—this helps eliminate the personal variable in a quest for the best possible solution; Concentrate on underlying interests rather than arbitrary numbers or stated positions—this helps to thoughtfully develop mutually beneficial options; Creatively invent new ways of defining and approaching the conflict—this helps to grow rather than simply distribute the potential pie and pool of benefits; and Establishing fair and objective criteria for evaluating the outcome of the negotiation—this helps to break down barriers and develop a common standard for success. Other useful negotiating techniques include finding common ground for meaningful dialog, remaining professional by resisting personal or petty quarrels, emphasizing the positive possibilities of a solution instead of making threats or resorting to intimidation, defining moral commonplaces where parties can agree on certain overriding values that govern the exchange, and seeking to establish "superordinate" goals that supercede individualized concerns to unite the participants in a common cause (e.g., what is best for the organization as a whole rather than individual departments). As these strategies suggest, negotiation is both a science and an art that can be enhanced to better facilitate positive conflict management outcomes. Our story is by a manager who learned to become a more effective negotiator through the application of some of the above principles.

In Action [Case Study]: I had extreme difficulty negotiating business deals at work. I usually felt too competitive and adversarial and feared being seen as losing the negotiation. This is a "distributive" bargaining technique concentrating on dividing up a fixed pie where someone wins and someone loses. As a negotiator I assumed that I could only improve at the other party's expense. In contrast, integrative negotiators use problem-solving techniques to find "win-win" solutions rather than forcing a choice between the parties' preferred solutions. I believe that I use the distributive method because of what was expected of me. *I have always been coached to take a "hard line" or to "split the difference" when I negotiate. As a woman I also found that if I appear soft, that the other party would* *try to take advantage of me. However I realized that by using this distributive negotiating method I was hurting my company and myself.* I found that the hard line negotiation tactic was often ineffective and frequently counterproductive, not to mention extremely stressful. This hurts my performance and the stress significantly affected my as well as the firm's well being. Management theory gave me the groundwork to change. I implemented the following methods in my last negotiation with a corporate buyer: (1) Before negotiating I found a bigger purpose (superordinate) goal where my interests were satisfied and where there was a benefit to both sides. This required me to look at the big picture and understand both positions in order to come up with a common ideal. Although this took a long time, I found that the process made me a better negotiator. (2) I also tried to take the negotiating process less personally. This was difficult for me because I am so competitive. However, my competitiveness sometimes made me unreasonable. By focusing less on myself and more on the goal I found that I got a better, quicker, and less stressful deal completed. (3) Importantly, I also defined success in terms of gains, not losses. I presented the goals and outcomes as half full, not half empty. This left everyone involved in the process more satisfied. The development of better negotiating skills has not been easy. But I found as I changed from a competitive stance to a conflict resolution with a common goal, that my negotiation become easier, more successful, and less draining on my emotions. I also resisted when the buyer used negative attacks by pointing out that we need to focus on the common goal, rather than individual needs and opinions. I believe that these steps improved my negotiating skills and outcome.

Walking the Talk: Select a situation in your life where you were engaged in a negotiation process. (1) **D**etermine whether you negotiated in more of an integrative versus distributive manner. (2) **E**valuate the degree to which you achieved an optimal resolution. (3) **A**nalyze why you were, or were not, able to negotiate as effectively as you might like and specifically how different strategies could help you improve on this. (4) **L**everage these insights to enhance your negotiation ability and develop effective negotiation skills.

> To negotiate more effectively, I will...

SECTION III

Macro Management (=Us): The Organizational

For Building More Productive Workplace Environments

You + Them **= Us**

CHAPTER NINE

Forging High-Performance Teams

Chapter nine examines management theories about teamwork and the management skill of creating the conditions for high-performance teams to flourish. In the modern workplace organizations are forming workgroups, often labeling them as "teams," with an exceedingly high frequency. The lure of teams is partly a result of a rapidly evolving, highly competitive, and increasingly interdependent business context that is demanding greater flexibility and responsiveness of organizations. Groups are often used because they are seen as promising vehicles for responding to these demands. As a result employees are spending more and more of their time working together to complete assigned tasks. The sad irony of this is that few of these groups are managed appropriately so that they truly become teams. Let us be very clear about this, a group and a team are not the same thing. A group is a collection of two or more people who come together for a shared purpose. A team is a special type of group that actually achieves synergy, with its whole greater than the sum of its parts. This type of teamwork requires the proper environment that creates the conditions for this process to occur. Although there is no magic formula for forging productive teams, adherence to sound principles and practices will increase the potential for achieving synergistic results. Properly managed a team of well-aligned novices will often outperform a group of all-stars, and this is well documented in the triumphs of entrepreneurial upstarts, home-grown business ventures, and even underdog sports franchises who fostered true teamwork over more entrenched and better funded, yet less synergistic, organizations. Therefore in this ninth chapter we look at how firms can better establish the context where teamwork can flourish.

9.1 Appreciating the Importance of Group Dynamics

Ask Yourself: Can you predict the performance of a group by looking solely at the credentials of its individual members? Could you understand its functioning by simply adding the different human resources in some sort of equation? Or instead are there some interesting things that just tend to happen when people get together that can add or detract from members' potential? How can managers better appreciate the importance of these processes to create the context for well-managed workgroups?

Management Theory: In modern times it is important for organizations to create a facilitative climate where groups can thrive so to get the most out of their workers. Yet all too often when managers bring people together they neglect key ingredients for this and produce results that are (to put it kindly) less than optimal. Thus, it is critical for organizations to appreciate the importance of establishing the proper environment that can help turn groups into teams. Management theory tells us that a group is more than just the sum of its parts, and the interaction of its members often produces peculiar outcomes that are impossible to predict from looking just at its components. This is because people think and act differently in a group than when they are working alone. Organizations can influence these social structures to improve the way work is organized and conducted. For example, we know that when people are grouped together they morph to fill distinct "roles," act in accordance with "norms" and "status" relationships, form clusters of different "sizes" and degrees of "interdependence," and develop levels of "cohesiveness" that work to either enable their collective process gain (i.e., "synergy," or 2+2=5) or loss (where 2+2=3). Influenced properly these group attributes can increase the knowledge, communication, creativity, development, motivation, resource utilization, strategic flexibility, and performance of a firm. Used poorly they can slow down processes, magnify errors, neutralize talent, and skew perspectives. Our story is about a manager becoming more appreciative of these group and team processes at his firm.

In Action [Case Study]: I recently witnessed firsthand how the implementation of good group management techniques increased productivity of our department. This year our productivity was lagging for the longest time but, in the last four months, we experienced unprecedented progress in beating deadlines and surpassing expectations. *There is no doubt that our performance and satisfaction have increased due to the efficient management of the groups.* Following are the changes made by our management that resulted in such a positive improvement: Organization—We used to have two unit coordinators and two team leaders. That structure did not work well because two leaders had constant arguments and disagreements. It got to the point where employees started to take sides and whine about one

manager to another. Instead we now have one team leader and have unified behind him. Roles—Our management was not very specific about
what was expected of us before. We dealt with continuous uncertainty
in the matters of responsibilities (what do we have to do during the day),
vacation time (when are we taking vacation and how many days we actually have), work hours (when to start and when to go home), dress code
(how to come to work), communication (whom to report to and what
is the formal procedure). But lately we had our roles better defined for
us. As a result, we do more actual work in the same time. Norms—We
used to surf the Internet a lot, spend hours on the phone and generally
goof around. The management either did not know or did not care. A
few months ago they made a 180-degree turn, and we are now forced to
abide by more professional standards and limit our phone and Internet
use. Status—We are called an "Elite Group" now because we work on
a new, improved, system and bring the most profits to our department.
We get extra praise from our managers, and employees are now willing to go extra mile just to keep the status. Size—Our two groups of
eleven and ten people were broken down by our organization into three
equal groups of seven people each. That structure works out well as our
team meetings take less time, we get more personal attention, and our
response time has shortened. Cohesiveness—The previous adjustments
plus physical separation from others and smart seating allocation made
us create close-knit groups. We now have some people always going to
Chinatown for lunch, getting together to discuss issues, and going to a
bar to play pool after work. In other words, encouraged by our firm we
found common ground within the teams and thus became more satisfied
and productive at work.

Walking the Talk: Select a situation in your life where you worked with
other people. (1) **D**etermine whether you were acting as a group or merely
a collection of individuals. (2) **E**valuate the degree to which your thoughts
and actions changed as a result of the group dynamic. (3) **A**nalyze why you
performed better or worse because of this. (4) **L**everage these insights to
better appreciate the impact of groups and the importance of creating the
conditions where they can flourish.

> To increase my appreciation for well-managed group dynamics, I
> will…

9.2   Achieving Team Synergy

Ask Yourself: Is a group the same thing as a team? If not specifically how are they distinct? Unique characteristics? Different processes? How can managers fully unleash the potential of their groups and turn them into true teams?

Management Theory: It is vogue in management circles to speak of teams as a way to improve workplace productivity. However, merely calling a group of employees who work together a "team" does not necessarily make them one. In fact, a large body of research demonstrates that there are specific and significant differences between work groups and work teams. Throughout this chapter we present many factors that can help a group's success, such as effectively managed team roles and norms, as well as those that can hinder it, such as groupthink and social loafing indicate. The fact of the matter is that group performance might sometimes be more or less than the combination of its members' potential. Thus although many use the terms interchangeably, it is more correct to say that a team is a special type of group; a group becomes a team when its combined output surpasses the mere sum of its parts. Groups are mere assemblies of individuals that may or may not result in process gains. Specifically, teams happen when members are able to synergistically combine resources and information, coordinate activities and contributions, work together interdependently, harmonize different abilities and contributions in a complementary manner, self-manage and regulate their efforts, and do all of this in pursuit of a common goal. To create the conditions for teams, organizations must work to encourage members to truly rely on one another, recognize and harmonize their diverse insights and different skill sets, learn from and enhance each others core capacities, and orient their combined efforts in a complementary quest for the greater good. Not all groups achieve this level of superior performance, but, managed successfully, groups may indeed rise to a level where they are able to perform as synergistic teams. Our story is by a manager who draws from her experiences to find the critical distinction between a run–of–the–mill group and a synergistic team.

In Action [Case Study]: All too often it seems that "catch phrases" sweep through the ranks of management without the underlying concepts being understood by their proponents. I fear that the teamwork concept has become one such catch-phrase especially in the case of my current employer. Teams, teams, teams, my company is teaming with teams. There are signs, speeches, banners, and endless e-mails all praising the virtue of teams. But are there any teams to be found? No. But we do have an abundance of groups masquerading as teams. That is to say that they are called "teams," which unfortunately leads management to believe that there really are teams. It just seems to me that nobody has taken the time to learn the teamwork concept and what the model entails before they set about implementing it. A team is not just a bunch of individuals working in the same place. It is a group of people having the similar interests and aspirations and whose members complement each other. It is a magical thing, but it does not come out of the blue. To change this in my company, I would hearken back to my school days as a soccer player. We had strong individual players but because we did not get along well with each other our performance was suffering. Our coaches tried to make us behave more like a team through activities such as picnics and parties. However their efforts were in vain until one faithful day when we were traveling together near a village on the bank of a mountain river. I recall that in the second week it rained continuously and the river had flooded the village. *Looking back, I clearly recall that that night was the moment when our group turned into a team.* Hand in hand we helped and rescued some of the victims' animals, furniture, and other household items. After facing that calamity together we began to realize that the other girls had their unique strengths. It was the time when we discovered ourselves and our potential as a team. What the whole year was not able to bring, brought a single night: the cohesion our team needed. Starting then, our play performance improved because we felt that regardless of mistakes we made we had the support of the other team members. Instead of yells and accusations, now we were receiving advice and encouragements. Everyone's satisfaction increased and we were all attending practices. As far as the turnover was concerned, one year before three players left the team and the coming two years nobody left. And as recognition of our efforts our team ranked first among all club teams, an unprecedented, deserved place.

Walking the Talk: Select a situation in your life where you felt like you were on a team. (1) **D**etermine whether this was merely a group or truly a team. (2) **E**valuate the degree to which it had the characteristics of teams and was able to synergistically bring together its members to improve their combined productivity. (3) **A**nalyze why this happened and specifically how management did or could have enabled teamwork. (4) **L**everage these insights to enhance your ability to develop and manage high-performing teams.

To truly achieve team synergy, I will…

9.3   Managing Formal Groups into Teams

Ask Yourself: Why do organizations combine tasks in an official manner and formally assign them to groups? What is their rationale? Their purpose? Their peculiar potentialities and challenges? How should managers best guide them to become teams?

Management Theory: As suggested in the earlier section, establishing the conditions for teams to flourish brings many advantages for an organization. They have the potential to integrate different perspectives and pool diverse talents in a complementary manner to tackle complex problems that might be beyond the scope of single individuals working apart. It is for this reason that formal groups are often officially incorporated into the design of firms to execute explicit tasks and objectives. What distinguishes these legitimately sanctioned collectives is their authorized designation and official charge within the confines of larger strategic objectives and organizational hierarchy. Formal groups can have varying duration—they might be permanent fixtures within the organizational structure, where the individual job descriptions are subjugated to group demands, or temporary "task force" creations centered on the limited life spans of specific projects or products. Formal groups can also occupy different locations within the horizontal and vertical command structure—they might be tied into existing divisions and reporting mechanisms or kept largely independent and self-managing. Notwithstanding, it is the official nature of their existence that distinguishes them from other types of groups and thus mandates specific managerial skills and competencies to turn them into teams. For example, because they are formal entities, these workgroups must reconcile their official charges with both the job responsibilities of its individual members and larger purposes of the firm. In essence well-managed formal teams are the prototypical "meso" structures housing the micro individual actors to support macro organizational objectives. To meet these often-conflicting requirements, managers must simultaneously integrate the smallest and largest aspects of a company by balancing individual employees' needs with those of the organization. Our story is by a manager who has attempted to do just this within his organization.

In Action [Case Study]: According to management theory, groups can be either formal or informal. *At work I have the opportunity to simultaneously be part of many formal groups, many of which were not managed well.* As a manager I am primarily a member of my command group, as depicted in our organizational chart, where I am confronted with differing role expectations. My subordinates expect me to represent their interest to upper management while my boss expects me to enforce the organization's policies. I have also participated in formally appointed task force groups. Generally, I found that they can become inefficient when members fight for items on their respective agendas or never coming together toward common goals. For example, I currently serve on a task force to change over a certain supply chain management product. At present, all of the corporation's customers are utilizing information in a particular format that is badly out of date. A Task Group was formed to implement the change. On the team were the product manager VP and AVP, customer service VP and service rep, sales VP and sales Rep, and line officer VP and technician. Each set of participants reported to a different command structure. The first pair was responsible for the product and wanted the change to take place as soon as possible (these are people who said it will be seamless—I do not think so!). The second pair would be responsible for notifying the customers of this change. The third pair would sell the product and help the customer coordinate with the installation of the product. The fourth pair (including me) would oversee the relationships. After two months, the customer service representatives said that the first group of customers was changed over, but the product managers said that no one was using the new format. The line officers found out that customer service called each customer and reported that it seems OK (job completed in rep's mind). The line officers uncovered that the customers were actually having serious problems such as not enough memory on their computers and complications connecting to the system. I recognized these difficulties and recommended that the group meet next week to come together on its assessment criteria and discuss a strategy that all would play a part in. As I said before, formal groups will only be successful if it can rally its individual members to align their role responsibilities and work together for the common goal of the project. You can be sure that I will be educating people on this at our next meeting.

Walking the Talk: Select a situation in your life where you worked together with others in an officially sanctioned interaction. (1) **D**etermine whether this indeed had the characteristics of a formal group. (2) **E**valuate the degree to which the formal group completed tasks and achieved organizational objectives. (3) **A**nalyze why it was or was not able to work and how its success could have been enhanced. (4) **L**everage these insights to better manage formal groups into teams.

To better manage formal groups, I will...

9.4   Managing Informal Groups into Teams

Ask Yourself: Why do groups sometimes form on their own independent of or despite formal organizational dicta? What is their rationale? Their purpose? Their peculiar potentialities and challenges? How should managers best guide them to become teams?

Management Theory: Casual connections and social interactions inevitably form within the work context of organizations. Whether around the preverbal water cooler or fax machine, or across department floors and over cubicle walls, people will talk and associations will develop that are outside the boundaries of prescribed authority relationships. These emergent collectives are referred to as "informal groups" and represent different types of dynamics, with different characteristics and objectives, than their more formal counterparts. Among their distinguishing characteristics are that informal groups are neither officially structured nor part of the sanctioned hierarchy of authority. Instead they tend to form spontaneously and for reasons other than of organizational charges or mandates. For example, informal groups exist not to accomplish a task per se but more frequently to provide personal enjoyment, a sense of affiliation, social support, and perhaps basic feelings of belongingness. They involve voluntary participation as opposed to being a required part of ones job. They often cut across authority lines and boundaries and are based more on shared interests, mutual friendships, external relationships, or other types of interpersonal attraction. They may or may not have anything to do with the organization's mission or strategy. Some see the emergence of informal groups simply as the result of the large and growing portion of people's lives spend at the office and their close working proximity to one another combined with a natural human need for social connection. Yet even if they do not play an official role in the organization, their widespread proliferation and potential to impact the attitudes and behaviors of its membership require a careful understanding to channel their energy into productive directions. Our story is by a manager tapping into some of the advantages of an informal group within his department.

In Action [Case Study]: One of the basic needs of the human being is to associate with others. As in life itself, organizations provide an environment where people look for others with similar interests, backgrounds, or problems to gain support and security. In my department, our informal group is made up of about fifteen managerial professionals. We all share the same job description, same issues, and same problems. Our activities include lunching together, communicating via e-mail, and spending occasional breaks together. Since each manager works separately in the department, this informal group is their only mean for professional association.

Among the many advantages of being in the informal support group, the most important is a basic interaction with people who have similar challenges and common ground. This gives us an opportunity to share news, latest rumors, and the new developments in the company. Besides a chance to interact, support and understanding is one of the most important reasons for group's existence. Within what has become an essential support network for us, everyone knows what everyone is talking about and what everyone is going through. It makes you feel that you are not alone and together we would be able to live through tough times. Besides psychological support, the group provides a sense of security and stability. You know that others will help you deal with your problems. Senior management is much more receptive and respectful to the members of our emergent "team." They realize that the network is helping our satisfaction and even performance, since we share information and tips with each other, so they have no problems with it and even started sending over special snacks to the break-room for us to encourage our interaction. Since several members are well known and respected, we have a certain status. Being a member gave me additional respect and recognition from others in the department. Satisfaction is definitely affected in a positive way. We enjoy work a little bit more and worry about issues a little bit less. We have someone to make our work experience more pleasant and rewarding and help with our problems. The existence and activity of our team has definitely resulted in much lower turnover than industry or organizational averages. We have a safe haven where we are understood and feel confident and secure about our future in the organization. There will be little motivation for us to leave a job that provides this kind of support and security.

Walking the Talk: Select a situation in your life where you came together with others in an emergent interaction. (1) **D**etermine whether this indeed had the characteristics of an informal group. (2) **E**valuate the degree to which the informal group satisfied the needs of its members. (3) **A**nalyze why it was or was not able to work and how its success could have been enhanced. (4) **L**everage these insights to better manage informal groups into teams.

To better manage informal groups, I will...

9.5   Supporting Team Development Processes

Ask Yourself: How do teams form and develop over time? Are there distinct processes and phases that tend to occur? Patterns that tend to repeat themselves? What are the central management challenges at each of these stages?

Management Theory: Groups tend to mature over time and pass through discernable phases of activities. Interestingly each stage brings with it different managerial challenges, but since the stages do not always happen in a set order and can even overlap or regress backward, it may be difficult to know what a group needs at different times. According to management theory, development encapsulates five distinct types of stages: Forming, Storming, Norming, Performing, and Adjourning. A group can fail to become a team at any one of these points, and so organizations need to create the conditions to help the team continue to mature and progress to greater levels of effectiveness. For example, in the initial forming stage a primary concern is resolving the initial uncertainty that come with its creation and managers must clarify its goals and expectations. Second, in the storming stage a primary concern is mitigating the emotions and disagreements that may occur over personal preferences or power relationships and managers must resolve these issues in a productive manner. Third, in the norming stage a primary concern is the achievement of a cohesive unit and managers must work to make sure that these bonds facilitate commitment and a positive camaraderie. Fourth, in the performing stage a primary concern is directing the team toward task completion and managers must foster effective and even innovative behaviors to accomplish objectives. Finally, in the adjourn stage a primary concern is the disbanding of the team and managers must help members transition back to their different individual paths. Together these dynamics suggest a complex and flexible role for the manager to track and facilitate group development. Our story is by a manager reflecting on the degree to which these processes were executed successfully in her organization.

In Action [Case Study]: Following management theory, I can confidently say that my team has rather closely followed the classic five-stage group-development model. Furthermore, I now realize that I have not only gone through all five stages, but I have also experienced a reverse of these stages where it eventually failed to stay a team. To begin, the formation of my task group was the decision of the senior vice president and was largely based on the most profitable business opportunity facing the firm. The first stage, forming, was rather prolonged. Since job training utilized "sink or swim" teaching techniques it took us some time to acquire the "tools of trade." After finally being admitted to the group, our big heads caused us to have intense arguments that caused tension along with hostility. We almost did not make it through this storming stage. Once the "edges" were filed off, close relationships emerged and question such as—"What do others need me to do?" unified us toward common goals. At the norming stage, power structure was well defined and individual members' behavior was consistent with a shared set of expectations. The performing stage, in my experience, has gone a complete 360-degree turn. At first, our group was performing exceptionally well and was a true team with high positive synergy. Questions such as—"How can I best perform my role?" were dominant. Interpersonal relationships at that point could not have been better. I could sense what the employees needed even before they had to ask for it. Unfortunately, however, later additions of two additional employees to the group from another division completely undermined the prior achieved synergy and regressed the group back a couple of stages. Personal differences and challenges to task roles introduced by the new employees undermined the group's chemistry and fostered rapid decline in performance of individual members and the group as a whole. Several months since the additions, losses began to mount. We needed to shift gears and get into a re-norming management mindset but for some reason we were unwilling or unable. The group eventually failed and abrupt adjournment soon followed. *One can see from this that the group was able to mature into a team but the subsequent mismanagement of its development had direct negative effects on our performance.* Initially efficient intra-team operations increase productivity and satisfaction while lowering absenteeism and turnover. When we were faced with the new members and new challenges we did not succeed. The team could have been salvaged had we applied the lessons of our first storming period and better adapted our management to meet the needs of its development.

Walking the Talk: Select a situation in your life where you witnessed the evolution (or de-evolution) of a group. (1) **D**etermine whether the group progressed through the above stages and in what order. (2) **E**valuate the degree to which it successfully developed into a team and fulfilled the requirements of each activity. (3) **A**nalyze why it was able to successfully pass from one stage to another, or not, and how this could have been enhanced. (4) **L**everage these insights to develop the skills needed to effectively shepherd the team development process through its different challenges.

To better manage team development processes, I will…

9.6   Establishing Effective Team Roles

Ask Yourself: Do people usually take on different roles or responsibilities when they work together? If so which types of roles are most important for achieving group success? Are there problems that can develop if roles are not properly defined and designed? How should roles be best managed to turn groups into teams?

Management Theory: Just as a motion picture or theatrical production relies on an interaction of people acting out their different parts, so too are groups a product of their members' various roles. The concept of a group role refers to the set of behaviors expected of a position, and hence of the person occupying that position. Roles can be formally appointed, such as those designated by higher-ups with a title and office, or more emergent as people step up to take on different responsibilities needed for the group to develop and succeed. What is important to note here is that not everybody does the exact same thing in a group—that is, they play different parts or occupy different roles. For example, some people might play the performance-focused task-master who initiates actions and keeps the group moving on schedule whereas others could act as the relationship-oriented bonder who maintains positive feelings and keeps morale up and spirits high. Without someone playing the task role a group would accomplish little, yet without someone fulfilling the interpersonal role the group would become fragmented and potentially implode, hence both are necessary for the group to succeed. Over time group members assume established role identities that define their expected contribution to the group. If the roles are allocated and managed well, they can combine to create a positive team interaction. However, all too frequently problems emerge such as when roles are too vague to give proper direction (role ambiguity), too onerous to handle (role overload), or do not match the expectations of their colleagues, values of the person, or mesh well with the other roles the person plays in their life (role conflict). It is therefore prudent for organizations to clarify the nature of roles, allocate particular roles to those members whose skills fit them better, and reconcile roles with both the interests of the team as well as personal goals of the role occupant. Our story is by a manager reflecting on the promises and challenges for their organization in properly defining roles for their work team.

In Action [Case Study]: Organizations design high-performing teams to successfully match and train people to needed roles. In my professional experience I have had the great opportunity of working on a work team such as this. Our mission was to provide seamless support and service to a major security agency. This work team had five members who filled positions that all required different primary skill sets to execute different responsibilities. Role one necessitated quick analytical thinking under high amounts of pressure. Role two required quantitative skills. Role three required presentation and customer service skills. Role four required methodical and analytical thinking. Role five consisted of the "glue guy" who held the group together and kept us working together smoothly. Each team member was chosen for the skill sets needed for each of these positions, and each team member was given the role that best fit his or her strongest skills. *My firm's strategic allocation of roles to those team members who have the most developed skills needed to excel in such a position is logical to meet the end of performing as a successful team.* This work team of which I was a member performed exceptionally. There was plenty of proactive communication between all members, and we were fully aware of what was going on with regards to all operational issues and concerns. There was strong trust, consistently high responsiveness, excellent morale, and good quality work. Employee' productivity was high because of the good job-personality-skill fit. The complementary nature of our roles created a high degree of success and our personal bonding ensured job satisfaction for all. But these positive implications did not last forever. One important lesson that I learned from this experience was that the pigeonholing of each team member made them complacent in their roles because of the lack of an environment that fostered learning. Even though this team was initially successful, the amount of work that filled the day overloaded some members and began to lower team morale. Absenteeism also rose and even our glue guy could not prevent members from posting for other positions within the company. Had I had the knowledge that I know now, I think that I would have implemented a cross training program to provide a buffer against role overload during peak times. The intra-team learning would also, I believe, increase job satisfaction as the scope of each member's role expanded and the cohesiveness of the team would be strengthened.

Walking the Talk: Select a situation in your life where you belonged to a group. (1) **D**etermine whether you and the other members played distinct roles. (2) **E**valuate the degree to which these roles were well defined, designed, and distributed. (3) **A**nalyze why the role assignments worked, or not, and how any role-related problems could have been remedied to form a true team. (4) **L**everage these insights to develop better role-management skills.

To establish and develop effective team roles, I will…

9.7 Establishing Effective Team Norms

Ask Yourself: How does a group decide what constitutes "normal"? Does normal mean the same thing in every group? What factors determine how these standards of behavior are determined? What happens when norms are not obeyed or improperly defined? How should norms be best managed to turn groups into teams?

Management Theory: The word "normal" describes what attitudes and actions are deemed appropriate in a given social context. From the word normal is derived the concept of norms that describes the acceptable yet often unwritten standards of group conduct. Normal is not always the same in every group. For example, the correct ways of working (performance norms), dressing (appearance norms), and interacting (social norms) in a professional work group may not be particularly appropriate when you go out with friends, participate on an athletic or musical squad, worship in the community, or sit around the table with family. And norms can even vary between groups in the same organization, where for example formal attire and conservative behavior might characterize one department whereas a more social or free-wheeling attitude could be commonplace in another. Groups develop their norms based on a variety of factors such as backgrounds of its members or the demands of their jobs. As such they tend to become part of the mental schema of participants and influence the way that they think. If effective, they can increase the predictability and identity of a team, reduce misunderstandings, minimize embarrassing situations, provide direction, and clarify that values are most important to accomplish its objectives. Ignorance or noncompliance with norms often leads to sanctions or outright ostracism by its membership thereby reducing an offending employee's satisfaction and harming their and the group's overall productivity. It is important to note that norms can be more or less productive (e.g., work hard and be on time) or unproductive (e.g., its ok to slack off or be late) so strong norms are not always a good thing—their strength combined with direction can either propel or inhibit performance. Therefore how as group defines "normal" can enable or retard the translation of a group to a team. Our story is by a manager who learned some of these lessons by observing the norms of different departments.

In Action [Case Study]: Even though we all are a part of the same department, there is clearly a big difference in the way different groups operate. I believe effective norms are what make the groups different from teams. However it is not always easy to learn and adjust to new ways of working. An example would be one of the more "social" departments that I have been a part of. I remember that there were a couple of people who did not join in our activities, and only a few weeks passed by when one of the people asked for a transfer and the other resigned because they did not fit in with the norms. Another example would be in a different division where someone violated our top norm of integrity. I remember being asked to support one of the new salespeople joining the group named Donna. A co-worker had warned me to be careful with her because she came from a different group that had a reputation for backstabbing norms and taking credit for others' work. At first I did not take much stock in the warning. However, an event took place that aroused my suspicion. Donna had given me two customer reports that had incomplete information. One of them could not be executed and the other led to an embarrassing error. I was left holding the bag and had to smooth the situation over with a perturbed client. I had contacted Donna for clarification and she was evasive in her answers. It was obvious that this was not her original work. The administrator who had previously warned me about her overheard me grappling with this and said, "see." *Needless to say Donna did not last long on our team or she might have compromised the very norm that allowed us to succeed so well. She betrayed our number-one norm so nobody would make her work a priority or do any favors for her and she was eventually forced out.* As this illustrates setting effective norms and complying with them is critical to organizational success. These experiences taught me another important lesson, to not assume that all norms are the same. In my firm it is important to be flexible because it is very common to be rotated to different groups. When you join a new group you should find out and respect their norms, especially if it is important to their proper functioning, or performance will suffer and satisfaction will be low and could lead to voluntary or involuntary turnover.

Walking the Talk: Select a situation in your life where you belonged to a group. (1) **D**etermine whether you and others were subject to norms. (2) **E**valuate the degree to which these norms influenced your thought and behaviors. (3) **A**nalyze why the norms improved, or inhibited, effectiveness and how any problems could have been remedied to form a true team. (4) **L**everage these insights to develop better norm-management skills.

To establish and develop effective team norms, I will...

9.8   Combating Groupthink

Ask Yourself: Are the tightest groups always the most productive and effective? Or can employees actually become too close that they go along with bad decisions because they fear "not rocking the boat"? What are the potential dangers of overly cohesive members acquiescing to the larger group identity? How can managers prevent this type of "group-think" behavior from blocking progress to becoming a team?

Management Theory: The previous discussion highlighted the powerful influence of norms on standardizing the thoughts and actions of group members. Whereas encouraging a collective mindset and consistent behavior has its advantages, too much cohesiveness can actually wash out individual contributions and produce pressures for conformity so great that nobody dares rock the boat even if this means allowing poor decisions or wrongful actions to go forward. Management theory describes this problem as "groupthink," where groups' concurrence-seeking dominates critical thinking and prudent planning, where a desire to not "make waves" is stronger than that to come up with the best possible decision, and where group harmony is deemed more important than good judgment and effective performance. Groupthink can infect and destroy a team in many ways: It squashes minority views, punishes dissent, pressures free-thinkers, and overwhelms unpopular but valid opinions. Groupthink has several enablers: censorship of dissenting ideas, insulation from outside expertise and perspective, powerful members who push their own agenda, exaggerated beliefs in the group's capabilities or morality, excessive regard for group unity, overly positive views of their self-image, and the collective rationalization and shared stereotyping of decision situations. Despite these dangers, groupthink is not inevitable and good management practices can minimize or prevent it. For instance, organizations can encourage leader impartiality, inject dissenting views into group discussions perhaps through devil's advocacy or subgroup debates, establishing a climate of openness and acceptance, allow members the time and encouragement to adequately consider alternative approaches, bring in objective voices and outside experts, and emphases the value of open dialog in reaching optimal decisions. Our story is by a manager's struggles with groupthink.

In Action [Case Study]: One of the biggest problems my former company suffered from was "groupthink." The problem with "groupthink" is that once the group makes an assumption they tried to resist changing direction even though there was strong evidence to indicate it was incorrect. One glaring example was when our advertising team created a promotion plan for a new product launch. Due to the limited budget, the group agreed to skip the market research because they believed they knew enough to assume most of the target market's basic characteristics by their collective wisdom and common sense. *As the project moved forward, one of the members realized that was a deadly mistake, but to keep the consensus within the group, he did not mention anything.* When another member realized the seriousness of the problem and requested the group to start over, the group, pressured by the deadline and desire not to offend fellow group members, resisted the idea and forces them to keep quiet and move forward. This resulted in a disastrous launch and ultimately low firm performance for the quarter, low employee satisfaction, and turnover of some of the best workers in the company. I learned from this experience and have applied it to my current job. I work for a Fortune 500 firm and was recently put in charge of a group of five members. They have been with the company for more than fifteen years and know each other very well. They have attended each other weddings, kid birthdays, and parties. I have learned that they are called the company's legacy team and do everything together. These people think exactly alike. For example, they constantly keep saying "if it doesn't break don't fix it" and rarely take any chances or do anything different. Maybe this is why they receive many complaints for slow response to new business needs. I tried to apply the lessons of my past experience to reduce groupthink. I encouraged them to attend our human resource's refresher training and started sending them one by one to take advanced classes to encourage their independent thinking and, and when they came back, bringing into the group the new skills and perspectives they have learned. I have also spoken to them about the value of treating work as a constant learning and growth experience. So far they have received this well but to be honest some seemed a little wary of getting out of their comfort zones. I know that I will need to continue to reinforce this message and support their growth to prevent groupthink.

Walking the Talk: Select a situation in your life where you were in a cohesive group. (1) **D**etermine whether you experienced any groupthink. (2) **E**valuate the degree to which any groupthink enablers negatively affected performance and hindered true teamwork. (3) **A**nalyze why you were or were not susceptible to groupthink pressures and how these problems might have been reduced. (4) **L**everage these insights to enhance your ability to deal with and prevent groupthink from harming group performance.

To combat groupthink, I will...

9.9   Combating Social Loafing

Ask Yourself: Are the biggest groups always the most productive? Or can adding people to a group actually reduce the effectiveness of group processes? Why do people sometimes take advantage of larger groups to hide from view, shirk responsibilities, and free-ride on the backs of their colleagues? How can managers prevent this type of "social loafing" behavior from blocking progress to becoming a team?

Management Theory: It has been said that "two heads are better than one" but management theory points out that this is not necessarily true. Whereas adding more members increases a group's potential output it can also, if poorly managed, destroy teamwork and inhibit overall performance. This problem is known as social loafing and it occurs when people exert less effort when they work together than when they work alone. In essence, the group output is less than the combined potential productivity of each member. It is especially ironic because, instead of the added human resources boosting team performance, the larger size in effect does the opposite. We see social loafing when employees feel disconnected, shirk their duties, withhold their participation, hide in the background, and simply coast along. Social loafing is more likely to happen in the following contexts: Employees feel like they can blend in and that their efforts are not identifiable or will not be assessed, norms are very individualistic and people look out only for themselves, workers think their contributions are unimportant or meaningless, expectations exist that other will loaf, or the task at hand is seen as so simple or uninteresting that it does not warrant their full effort. When employees withdraw or reduce their contributions, then the total output is bound to suffer. This dysfunction is akin to the economic concept of the free rider who obtains benefit from a group without contributing their fair share. Thus it is incumbent on organizations to directly combat the enablers of social loafing by engaging all members fully in the group task, maintaining a sense of personal responsibility and accountability, and reducing the type of self-centered attitude which could encourage employees to take a free ride. Our story is by a manager trying to combat social loafing in the workplace.

In Action [Case Study]: Social loafing is the tendency for individuals to expend less effort when working collectively than when working individually. It challenges the logic that the productivity of the group as a whole should at least equal the sum of the productivity of each individual in that group. I have experienced social loafing at work and this experience has led me to pay closer attention to understanding and managing work teams theories. At my job four of us were recently assigned to support and analyze a global trade initiative. We had four weeks to finish the report. I e-mailed everyone and encouraged every member to complete their initial research in a week then we would meet to discuss the major issues. At our first meeting, two of us showed up with research results and the other two complained that they were too busy with other jobs and did not even come. I followed up with e-mails and phone calls, but one of them still never replied to any messages. The three of us were upset about the "free rider" and we began to have low morale. The project was not even half finished a week before the deadline because only a few of us were actually doing their share of the work. When we all finally found the time to meet together, the two hardest working members started to complain and refused to donate any more time to the so called team. The worst "free rider" was basically forced to finish up the report within only a few days remaining. One day later, the "free rider" started to complain the amount of work he was forced to face and claimed that he won't be able to finish it before the deadline. The unhappy group players gathered after normal work hours and did some emergency planning. We distributed the remaining tasks among us and asked the free rider to fine tune the report. *The project was barely finished on time and its quality was so discounted that it was actually worse than any of us would do if we were working alone! The group members were reprimanded by the VP for this and we realized the seriousness of social loafing.* I will never forget this disaster. The next time I will be sure to minimize social loafing by holding each person accountable, educating them about the problems of loafing, and promoting a shared commitment among each member to contribute to the team to reach the maximum output.

Walking the Talk: Select a situation in your life where you were in a large group. (1) **D**etermine whether you experienced any social loafing. (2) **E**valuate the degree to which specific social loafing effects appeared and hindered true teamwork. (3) **A**nalyze why you were or were not susceptible to social loafing pressures and how these problems might have been reduced. (4) **L**everage these insights to enhance your ability to deal with and prevent social loafing from harming group performance.

To combat social loafing, I will…

9.10   Guiding Cross Functional Teams

Ask Yourself: Can teams be used strategically to integrate different disciplines and divisional interests? Bridge traditional boundaries within a firm? Represent diverse organizational perspectives and overcome narrow mindsets to more effectively and efficiently accomplish complex tasks? How can managers facilitate this type of cross-functional integration?

Management Theory: A cross-functional team is designed to foster integration across organizational boundaries by combining members from different areas in a single unit so that they complement rather than compete with each other. The underlying rationale of a successful cross-functional team is holography—representing the complexity of the larger firm, including essential interests from different functional or divisional parts of the organization, in a smaller group format. In this sense a holographic team can bring to bear the knowledge and concerns of all relevant parties in a more manageable setting. This mirrors the logic of representative democracies and corporate boards where a requisite diversity of perspectives is sought on a more microcosmic level. When workers are given the opportunity to come together in cross-functional teams they can exchange information and coordinate tasks that could benefit from the early insights, diverse knowledge, and continued involvement of all facets of a work process. For example, manufacturing and marketing employees might contribute early on to insuring that a new product will be easily produced and sellable whereas R&D and finance might help decide if late-stage additions are feasible and profitable. Because of these advantages, cross functional teams are often used to manage highly innovative projects that require a great deal of collaboration and speed. However, cross functional teams are not panacea. Sometimes they are teams in name only insofar as such a diverse membership can create communication challenges and cause dysfunctional conflict. After all, the more far-flung a group's membership the correspondingly greater the possibility that they will experience misunderstandings, mistrust, and disagreements that might impede or derail a project. Thus organizations must help group members to harmonize and integrate their diverse perspectives so that true team synergy can be realized. Our story is by a manager using a cross functional team to aid research and development activities.

In Action [Case Study]: Recently, my company decided to implement cross-functional teams of specialists accordingly to the type of product that a particular customer buys. This approach allowed us to speed-up and generate new pricing and design solutions that would significantly improve performance and increased sales. Traditional selling process in our industry usually involves only one sales-person per customer. The single salesperson then is the only liaison between company's administration (pricing decisions), R&D (design studio), quality control, traffic department (logistics), and customer's buying team. *Creating a cross-functional team of salesperson, designer, and pricing decision maker allowed selling team to eliminate inconsistent service and very annoying mistakes and delays to the customers.* The selling team was able to work together to define product-development strategy and pricing on the very first meeting with the customer (complementary skills). Since there was a designer on the selling team who can consult customer's product design directly, customer satisfaction shot up drastically. Since customers felt that their customized platforms were a definite success, they placed increased orders for coordinated products (increased sales). A representative of administration on the selling team was in the position to make pricing decisions on-the-spot that allowed customer to receive an instant feedback for inquiries and speeded up sales closure. Design and product development were kept in the loop about the intersales territorial situation; and therefore, were able to direct relationships with a particular customer in the desired direction. A salesperson on the selling team carried all coordinating and follow-up functions to make sure everyone delivered a consistent product and act as a "customer's advocate." One of the key customers was so impressed with our new cross-functional sales team design that she spoke of it at her company's annual stockholder meeting. Now two other divisions of this large account started placing numerous orders with our team: our company tried to get that market for years with no success. However the success of the teams was not determined by simply combining different professionals in a group, but by improved communications with customers and among departments. Collective team effort exceeded by far the sum of personal efforts (synergy) and business has never been better.

Walking the Talk: Select a situation in your life where you worked on a project with others across organizational boundaries. (1) **D**etermine whether the group was holographic and represented different functional perspectives. (2) **E**valuate the degree to which the interaction was or was not successful at bringing together members' divergent perspectives to synergistically integrate their areas into a common product or service. (3) **A**nalyze why this did or did not happen and how management could have further enabled cross-functional collaboration for true teamwork. (4) **L**everage these insights to enhance your ability to manage cross-functional teams.

To better establish and guide cross-functional teams, I will…

CHAPTER TEN

Designing an Enabling Structure and Culture

Chapter ten examines management theories about designing an organization and the management skill of creating an enabling structural and cultural context. First, the formal design of an organization is represented by its structure. Just as a person's physical anatomy influences his or her capability to enact different strategies, so too does an organization's configuration influence the actions of its employees. However organizations can play the proverbial Dr. Frankenstein by redeploying or adding/subtracting resources and altering the manner in which they are linked together to build a variety of distinct systems. These organizational schemes will then alter the workplace environment to trigger different types of behaviors. For instance, firms can break up jobs into smaller or bigger pieces, connect them more or less closely, establish many or few rules, and concentrate more or less power at the top. These design decision will in turn enable drastically different officially sanctioned patterns of work such as those observed in the highly programmed apparatus of a bureaucratic machine or the fluid and flexible laboratory of an innovative pioneer. Second, supplementing a firm's formal structure is its informal configuration of organizational culture. Some refer to it as the organization's personality or "invisible" structure. Corporate culture is based on deeply held beliefs of a firm, manifest in its core values, and shows up in its rites, rituals, stories, and symbol artifacts. Even if a particular rule or relationship is not formally documented in a structure or specified on an organizational chart, it might be governed just as purposefully by the firm's particular value system. Therefore in this tenth chapter we look at what managers need to know about organizational structure and culture if they are to understand the contextual influences on work behavior and proactively manage these arrangements to best build their environments for success.

10.1 Appreciating the Importance of Structural Context

Ask Yourself: To what extent is your workplace behavior influenced by your organization's structure? Might the same person act differently if they were employed by one organization versus another? Why does an organization's design exert such a powerful influence over its employees? How can an organization construct an environment to best enable desired actions and support their strategic goals?

Management Theory: An organization's structure is the formal system that provides the map for how its parts fit together. It dictates the means by which people are assigned to tasks, are allowed to exert authority, are required to coordinate activities, and are held responsible for their actions. As such one fundamental characteristic of structure is the degree of control that it exerts to focus behavior and guide the actions of its employees. Designed effectively, an organization's structure (its frameworks, or what it can do) will allow it to successfully pursue its strategy (its objectives, or what it wants to do). A second characteristic of structure is the degree of predictability that it establishes to promote stable sets of working relationships. Designed effectively, an organization's structure will create an internal environment that reduces uncertainly so employees know what to expect when executing their job. A third characteristic of structure is the degree of interdependence that it creates to delineate how different people and resources are expected to interact. Designed effectively, an organization's structure will allow employees and tasks to come together in choreographed manner with defined linkages and boundaries. Overall structure seeks to organize activity to enable levels of efficiency and effectiveness beyond what might be produced by the same parties acting under different arrangements. It is important to note that different firms, even those operating in the same industry or niche, will vary in how they establish a structural system. Structures will also (or at least should) evolve as the organization confronts different business environments. As such a well-designed structure properly oriented to support a firm's internal and external objectives can connote a key source of competitive advantage. Thus managers must understand the wide variety of forms an organization's structure can take and its subsequent influence in shaping behavior and impacting success. Our story is about a manager's direct experience with the outcomes produced by different structural contexts.

In Action [Case Study]: Same industry + same position + different structure = different experience. This summarizes my managerial experiences within two organizations that have proved to be quite insightful. My first position was as an entry level manager for a "new age" firm on the coast. Now management theory tells us that there are benefits to having a formally structured organization and from this experience I could not agree more. *Having worked in a company with little formal structure, I found myself lost in the shuffle, as did many of my colleagues.* None of us were able to identify with the company goals and objectives because there was nothing established to follow. It was even unclear who I was supposed to report to on a daily basis. I frequently could not get assignments delivered to the correct areas because there was no defined area or person and, like most of the other employees, felt very confused. Although certain companies pride themselves on having a vague or relaxed structure, there need to be clear guidelines and boundaries or else no matter how creative you are the employees and the productivity suffers. Now contrast this with my present position where I was subject to six weeks of training held at the regional corporate headquarters. During this time, new managers received instruction from corporate departmental and divisional managers as well as met with the regional vice presidents. The end of this period culminated with each manager performing an hour long presentation on the company's regional organizational hierarchy and their place in it. When I transferred out to my actual job the reporting mechanisms and structure followed the training to a tee. The vertical and horizontal differentiation was clear. Everyone knew their position's responsibilities and requirements. We operated like a finely oiled machine. Needless to say in my current organization I am more productive and satisfied, do not miss work very often, and do not intend to leave any time soon (whereas the first organization had a huge turnover problem). Both of these companies are in the "creativity" business but the second one did not sacrifice organization and is much more profitable.

Walking the Talk: Select a situation in your life where you worked in an organization. (1) **D**etermine whether the organizational structure had an impact on you. (2) **E**valuate the degree to which your actions and perspectives were influenced by the structural system. (3) **A**nalyze why the structure was able to exert such a strong effect and how it affected your performance and satisfaction. (4) **L**everage these insights to develop an enhanced appreciation for the impact of organizational structure.

To better appreciate the power of organizational structure, I will…

10.2 Constructing Appropriate Differentiation
and Integration

Ask Yourself: Why does your organization define and design your job one way versus another? How do firms determine which parts of projects different people will work on? How do this division of labor affect their employees' efficiency and effectiveness? Also, how should an organization best put these specialized pieces together so that they fit together as an integrated whole and not work against each other?

Management Theory: Structure can be partly understood by the way it separates tasks into positions and correspondingly coordinates these parts to support each other. The first of these challenges is called differentiation whereas the second is called integration. Differentiation involves the division of labor where the organization structures vertical (management authority) and horizontal (functional expertise) roles for different people based on the specialized backgrounds and knowledge that they bring to the organization. Vertically, an organization might employ many managers in a tall controlling hierarchy or fewer empowered people in a flatter, flexible structure. Horizontally, an organization might separate jobs into functions to establish technical expertise, divisions to establish product or customer expertise, or geographic centers to establish location expertise. Each of these design decisions brings different advantages and challenges. In addition, the more specialized an organization becomes the more sophisticated the mechanisms managers need to coordinate its activities. Without sufficient integration, the differentiated parts might develop a myopic subunit orientation focusing only on their own goals to the possible detriment of overall organizational interests. Thus organizational integration seeks to align interests by connecting its parts in formal ways to reconcile differences and blend knowledge areas. It can be accomplished through the structuring of basic reporting relationships or via more intensive, and expensive, methods such as liaison positions, task forces, or entire integrating departments dedicated to bridging diverse corporate interests. Taken together, the most important thing for managers to be aware of is that they must balance differentiation and integration to form systems with sufficient depths of expertise as well as the matching capability to link them toward common ends. Our story is by a manager involved in the structural integration of two specialized departments to better coordinate processes.

In Action [Case Study]: The establishment of integrating departments is used when inter-organizational relations are completely fragmented in terms of goals and scope yet their differentiated functions need to work together for the company to succeed. About a year ago, I was involved in integrating two departments into one. The department that I run was responsible for managing supply chains, collecting payments, and reconciling invoices. A large percentage of our activities were dependent on information that was provided by another department called Marketing Sales and Support. Historically, there always seems to be some tension between the two departments since we did very different things and there was a high level of interdependency between us. They wanted to make as many sales as possible using the most liberal payment plans available and involving the maximum number of packaged services in our portfolio. They were sales experts and without them our firm would die for lack of revenue. We needed more measured approaches to assure adequate quality control, logistical processing, and profitability criteria. We were process experts and without us we would bleed to death due to cost inefficiencies. Obviously the two divisions were both essential but frequently at odds working under different mandates. It seemed like a constant tug-of-war between me and the other division manager. This tension was distracting us, hurting performance, and lowering morale. This spring a new COO came on board and I used the opportunity to point out the intergroup relation problem and propose methods to fix it to better integrate our functions and achieve the larger firm goal of efficient and effective operations. *The coordination of the two differentiated areas with an integrating department was deemed the best option for syncing the functions and made good business sense.* Several full time positions were reoriented and regrouped to form a bridge between our two functions. They worked to make sure our systems were integrated so we could know what the other was doing. They also made sure we worked with rather than against each other. As expected, the transition period was not very smooth because there were different people to deal with and procedures to follow. However, after a few months there was a noticeable improvement in performance and customer service and a smoothing of relations. We were extremely satisfied that all parties were finally working toward the same goal.

Walking the Talk: Select a situation in your life where your job was affected by differentiation and/or integration. (1) **D**etermine whether division of labor and integration mechanisms were present in the organization. (2) **E**valuate the degree to which your role was appropriately specialized as well as properly coordinated with other jobs and areas in the organization. (3) **A**nalyze why these design decisions were important in shaping action and how they affected your performance and satisfaction. (4) **L**everage these insights to better design and manage differentiation and integration.

To appropriately design and manage both differentiation and integration, I will...

10.3 Constructing Appropriate Formalization and Centralization

Ask Yourself: Are there rules and regulations that you must follow at work? Why? What are the advantages of establishing more or less formalized governance structures? In addition, who makes the important decisions where you work? Why? What are the advantages of establishing more or less centralized governance structures?

Management Theory: Structure can also be understood by the way it standardizes activities into prescribed routines and allots decision-making power to different parts of the hierarchy. The former of these challenges is called formalization whereas the latter is called centralization. Formalization entails the establishment of rules, policies, and standard operating procedures to increase the predictability and control over its operations. For example, through high formalization a firm can standardize jobs' inputs (e.g., strict criteria for hiring and obtaining other resources), process (e.g., detailed steps to be taken when performing ones job), and/or outputs (precise metrics for orienting and assessing performance). Whereas there are control advantages to rigorous standards there are also tradeoffs in the amount of flexibility afforded to managers to exercise their judgment and adapt to changing circumstances. Related to this is the concept of centralization. This refers to the degree to which authority to make important decisions is concentrated in one place, usually at the top of the hierarchy, or distributed throughout the organization. For example a decentralized approach to organizational structure delegates decisions to their most appropriate levels. Alternatively a centralized approach seeks to establish a shared vision, maximize control over the organization's direction, and create an internally consistent approach to operations. Despite its advantages centralization carries many potential costs such as frequently overloading top managers with too many responsibilities, alienating lower level managers and employees with roles that involve little input or judgment, and creating a less-responsive managerial approach removed from local trends and conditions. Taken together, the most important thing for managers to be aware of is that they must balance the degree of control they exert through formalization and centralization with the need for flexibility and responsiveness that often come from a more informal and decentralized approach. Our story is by a manager reconciling how his workplace differs from other companies on these dimensions.

In Action [Case Study]: In my fifteen years of management experience, I see that there has always been very low formalization and centralization in my firm. After a brief training period in which we learned about the company's products, we were virtually on our own and sent out to direct our staff and deal with customers. I had former classmates who after earning their MBAs were put through rigorous orientations and were given thick manuals of rules and standard operating procedures to follow at all times. Not me. In other firms managers get their marching orders from the corner suite and must go through extensive approvals to make a decision of any significance. Not me. *My firm's lack of formalization and highly decentralized atmosphere led to a greater sense of freedom but also a lot of uncertainty and variability on how each manager ran their department.* The practically lawless anything-goes atmosphere trickles down to the sales professionals who we "supervised." They literally go weeks at a time without actually reporting into the office, simply sending their sales orders in to be processed. They are able to exercise a great deal of discretion in their jobs (low formalization) and make decisions on the spot (low centralization) with little oversight. As a result, the company sees very uneven returns and experiences much turnover. There is also the constant danger of a lawsuit or damaged reputation due to inappropriate behavior. In contrast some competitor firms plan out their employees' schedule and have strict rules to protect the company image. This is good for quality control but also has some drawbacks like not letting your people adapt to different situations and customer demands to make the sale. A friend at another firm told me a story about how his manager placed a huge inventory order to stock up for last Christmas. He did not involve anyone in the field. If his decision were less centralized, he would have found out that it was way out of line with the prevailing sales climate. His centralized decision cost them a lot of money. I am not sure which of our company's approaches is better but believe that there must be a balance of freedom and control. Too much or too little of either can spell big problems.

Walking the Talk: Select a situation in your life where your job was affected by formalization and/or centralization. 1) **D**etermine what rules and decision-making mechanisms were present in the organization. (2) **E**valuate the degree to which your role was appropriately standardized and empowered compared with others in the organization. (3) **A**nalyze why these design decisions were important in shaping action and how they affected your performance and satisfaction. (4) **L**everage these insights to better design and manage formalization and centralization.

> To appropriately design as well as manage both formalization and cen-
> tralization, I will...

10.4   Designing and Managing a Bureaucratic Structure

Ask Yourself: What thoughts come to mind when you hear the word
"Bureaucracy"? Why do organizations establish these types of objective,
unified, and stable structures? What are their benefits and drawbacks? Do
you enjoy working in them? How can a bureaucratic structure be best
managed?

Management Theory: Few worlds evoke such universally negative
reactions as the dreaded "B" word—bureaucracy. Ironically it was origi-
nally conceived as an optimal organizational form unique in its capacity
for efficiency and effectiveness. The ideal Weberian Bureaucracy (note
the capital B) was seen to possess several characteristics: (1) Rational-legal
authority derived from scientifically proven rules with power embedded
in formal positions rather than particular persons, (2) Roles held on the
basis of objective technical competence rather than status or connections, (3) Clearly specified vertical and horizontal lines of authority and
responsibility between role-occupants, (4) Unity of the chain-of-com-
mand whereas each role is under the control of another in the hierarchy,
(5) Behavior governed by well-defined rules, standard operating procedures, and norms, and (6) Administrative rules and decisions formally
documented and stored in writing. Such a structure would in theory
enable logical and orderly activity. If this is the case, then why do actual
bureaucracies (note the lowercase b) connote such pessimistic imagery?
Part of the reason must lie in its stronger fit with predictable, stable
environments and weaker one with those that are more dynamic. Yet
much of its bad rap is also due to poor implementation of its principles
or exaggeration of its tendencies; for example, blindly following rules,
clinging to literal (i.e., "red tape") versus intended protocol, suppressing innovation and creativity, oversimplifying tasks, and dehumanizing
jobs. A central insight for managers is that organizations can suffer from
too much, little, or a poorly implemented bureaucracy. Organizations
must therefore (a) in its initiation, utilize this machine-like structure for
appropriate situations and strategies and (b) in its implementation, seek

to maximize its advantages while mitigating its dysfunctions. Our story is by a manager who compares the different experiences of working in a more versus less bureaucratic climates.

In Action [Case Study]: I would like to compare the organizational structures of two places where I worked, the U.S. military and a small private high-tech contractor. The military employer was a definite bureaucracy. Operating tasks were highly routine and handled by specialized roles. For instance, I was a radioman on a submarine. My job was to operate the communications equipment. However, I did not operate the nuclear reactor, nor fire torpedoes or launch missiles. Like many large private organizations we had a comprehensive rule book that must be adhered to by its personnel. The personnel were required to conform to centralized direction and "obey orders" as opposed to going rogue and making their own decisions in the field. *We had very formalized rules and regulations, centralized authority, narrow spans of control and decision making that followed the chain of command. Good thing!* It would not be a good idea to start launching missiles or torpedoing ships just because someone felt like it! I was officially part of the Navigation/Operations department. The Weapons department handled torpedoes, missiles, and so on. Engineering took care of the air, water, and power. Supply handled food and parts. The structure enabled us to perform standardized activities in a highly efficient manner, a mechanistic model. This is in stark contrast with my current position with a high-tech private contractor. The company is utilizing a less bureaucratic and more flexible team structures. I am a service group manager working with the government division manager. This clearly shows two distinct lines of authority in a dynamic environment that constantly adjusts to service the needs of the customer. The unity-of-command concept is splintered. Role conflict and ambiguity arise. But, the more flexible structure does facilitate coordination of multiple and interdependent activities and gives me the freedom to apply my best judgment to a problem. In addition, due to our dynamic environment the company is utilizing teams on projects spanning multiple departments. The work bureaucracy in the military was well fit for its environment and led to high performance, but I feel that for many employees it reduced job satisfaction and more people got out than reenlisted. Conversely, with participative decision making at the small private firm job satisfaction is higher. I am still getting used to this new environment. I would not say I miss working in its bureaucracy as much as that I was comfortably used to it.

Walking the Talk: Select a situation in your life where you worked in a bureaucratic organization. (1) **D**etermine whether the firm conformed to the six principles of Bureaucracy. (2) **E**valuate the degree to which the structure fit or did not fit with the firm's strategy and environment. (3) **A**nalyze why it was more or less able to capitalize on the design's strengths and reduce its dysfunctions. (4) **L**everage these insights to appropriately design and better manage within a bureaucratically oriented context.

To properly select and construct a bureaucratic structure, I will...

10.5   Designing and Managing an Organic Structure

Ask Yourself: What thoughts come to mind when you hear the word "Organic"? Why do organizations establish these types of flexible, multidimensional, and dynamic structures? What are their benefits and drawbacks? Do you enjoy working in them? How can an organic structure be best managed?

Management Theory: Complex organizational structures are not only differentiated, integrated, centralized or formalized but instead are at the same time varying degrees of all of these. Insofar as the ideal Bureaucracy paints a picture of how these multiple dimensions converge into a distinct structure, it is also useful to explore how the opposite extreme might appear (keeping in mind that organizations often adopt nuanced combinations and hybrids of these forms). Management theory contrasts a pure mechanistic bureaucracy with, at the other end of the spectrum, a correspondingly flexible, evolving, interlaced, ad-hocracy. This "organic" form stands in stark contrast to its bureaucratic brethren—it enlarges the scope of highly differentiated positions, increases the intensity of integrative mechanisms, expands the decentralization of decision-making authority, and augments the ability of its employees to utilize their judgment via mutual-adjustment. Whereas mechanistic bureaucracies are best fit with stable efficiency-related contexts, organic forms enable greater effectiveness under more dynamic, innovative conditions. This implies a contingency approach to organizational design where structure is adapted to the predominant internal (e.g., strategy, technology) and external (e.g., environment, institutions) demands facing the organization. One mechanism that organizations often employ to increase organic qualities is to adopt a matrix-like structure that overlays multiple governance mechanisms on its operations. For example, in a simple two-dimensional matrix structure, both functional and product hierarchies interact to simultaneously govern operations. This dual responsibility builds more complex and interlaced integration channels to broaden perspectives and increase flexibility. Matrix connections can be quite useful in overcoming functional silos and bringing people together but can also create confusion if not coordinated properly. Our story is by a project manager evaluating the advantages and disadvantages of moving from a bureaucratic to a more organic, matrix-like structure.

In Action [Case Study]: My corporation has changed from a bureaucratic to a more organic matrix-like structure as its basis of operation. This works better for the company because we handle many projects that require multiple combinations of functional specialists on a dynamic basis. For a given project, there is now a product manager who must work with functional managers to staff and complete a team. The best way to complete the project is left to the team leader and members who come on and off the project as needed. The flexible, evolving web-like structure allows the company to better handle peaks and valleys in workloads because functional employees' expertise can be applied from project to project based on current task needs. The company can maintain a constant level of specialists and apply them in a way that makes the best use of their skills. When a project manager identifies the need for a certain expertise, the functional manager can assign a specialist to the project and then relocate that person as necessary to support other projects. This also creates a con though, since it is often stressful to be moved around just as you have become accustomed to a project and to not know where you will be working from week to week. *The organic matrix-like structure in our company helps to keep all functional departments involved and working together.* Management theory warns that one problem that arises out of this type of structure is that there is a dual chain of command, with functional employees reporting to both their functional manager and their project manager. I have seen this but hope that as the company gains experience with the arrangement the ambiguities will lessen. The effect of this kind of organizational structure has on the bottom line varies by individual. Someone who likes stability of assignments will not be satisfied in this atmosphere because there is a lot of reassignment and moving around that goes on. They need to learn how to break out of their narrow silos and comfort areas to look at the big picture of things. If not, they will be prone to higher levels of turnover and lower levels of productivity. Someone who likes constant change will likely do well and be very productive.

Walking the Talk: Select a situation in your life where you worked in an organic organization. (1) **D**etermine whether the firm was built around an emergent and flexible framework. (2) **E**valuate the degree to which the structure fit or did not fit with the firm's strategy and environment.

(3) **A**nalyze why it was more or less able to capitalize on the design's strengths and reduce its dysfunctions. (4) **L**everage these insights to appropriately design and better manage within an organically oriented context.

> To properly select and construct an organic or matrix structure, I will...

10.6   Constructing a Coherent Culture

Ask Yourself: Do organizations have a "personality"? What is this thing called organizational or corporate culture? How do you see it? Build it? Learn it? Manage it?

Management Theory: Management theory describes an organization's culture as its set of shared meaning and values within a system that work to influence the daily thinking, behavior, and interactions of its members. This definition has several important components. First, culture is shared. It is a collective understanding that connects employees to each other in a common framework and corporate philosophy. The links that culture creates work to institutionalize its central tenets throughout the organization. Second, culture is about meaning and values. It promotes a fundamental worldview and methodology for making sense of things. As such it embodies distinct business principles and priorities about what ends are good and what means are acceptable. Third, culture affects the everyday work environment. Its deep-seeded corporate assumptions and values rise to the surface and can be seen in the language that people use (how they dress, talk to each other, use acronyms and jargon), repetitive rites and rituals that they follow (orientation, bonding, promotion, and exit ceremonies), stories that they tell ("heroes" who were rewarded for conforming or "villains" who were punished for going against the grain), and symbols that are displayed (decorations, artwork, office designs, prominent charts, or banners). Fourth, culture is about influence and control. It orients its members in a certain direction. As such it is a mechanism that ideally will adapt with environmental demands to both support and enforce a positive (versus destructive) corporate vision. Often people operating within a culture will take it for granted and unconsciously internalize it to such an extent that the culture will appear normal without any question or doubt. Our story is by a manager who describes the power of culture on their organization and learns to pinpoint the tell-tall signs for detecting it.

In Action [Case Study]: At my current job, the company culture is about lowering overhead and cutting costs. *All the cultural characteristics that help institute "cost cutting" are applied across the board and show up everywhere you look.* If the firm were a human, its personality would be like a cheap old man who never spends a dime unless absolutely necessary. E-mail inboxes are constantly filled with organizational announcements reminding us to turn off our equipment at the end of the day, not to waste supplies, and to get every last drop out of resources. Lean and mean, lean and mean, that is what we hear all day and see postered all around the office. We are constantly understaffed so managers are asked to take on a significant amount of additional responsibility. The CEO does not have a personal secretary; we hear this story all the time, so why should any of the managers need one. The walls in people's offices are bare, and the computers have not been replaced in years. One time my colleague brought in an art print to hang up, and his director made a sarcastic comment about him being Rockefeller or something. For those attending our corporate picnic, we had to pay a fee and bring a dish. There are company-specific acronyms that are used to facilitate cultural membership such as "stretchy", this is when you get every last bit out of something, and "crabby", this is fighting for every last inch of cost savings. At work it is all business and nobody talks about themselves. If it is your birthday, the director might give you a card but certainly no bonus or even a token gift. As more of the cost cutting is expanded, we are seeing the migration of more jobs overseas. All of this has resulted in a distinct attitude of the firm. When people come to work they are paying close attention to what changes are going to be mentioned in their e-mails. The phrase "TGIF" is meant from the heart as opposed to being something that is just lightly used in a conversation on Fridays. Offers to share knowledge rarely happen and we never get sponsored for industry conferences. It is amazing how picking up on the cues from one dominant trait, cost cutting, revealed the entire personality of the organization and explained the attitudes of the people that work in it.

Walking the Talk: Select a situation in your life where you felt part of an organization's culture. (1) **D**etermine whether there were observable cultural markers in the workplace. (2) **E**valuate the degree to which these artifacts were used to communicate a coherent cultural framework. (3) **A**nalyze why the stories, rites, rituals, language, and symbols were more or less effective in promoting desired behaviors. (4) **L**everage these insights to better construct and detect cultural nuances.

To better construct and detect an organizational culture, I will...

10.7 Shaping Deep-Level Values and Assumptions

Ask Yourself: Where can you find the heart of an organization's culture? What less tangible factors lay beneath the surface of artifacts and observable indicators? How does one shape these fundamental assumptions and core values? Manage them in the proper direction?

Management Theory: As suggested in the previous discussion, an organization's culture exists at several levels. In the workplace there can be seen observable artifacts. Yet the essential core of a culture, just as that of an iceberg, lies beneath the surface and is not easily seen. Often molded by the founder, the basic assumptions of a culture define the primary mission of an organization, the rationale for its existence, taken-for-granted truths on which the enterprise is established, and elemental beliefs about how to succeed in its environment and lead a profitable existence. The assumptions are in essence the organization's central philosophy—shaping their logic about what works, ethics about what is good, epistemology about what things mean, aesthetics about what is satisfying, and metaphysics about what is important. Born from these assumptions are the values that in turn govern relationships and guide activity. They provide a sense of stability and identity among its members and lay out the unwritten codes of conduct that they are expected to conform to. Taken together, these assumptions and values comprise the heart of an organization's culture. For example, an organization that adopts a philosophy of efficiency and seeks to promote it through the values of caution and frugality would look quite different from another that was run based on a philosophy of innovativeness and supported by values of risk-taking and creativity. Just as an in chapter one where we discussed how an individual's unique personality influences their outlook and activities, an organization's unique culture similarly influences their collective attitude and performance. Our story is by a R&D manager witnessing the subtle yet powerful influence of deep-seeded cultural assumptions and values on the strategy.

In Action [Case Study]: Organizational culture is the shared meaning held by and continually being reinforced in the minds of its employees.

Obviously, the implication is that at my and other companies, the learning is not a function of some initial indoctrination but the result of ongoing company philosophy to demonstrate values over time. One of my company's core values is a low level of risk tolerance. The company was recently working on a drug to prevent blood infections in emergency surgeries. Many people felt that it would have been very lucrative since it could be used in every hospital emergency room and no other drug like it exists. Even though we had made great progress in development, the company decided to abandon the project. They felt it was too risky since it was so unlike any of the other drugs they have developed. Many felt that this decision was not the right one since the company is doing very poorly financially and has so few drugs in the pipeline. However this is who we are. We focus on the sure bets and leave the long shots to other firms. This is what our company founders believed was the recipe for success and it still guides us today. But I have my doubts as to whether this culture would serve us well in the new competitive environment. *I felt that it made a negative statement to employees about risk taking at a time when the company desperately needs to branch out and be innovative.* The principles on which our company was founded permeate all aspects of the firm so to change them would be a significant undertaking. For example, to complete new or experimental drug development would require so many forms and approvals that it would never get done. Even to hire someone who worked in these areas would never happen. Therefore open positions are usually filled from within the company rather than from the outside. This reinforces the culture rather than encourage new thinking, and this could hurt performance in the long run.

Walking the Talk: Select a situation in your life where you were influenced by an organization's culture. (1) **D**etermine whether there were definitive philosophical and principled foundations underlying the culture. (2) **E**valuate the degree to which these core assumptions and values shaped the organization's personality in a certain direction. (3) **A**nalyze why they were more or less effective in promoting desired behaviors and how this could be better managed. (4) **L**everage these insights to better shape deep-level cultural assumptions and values.

To better shape deep-level cultural assumptions and values, I will…

10.8   Guiding the Socialization Process

Ask Yourself: How do you become accepted into an organization's culture? What practices do organizations use to indoctrinate and integrate newcomers? Keep veterans committed? Reorient those moving from one area to another? Do these varying approaches to socialization have different advantages and downsides?

Management Theory: The process whereby employees learn and internalize information about an organizational culture is called socialization. Through socialization (new) employees learn the "right" values and ways of dong things to become productive members of the organizational society and accepted as "insiders." In general organizational socialization takes one of two forms. First, socialization promoting an "institutional" orientation tries to produce a standardized and consistent attitude toward the culture where employees conform to existing paradigms and follow set protocols. Basically everyone is taught to think and act in the same way resulting in highly controlled and efficient operations. This is often done through collective and formal training programs that follow specific steps at fixed time intervals and employ seasoned insiders to guide them, connoting respect and acceptance only when the employees have been "cloned" to sufficiently blend in. Alternatively, socialization promoting an "individualized" orientation tries to produce a unique and customized attitude toward the culture where employees feel free to experiment creatively within the overall rubric of the firm and truly express themselves. Basically everyone is taught to think and act through their own personal interpretations resulting in highly flexible and innovative operations. This is often done through informal on-the-job training that adapt to the real-time experiences of the employee that supports them, and they allow them to learn as they go to marriage their unique styles and perspectives to the overall firm approach. As is evident institutionalized or individualized approaches connote different degrees of control and flexibility. Notwithstanding, they both aim to harmonize individual with organizational personalities. If socialization is successful the employee will be accepted into the culture but, if unsuccessful, the relationship could be short-lived. Our story is by a manager who describes his experiences with each of these types of organizational socialization processes.

In Action [Case Study]: I feel that at my firm socialization happened twice. The first transition occurred when I entered the management training program and was put into what many of us describes as "boot-camp." The next one followed about ten years later when I was promoted and relocated to the corporate headquarters. *When I initially joined the firm and encountered their orientation boot-camp, I learned in an institutionalized manner* *how to adapt to this environment if I wanted to succeed and climb the corporate ladder.* The rules, regulations, and customs were implemented stringently. After a while, I learned to endure and follow the code in which everyone else was a part of. No one was special, each individual had to adhere properly to instructions and policy, or they would receive strict reinforcement. The program was conducted in a lock-step order where everyone would go through the same training together. Once I finished orientation, I even became a trainer who socialized our new hot-shot recruits and taught them the ropes of the company. However everything changed some years later when I was moved up to the central office. I had to completely readapt to this new cultural environment. When I acted like I was supposed to, or so I thought, it was greeted with amusement among the senior execs. It was almost like a different organization but instead of a formal training program I was on my own and had to figure things out as they came up. This was more like individualized socialization. No more waiting for orders or asking permission for everything, you initiated action and used your judgment to make decisions. I could almost hear myself think "What? Think for myself and act to solve a problem by myself without ten different types of approvals or clear instructions?" It was hard to get the old habits out of my head because the routines were so ingrained but eventually, after a few missteps and the inevitable rounds of good-natured laughter and words of advice, I learned to change my approach. This is why I feel like I went through two different socialization processes. Each type was well fit to their different parts of the organization and both were effective in helping me learn the different cultures.

Walking the Talk: Select a situation in your life where you were new to an organization's culture. (1) **D**etermine whether the organization utilized a cultural socialization process. (2) **E**valuate the degree to which the process was more institutionalized or individualized. (3) **A**nalyze how the nature of this process influenced your ability to internalize the culture and why you were or were not able to become part of the culture. (4) **L**everage these insights to appropriately design and manage cultural socialization.

> To better design, manage, and execute cultural socialization, I will...

10.9   Facilitating Cultural Change

Ask Yourself: How do you change an organization's culture? Reorient its personality? Question its assumptions and redefine its values. Shift its artifacts? Get people on board to support the new direction? What are the major methods for and challenges to doing this?

Management Theory: Changing an organizational culture represents one of the most profound challenges a manager can undertake. This being said, knowledge of the factors that drive a firm's culture is essential to understanding how a manager might attempt to modify its direction. First, changing a culture can be approached by altering the makeup of the workforce through the hiring, firing, retraining, or transferring of employees based on their fit with the new system. Second, pay and promotional criteria can be reengineered to reward values more consistent with the new culture such as moving from fixed seniority-based metrics to variable performance-driven bonuses, short-term to long-term executive compensation packages, and individualized to group-measured assessments. Third, structures can be redesigned to change the formal patterns of interaction such as to concentrate or disperse decision-making authority, tighten or ease rules and procedures, and reconfigure reporting relationships. Fourth, socialization processes can be altered by, for example, moving from an institutionalized to an individualized process. Fifth, cultural artifacts can be managed by altering dress codes and office layouts, changing meeting protocols, and instituting new ceremonies and tales of corporate heroes. Yet despite the best intentions, organizational "personalities" are resistant to change and the longer and more successful it has been in the past the harder it usually is to modify. Managers must overcome of ingrained interest that may come from employees who benefited from or liked the old system, structural inertia that is designed to promote stability and consistency, and subcultures that are protective of their distinct systems. All in all, by changing the factors that feed a company culture and addressing barriers to change, managers can try to communicate different philosophies and construct a different cultural system. Our story is by a manager who experienced the promises and challenges of cultural change within the organization.

In Action [Case Study]: Organizational culture refers to a system of shared meaning held by members who distinguishes the organization from other organizations. However, culture can be a liability when the shared values are not in agreement with those that will further the organization's effectiveness. My company is in the communications industry and was not doing well against its newer and more modern competition. *Recently my firm decided to change its culture from emphasizing history and* *continuity to one where innovation and risk are valued. To stay competitive in the industry, the company had to find new ways of doing things.* The clients we serve want to see change, they do not want to hear "this is the way we've done it for the past 50 years." Top managers decided to embark on a path of cultural change through which they have coined the phrase: "Better, faster, safer, cheaper." People who have been with the company for many years are not readjusting well. They do not understand why it needs to happen. One person I work with is particularly concerned about these changes because he championed many of the standards we used for our work processes and now "his" methods are being challenged. He views it as a personal attack when someone comes up with a new idea about how to do something that he has done a set way for his whole life. I, however, think the company is showing initiative and a desire to do whatever they can to stay profitable in today's tough market. They seem to be recognizing the need for more systematic change efforts. They have even announced a new performance-based bonus system that is almost unheard of in this company where paying your dues and serving your time was the only way to the top. They have also brought in a new wave of recruits who are more entrepreneurial and energetic. Rumor has it that they are also considering flattening the hierarchy and streamlining approval processes so that it is easier to implement new initiatives. It is evident to me that when I joined the company it had one culture and now it is changing so I must either adapt or get out. Charles Darwin once said, "It is not the strongest that survive, nor the most intelligent, but those most adaptable to change," this certainly holds true in this instance.

Walking the Talk: Select a situation in your life where you were involved in a cultural change. (1) **D**etermine whether the change targeted different aspects and levels of the culture. (2) **E**valuate how people, rewards systems, structures, socialization tactics, and artifacts were used to facilitate the change. (3) **A**nalyze the degree to which the change was successful in overcoming personal, institutional, and other barriers. (4) **L**everage these insights to better manage cultural change.

> To better manage cultural change, I will…

10.10   Combining Structures and Cultures

Ask Yourself: What happens to an organization's structure and culture when it acquires, is acquired, or merges with another firm? How are their diverse systems reconciled? What are the major challenges to doing this? How does it affect the employees of the two organizations?

Management Theory: Organizations do not last forever in their current form. Just as humans grow and change to fit their surroundings so do organizational structures and cultures. As the previous discussion suggests sometimes this change is intentional and executed internally. This process is normally referred to as restructuring and may be engaged through the process of organizational development. Other times structural and cultural change is thrust upon an organization from outside. For example, dramatic shifts in a firms design can result from mergers and acquisitions, as when an organization purchases or combines with another to share resources and become a single entity. Even though many of these unions might make financial and strategic sense, they are less frequently initiated with a consideration of structural and cultural compatibility. Instead differences between partners can result in painful adjustments to the system or outright cultural clashes. Just like in a marriage, when two organizations wed it is important to reconcile differences and reach common understanding. Ideally this would be through a combination that adopts the best practices of each but, in the real world, frequently involves a series of compromises or the imposition of the "stronger" organization's ways and values on the other. Either way, employees are challenged to adjust to the new climate. To best manage this transition, organizations should pursue proven methods for facilitating these relationships, for example, proactive planning processes, high degrees of employee communication and involvement, extensive reorientation and training programs, and coalescence around a clear, shared vision for the newly created context. Yet in the end there is no getting around the stress and adjustment challenges that come with such transformations. Our story is about a manager recounting a seemingly endless cycle of structural and, in their view, superficially managed cultural reorganizations.

In Action [Case Study]: In the three years that I have been working as a software development manager in the same group at the same location, I have gone through at least three (and one more pending) major structural and cultural changes. My company (company 1) was bought by a larger firm (company 2). However they then sold us to another company (company 3). Now this new company has merged with another firm to form yet another corporate entity (company 4). Each of these companies had its own structure and culture. When I first joined my firm, the software development area of the company was organized by product differentiation. There was great interaction between all the members on the project. Our culture resembled a close-knit "family." Six months later we were acquired and reorganized to emphasize the customer and it resembled process differentiation. In this organization, there were four or five groups that were structured around the different operations processes of our clients. This structure was valuable because it allowed more communication across products, thus increasing the overall support that we provided to the customer, but did not help us in planning across processes. Their culture was very client-centered and used all the normal buzzwords to support this. However there were definite culture clashes between us, like when they urgently sent customer-requested changes and we did not want to violate the integrity of the original product design. Also we were used to significant amounts of freedom in our work but in the new firm we were required to do exactly as instructed. One structure promoted creativity while then other promoted control. The next reorganization occurred a year later when a different company bought the acquiring firm, and then we were folded into their structure and became functionally departmentalized. Now, there are separate system engineers, testers, developers, and so forth, with little consideration to either process or product. This has helped us improve our specialized skills but we no longer have a product manager who oversees the entire product, which is a major hole that has created a gap between the "team members" that contribute to a product. The first Christmas after being acquired, they sent to every employee a book written by a retired president about the story of the company, its people, and their "pioneering achievements." This contrasted with our history and expressed very different values that we were used to emphasizing. I can see many tensions coming from this. Now since the latest merger I have recently heard rumors of another reorganization toward geographic departmentalization. *Hmm... Do all mergers result in these continuous cycles of reorganization? Are they strategic or just change for the sake of change?* Yes different organizations have different approaches to structure, and companies in general should continuously reevaluate their structure and adapt it to their environment. However if organizations are naively chasing each fad and fashion or copying someone else's "best practice," then it makes little sense for us to go through so many major changes and have our managers experience all the stress and new challenges that it brings. While you are hoping to increase productivity as a whole through synergies, you may find productivity decreasing when the two cultures clash and they have difficulty working together.

Walking the Talk: Select a situation in your life where you were part of a merger or acquisition. (1) **D**etermine whether the merger resulted in structural and/or cultural transformations. (2) **E**valuate the degree of synergy between the organizations' structures and cultures or if there were fundamental incompatibilities to overcome. (3) **A**nalyze how the organizations attempted to address these challenges and why employees were or were not successful in adapting to the new systems. (4) **L**everage these insights to more harmoniously combine structural and/or cultural frameworks.

To better manage the combination of structures and cultures, I will...

CHAPTER ELEVEN

Executing the Leadership Function

Chapter eleven examines management theories about leadership and the management skill of leading organizations. There is perhaps no more important organizational role than that of leadership. Leaders are often vested with formal authority at the very top of organizational hierarchies and wield asymmetrical influence over its people and operations. However, leaders can emerge from anywhere in an organization, thus no manager is immune to its promises and pitfalls. In a nutshell, leadership is the practice of orienting and facilitating the progress of their followers toward the attainment of desired objectives. Let us unpack this definition. First, leadership is about determining objectives. Creating a vision. Establishing a mission. This is the strategic mandate of leaders who must set a direction for employees to pursue. Second, leadership is about orientating people toward this end state. Clarifying expectations. Gaining commitment. This is the enactment mandate of leaders who must define a reality for employees to internalize. Third, leadership is about facilitating the achievement of this end state. Inspiring progress. Showing the way. This is the implementation mandate of leaders who must move employees to actually get things done. Although some draw a distinction between leadership and management, it is more accurate to say that the two are inexorably intertwined because in the real world organizations are constantly balancing the forces of constancy and change across all levels and activities. Simply put, to be a successful modern manager one must be able to lead. Therefore in this eleventh chapter we look at how managers can master the leadership function to achieve maximum effectiveness.

11.1 Appreciating the Importance of Leadership

Ask Yourself: Does leadership really make a difference? Can superior leaders take an organization farther than it is otherwise able to go? Why?

Are there any conditions that might substitute for or reduce the effect of your leadership?

Management Theory: We often under-appreciate just how much of an impact a leader can have on their followers and organization. Leaders are the central and most visible actors who define, energize, and guide behavior as well as act as the stewards, shapers, and shepherds of an organization's resources. Throughout time those who have successfully seized its mantle and borne its burden have exerted great influence over the course of history. And because of the advanced technological tools available to today's leaders as well as the expanded reach of global relationships, effectively executing the leadership function continues to be of equal if not of greater consequence. Indeed numerous studies have documented the strong relationship between leadership and organizational performance. Its importance is also reflected in the vast amount of trade books as well as professional, educational, and training resources dedicated to leadership development. However, to be fair, sometimes the impact of leadership can be exaggerated. Situations beyond the control of leaders might exert a substantial limitation on their success. Their visibility might invite symbolic or even overly romantic notions of their impact on events. Structural arrangements might also be put into place that negate or substitute for the role of leadership, for instance, a strong corporate culture or well-defined team norms. Yet despite these caveat leadership continues to rank among the most critical factors in management and attract the attention of numerous researchers, executives, and coaches interested in improving their organization's success. The call of leadership is undeniably strong, its challenges certainly significant, and its potential impact considerable. Our story is by a manager who has witnessed first hand the degree to which leadership can make a difference in an organization.

In Action [Case Study]: I am a district manager for a retail company. Working under my former boss was the most pleasant management learning experience. I believe that he is still the only leader I had who was able to make me feel good about my job and allow me to perform at the best of my ability. I am one of those people who never feel like their work is good enough or that it is really worth it to do your absolute best. Even when I get results I do not think that the leader really appreciates it and that they are just using you to get what they want. But not with my former boss. He made me feel that I was important and my assignments were challenging and interesting. *No matter how uncertain and difficult the job, the treatment I had from my leader somehow made me feel that I could make things happen.* As long as I worked hard, good things happened one after and another. To this date, I still remember those days when I was fully loaded to get things moving as fast as I could, not because I expected any big cash bonus return, but because I admired my former boss' leadership abilities and did not want to let him down. In addition to his high confidence, intelligence, understanding, strong verbal skills, and industriousness, he observed and judged things with his own eyes; he understood and allowed differences among his followers; he was unconventional, consistent, and allowed you to have some mistakes. Most important of all, he knew who you were, what you needed, and how to get you work hard for him (the key to become a successful manager!). Recently a friend of mine from headquarters told me about how my boss was doing since we parted ways: he had been appointed director for a number of our overseas facilities: India, China, Philippines, Singapore, and Egypt. He was loved by everyone in every job he took and his divisions generated more profits. He has been successful everyplace he worked. I have not had as much success and our division has gone nowhere since he left. This says it all.

Walking the Talk: Select a situation in your life where you were influenced by someone's leadership. (1) **D**etermine whether this person truly was a leader. (2) **E**valuate the degree to which their leadership made a difference in your satisfaction, behavior, and performance. (3) **A**nalyze the reasons why they were able to affect you in this way. (4) **L**everage these insights to develop a better appreciation for the importance of leadership.

To better appreciate the importance of leadership, I will...

11.2 Tapping into Leadership Traits

Ask Yourself: Are good leaders born (versus made)? If so what are the core traits that they possess? Is there such a thing as a general, universally applicable leadership profile? Do you fit it?

Management Theory: The earliest and simplest explanations of leadership are that some people have the "right stuff" to be effective leaders whereas others do not. If this is true then it would logically follow that leaders are born and not made. Labeled by some as the "Great Man (or Woman) Theory" of leadership, it proposes that leaders are fundamentally different from other types of people and, because of this, an organization needs to know what their key innate characteristics are to properly choose its leaders. To this end, management theory has identified several types of potential leadership traits: Personality characteristics such as extroversion and assertiveness; physical characteristics such as height and appearance; attitudinal characteristics such as self-confidence and integrity; and specific abilities such as intelligence and social insight. Yet this is only part of the picture and does not provide a complete or balanced account of what leadership is about. Research has also suggested that a trait approach has certain problems. For example, for each trait associated with a successful leader that same exact trait can be also found in unsuccessful ones. It might also be the case that some traits only help to make people look like and be chosen a leader without actually enabling them to be a good one. Plus even the most useful traits are more or less functional depending on the situation. And even if some are found to be broadly desirable, these so-called traits might in fact be learnable behaviors that people can develop over time with the proper training. Therefore it is perhaps most accurate to say that some personal characteristics might increase the potential of leadership success but none guarantee it. Our story is by a manager who identifies desirable leadership characteristics in her division head and uses him as a model to grow as a leader.

In Action [Case Study]: My organization's leadership exhibits behavior that is consistent with the Trait Theory of Leadership. *Judging from my experience, our division was engulfed by the leader's personality attributes that propelled us to great results.* First, the energy emanating from our leader, let me call him Bob, was electrifying. Bob never seemed exhausted and always had a comment up his sleeve that made you forget of your weariness and put a smile on one's face. Bob's ambition was of equal strength. His approach was systematic and unrelenting. I can still hear him say, "Success is a marathon, not a hundred yard dash." Second, his honesty and integrity inspired our full cooperation. Interactions felt free of alternative motives thus paving the road for often-creative solutions to our daily problems. The third trait and often most noticeable by most everyone around Bob was his self-confidence. He was able to alter the direction of work and was never afraid to take an opposing side to other managers. This made him the richest resource of our division. The final quality, raw intelligence, was evident by his ability to predict trends in the industry before they even happened and most importantly in his constant desire to learn more about the market and the product. Bob's character, amenable manner, intelligence, and vast confidence made him an open book for everyone to learn from. I will continue to hold him as a role model for my personal leadership. To conclude, the presence of traits exhibited by Bob, I believe, are somewhat of a prerequisite to effective leadership. However, I further believe that the presence and full utilization of these traits are contingent on individual's self-awareness and being in the right place at the right time. Our organization was wise to identify Bob as a high-potential leader and develop and promote him. I was fortunate to work under him. During this time, my performance and job satisfaction were sky-high and absentee-ism and turnover were non existent.

Walking the Talk: Select a situation in your life where leadership was important. (1) **D**etermine whether the leader was effective or ineffective. (2) **E**valuate the degree to which their personality profile influenced their success. (3) **A**nalyze the specific aspects of their personal characteristics that enabled them to lead in a better or worse manner. (4) **L**everage these insights to identify these characteristics in yourself and tap into them when executing the leadership function.

To better identify and tap into my leadership characteristics, I will...

11.3   Displaying Charisma

Ask Yourself: Do good leaders have an electric or magnetic aura about them? Are they usually more energetic, confident, and optimistic? Do they rely more on emotional or logical inspiration? Are there any instances where this leadership style can be a bad thing? Can someone actually learn to become more charismatic?

Management Theory: Charismatic theory proposes that successful lead-ers have extraordinary, almost heroic qualities that enable them to arouse extreme loyalty, create high levels of personal admiration or identifica-tion, and achieve superior performance. Management theory has isolated several key behaviors and competencies of these larger-than-life "charis-matic" leaders. First, they are able to delineate a clear, compelling vision of the future and their organization's place in it. Second, they personalize the vision by providing appropriate behavioral expectations for employees and express the confidence that they can succeed. Third, charismatic lead-ers walk the talk by serving as a role model for their ideals thereby earn-ing followers' respect. Fourth, they are not afraid to break from tradition, acting boldly and courageously to take responsibility for establishing the desired reality. Together these actions have been shown to inspire follow-ers and boost their success and satisfaction across numerous outcome-based metrics. However a few words of caution are in order. Charisma may not be a trait per se but in fact a learnable behavior. For example, a person can boost their ability to portray charisma by showing more optimism, projecting an aura of confidence and command, better using emotional appeals, and creating closer bonds with employees. Also charisma may not be equally appropriate in all situations. For example, some organizations might benefit from a charismatic leader, such as those facing uncertainty and emotional situations, yet when stability and moderation are called for a charismatic leader might be detrimental to these goals. Thus sober and steady can be just as effective in the proper context. Finally charisma may not be an end in itself but rather a tool that can be used to achieve better or worse objectives. History shows us that charismatic leaders can perpetrate wonderful good or great evil, promote selfless causes or megalomaniacal greed, and lead their organizations to new heights or ego-induced failure. Our story is by a manager who witnessed first hand the potential benefits of a positively channelled charismatic leader.

In Action [Case Study]: I can truly say that the CEO of my previous firm embodied charismatic leadership. I can clearly remember on my first day at work he called me in his office and took the time from his busy schedule to explain the ins and outs of the department I would be running. He said that he would always be there to assist me whenever the need be and he really meant it. At lunch I was alone the first day eating in my office. When he saw me, he asked me to join him and other executives at a local restaurant. During lunch he "worked the room" but really connected with each person around the table and never made us feel like we were his subordinates. At his weekly addresses to the staff, he emphasized his vision for the future and what he expects from everyone from the executive team to the mailroom. He also mentioned that to achieve any target we would encounter obstacles and he would provide the resources for overcoming them. He praised two of his top managers for making their numbers ahead of schedule and commended everybody for doing a good job. Then he asked if anybody had any questions or concerns. He did not avoid answering the tough questions. When he walked down the hallway, he was like a tornado carrying everyone higher. I also noticed that he was the first one to come to work and he usually stayed late. Over a period of time I got to know him more, he was a man who took risk, calculated risk and whenever there was a new development in the marketplace he would take it upon himself to become an expert in the area. He always had an open door policy, a real one and not just some hot air, and he was like a fatherly figure to everybody in the organization. I truly miss working with him. *Off all my years working I have never found anybody in a leadership position as inspiring as him. We would walk through walls for him.* He had all the qualities of a charismatic leader, and we were all extremely dedicated to work under him. Now as I find myself taking on the leadership of my own organization, I can only hope that by having him as a leader I learned something so that I will be able to do for my employees, and my organization, what he did for me.

Walking the Talk: Select a situation in your life where you worked for a charismatic leader. (1) **D**etermine whether the leader was effective or ineffective. (2) **E**valuate the degree to which their level of charisma influenced their success. (3) **A**nalyze the specific aspects of charisma that they displayed and why they enabled them to lead in a better or worse manner. (4) **L**everage these insights to appropriately display charisma in your personal leadership behaviors.

To better and more appropriately display charisma, I will...

11.4   Meeting Task and Relationship Challenges

Ask Yourself: Is leadership more about who you are or what you do? How should leaders orchestrate tasks and employees to facilitate goal accomplishments? Establish bonds to forge productive and positive working relationships? Can leaders meet both of these challenges at the same time? What happens when either is missing? Can this "playbook" of effective leadership behaviors be taught?

Management Theory: Leadership is not just a noun but also a verb—a distinct pattern of action. In this sense leaders succeed or fail based not so much on who they are but what they do. Management theory posits several theories describing these leadership "playbooks" or "punch-lists" with long lists of suggested behaviors but, when boiled down to their essence, we can extract two themes: cultivating relationships and accomplishing tasks. First, leaders need to address the needs of their followers. They do this through consideration-like, employee-centered, people-oriented behaviors meant to establish positive workplace bonds such as showing respect, giving recognition, providing encouragement, and offering counseling. Second, leaders need to address the demands of their tasks. They do this through initiation-like, production centered, job-oriented behaviors meant to achieve organizational objectives such as providing direction, organizing work, setting standards, and giving guidance. Taken together a leader is seen as most effective when they simultaneously exhibit high levels of relationship and task leadership behaviors. By learning how to adopt a "high-high" leadership style, their performance will be superior to either a task-only authority-emphasizing "drill sergeant" style or a relationship-only country-club "best buddy" style. Even though there are some doubts that this style will work with all people in all situations (see section 11.6), the notion that people can learn how to execute better or worse leadership behaviors has had a significant influence on modern day management training and development programs. Our story is by a manager who compares working for a high-high leader who exhibited both task and relationship behaviors with another that in their view did not measure up.

In Action [Case Study]: I have experience working with employee-oriented style leaders who emphasized relationships and production-oriented style leaders who cared mostly about tasks. Once I was lucky enough to work for one who did both. About five years ago *I had a leader who not only set high standards and was well respected for his level of achievement and ability, he genuinely got along with everyone in the office and truly cared about the success of each employee.* This was very unique considering it is an industry based on individual success. He knew that we all had our own style of client gathering and different experience levels so he helped each of us differently to achieve high levels of performance. He was highly supportive and cared about us as people, asking about our personal lives and giving us advice on problems, which made us tight as a group and kept us positive during the tough, slow times. In November of that year my manager was promoted and took over a larger office. Our new manager brought more of a production-only leadership behavior and the change was very noticeable. His ultimate concern was just about completing the tasks and how much profit was brought into the office. Once when an employee was experiencing some personal problems at home, he showed no patience or sensitivity to her needs. The drastic change in management style had a negative effect on the employees in our office, especially the new hires. Their performance level began to deteriorate by the lack of new clients being brought in to the firm. Our motivation vanished and daily frustration was very high, which equalled a very low job satisfaction level. I started to make up client meetings to stay out of the office and others admitted to doing the same. Many of the employees in our office left after the management change. I later realized that I was willing to give a stronger effort with a manager who cared about us as both people and the success of the organization more than just one who treated us like disposable parts and cared only about the bottom line.

Walking the Talk: Select a situation in your life where you were a leader. (1) **D**etermine whether you had more of a task- or relationship-oriented style. (2) **E**valuate the degree to which these behaviors were effective. (3) **A**nalyze how your actions affected your employees and why you had any difficulty learning or meeting different leadership demands. (4) **L**everage these insights to develop an enhanced toolbox of leadership behaviors.

To better satisfy task and relationship leadership demands, I will...

11.5   Forming In- and Out-Groups

Ask Yourself: Do leaders always treat everyone in the same way? Give their followers the same amount of attention and support? Should they? If not what determines whether a leader will select you for their "in-group"? How should you select people for yours?

Management Theory: The idea of a high-high leadership style is given a slight twist by the leader-member exchange theory. It is proposed here that, in the real world, there is simply not enough time in the day or energy in their tank for a leader to do this for every employee. Thus leaders tend to form special relationships with a select subgroup of followers and put them in their "in-group" whereas the others are cast off into the "out group." Employees who find themselves in the leader's in-group are given more time, attention, and privileges, that is, greater relationship leadership. They are also given more trust, responsibility, and support, that is, greater task leadership. It should be of little surprise that workers in the in-group tend to be more productive and satisfied than those in the out-group. Management theory tells us that employees are more likely to get into an in-group not based on technical merit per se but by being (1) perceived as more competent and/or (2) seen as similar in interest or attitude to the leader. This suggests that it is often advantageous for a worker to mimic his or her boss to take advantage of a potential "birds of a feather" effect. It would also follow that active impression management could be useful for an employee to create a positive image of themselves, thus appearing worthy of preferential treatment. From the perspective of the leader, they should aim to make balanced decisions about membership in their inner circle based on actual competence and objective standards instead of falling victim to superficially and subjectively biased criteria. Our story is by a manager who reflects on being cast from a leader's in- to out-group and the lessons learned for improving their own leadership.

In Action [Case Study]: I recently had the unique experience of being in both the in group and the out group. In this way I saw both sides of the Leader-Member Exchange Theory. Don, the president of the corporation, chose me early in my career for his inner circle of advisors. We had similar ideas about how an exercise facility should be managed and both of us had the motivation to work long hours to reach these objectives. Don kept me informed on all activities of the business and got me involved in designing new programs for the facility. He would return from trade shows and keep me up to date on the latest equipment and findings in the exercise field. Later in my management career, Don began paying my way to trade shows and gave me free exercise clothing. However, a year and a half ago, I decide to scale back my ambition a little so I could start a family. I was immediately dumped into the out group. Suddenly information was hard to come by. Not only was I not part of developing new programs but when they were introduced I was not even informed on what they were. New equipment would arrive and it would be weeks before someone would let me know how to operate it. No longer did I receive inside information about the company and Don did not seem to have time to even acknowledge that I was still an employee. I began to feel alienated and made it a point to not waste any extra energy doing anything additional for the company and leave work as soon as possible. During my time in the in-group, my performance was high and I was very satisfied with no intention of leaving. When I was moved to the out-group my satisfaction decreased substantially. *Now, like most people, I can say with certainty that it is far better to be a member of the "in" group than not.* It seems to me that the danger here comes when membership in one group or the other is given for the wrong reasons. As my personal example above shows, it is sometimes conferred based on personality differences or things outside job performance. As managers, we need to be clear with ourselves about the factors that determine membership in our own "in" and "out" groups and that we apply those criteria fairly for the best interests of the employees and company.

Walking the Talk: Select a situation in your life where you were a leader. (1) **D**etermine whether you formed in- and out-groups. (2) **E**valuate the degree to which your differential treatment of them made a difference in the employees' satisfaction and performance. (3) **A**nalyze why and on what basis you formed these groups and whether it was driven by objective or subjective criteria. (4) **L**everage these insights to develop an enhanced approach to constructing and leading in- and out-groups.

To more appropriately construct and lead in- and out-groups, I will...

11.6   Adapting Styles to Situations and Contingencies

Ask Yourself: Do you always lead in a consistent way regardless of the particular circumstances? Or alternatively should you change the way you lead depending on the nature of your environment, tasks, and followers? Do people of varying abilities and motivations need to be led differently? How can a leader learn to better fit his or her style with the situation?

Management Theory: We provide further context on the idea of high-high leadership by considering the circumstances that a leader might encounter. Simply put, a contingency perspective posits that there is no "magic bullet" or one best way to lead. Rather the best leadership style that will lead to superior performance depends on the situation. At certain times, with certain people, and for certain jobs a task-oriented style will work best. In others it might make more sense to focus on a relationship style. And to complicate matters further there are even some conditions when both or neither would work well. At its essence, a situational approach to leadership suggests that leaders are successful when they do two things well: (1) Read their circumstances and (2) Adapt their behavior accordingly. The first competency demands diagnostic acumen, the capacity to figure out what style is needed. The second competency demands behavioral flexibility, the capacity to vary ones leadership approach by invoking the most appropriate style. Management theory provides several frameworks for helping managers meet these challenges. For example, one widely used theory focuses on the willingness and ability of the people being led. In this "life-cycle" model, leaders are advised to adopt distinct styles depending on the followers' level of maturity, specifically a "Telling" style high in task orientation for neophytes, "Selling" style for eager learners, "Participating" style high in relationship orientation for reluctant converts, and hands-off "Delegating" style for highly motivated and highly skilled professionals. Overall the message here is that there is no ideal profile or pattern of leadership—leaders today operate in a dynamic and complex business environment and therefore must increase their skill at both interpreting and adapting to whatever situation they face. Our story is by a manager who applied this very lesson.

In Action [Case Study]: Recently at my job, I was involved in a situation that demonstrated many aspects of situational leadership theory. My main responsibility as General Manager of Sales is to ensure that our sales force reaches the yearly sales target. During the first quarter of this year, the volume of our company was well below the goal. In particular, the sales of our new hires were extremely low. At our first meeting, I chose to use a participating approach to make the sales force feel like I was "on their side." I said things such as "How can we improve our sales result," and "What can I, as General Manager, do to help you achieve better results." After monitoring the results it was obvious that there were no significant improvements. I held a second meeting, at which I chose to use a "selling" approach to leadership. I gave directive behavior (i.e., going on sales calls with the new members) and also provided supportive behavior, by holding several late-night rap sessions. Once again, there were no improvements to speak of. I met with the other managers to get their advice and we determined that the employees had neither the ability to get the job done nor the willingness to put in the effort required to achieve successful results. I then held a third meeting in which I used a "telling" approach to leadership. I laid out specific guidelines for making sales calls and informed the group that any person who did not achieve a certain number of successful appointments per week would be put on probation. They were informed that if their sales results did not improve a period of retraining would begin (making it impossible to earn any commissions). This "strong armed" approach, although unpopular at first, was successful. The group began making more calls and meeting more clients, and in turn began to gain confidence. Result of the group improved drastically within the next month. It is clear from this example that the person who is trying to "lead" knows who their "followers" are. *The leader must determine what "stage of readiness" his followers are at, and choose the leader behavior that will work best.* I feel the reason I had to try a few different leadership approaches before reaching the appropriate one may have been because I was having a tough time reading what stage of readiness my followers were at.

Walking the Talk: Select a situation in your life where you were a leader. (1) **D**etermine the characteristics of the situation that you were in. (2) **E**valuate the degree to which your followers were both willing and able to perform the needed tasks. (3) **A**nalyze why and how the degree of fit between the employees and your leadership style influenced your ultimate success. (4) **L**everage these insights to enhance your diagnostic ability to read situations and behavioral flexibility to adapt your leadership style to them.

To better improve my diagnostic acumen and leadership flexibility, I will...

11.7 Defining Paths for Achieving Goals

Ask Yourself: Are you good at defining objectives? Making them personal? Helping people to achieve them? All of the above? How might an effective leader adapt the way they motivate followers along appropriate paths to accomplish organizational goals?

Management Theory: Consistent with contingency thinking, the "Path-Goal Theory" of leadership is centered on the idea that a leader must adapt to the situation to be successful. Specifically, it posits that leaders are accepted when they can satisfy subordinates' needs and are effective when they are able to identify and remove barriers as well as provide guidance for their employees to achieve results. Leadership is thus seen as a process of establishing performance parameters for employees who link their personal aspirations with organizational objectives (i.e., defining the goal) and then providing customized support to facilitate their successful achievement (i.e., clarifying the path). Here the critical leadership success factor is flexibility across four primary styles: Supportive leadership, which emphasizes concern and a focus on friendliness and relationships, Directive leadership, which emphasizes expectations and a focus on guidance and tasks, Participative leadership, which emphasizes involvement and a focus on consultation and empowerment, and Achievement-oriented leadership, which emphasizes quality and a focus on challenge and excellence. Leaders are advised to adapt their style based on the complex interaction of employee characteristics (such as personality, needs, motivation, and ability) and environment characteristics (such as tasks, roles, uncertainly, and structure). For example, employees with an internal locus of control will often prefer a participative style whereas those with a high growth need working on complex tasks might respond better to an achievement-oriented style. In addition, a directive approach can be more effective for those working on unstructured tasks while a supportive approach usually works well for those engaged in clear tasks. These are just a few of the model's many contentions. Whereas the path-goal model is quite complex its fundamental message is nonetheless simple: leadership is about adapting your style to motivate your followers to move from point A to point B. Our story is by a manager who learned to lead in precisely this way.

In Action [Case Study]: As president of a nonprofit organization, I became all of the leaders described by the Path-Goal Theory at different times to appeal to the needs of my members for the purpose of attaining the organization's goals. In my charity foundation, there existed a lot of animosity and low morale. The administration felt the members were not working together for the benevolent purposes of the organization and were getting lost in creating the "hip" fundraising events that the organization was known for. Staff members felt the administration was selfish and inattentive to their needs and that there was no sharing or delegation of responsibilities. Committee volunteers felt like workhorses of the organization and their personal satisfaction was becoming nonexistent. When I became president I wanted to fix these problems. *I realized the need to understand what people wanted out of joining the organization before I could get them to work toward what the organization and its beneficiaries needed. It was therefore necessary for me to accept that everyone, and subsequently every committee, required individualized degrees of supervision and guidance to optimize organizational and personal satisfaction.* I was a directive leader with the responsibility of laying out our overall strategic goals. The production committee was already knowledgeable of the technical aspects of events and desired only experience, so a supportive leader was all that was called for. With the research committee, I was an achievement-oriented leader since members wanted definitive challenges of their own and my desire to regain emphasis on the charity was one of their challenges. With the sales and marketing committee, I was a participative leader when incorporating members' experience, education, and ideas when promoting any events and the cause. When these leadership changes were made, positive outcomes surfaced. Everyone's performance increased producing abundant funds for all of our charities. Member satisfaction reached an all-time high. People were motivated to utilize their personal talents to further the original goals of foundation. Strong communication, mutual respect, and acceptance of each other in the organization were established, and we were all encouraged to sustain our commitment and participation. Attendance and collegiality at meetings has never been better.

Walking the Talk: Select a situation in your life where you were a leader. (1) **D**etermine the leadership styles you used to motivate your followers. (2) **E**valuate the degree to which these behaviors were more or less appropriate for the leadership situation. (3) **A**nalyze why and how the degree of fit between the context and your leadership style influenced your ultimate success in defining goals and clarifying paths for your followers. (4) **L**everage these insights to enhance your ability to customize your leadership approach.

> To better customize my leadership approach for guiding followers along paths toward desired ends, I will...

11.8   Aspiring Toward Servant Leadership

Ask Yourself: Should leaders be more concerned about their own or their followers' well-being? Their personal or their organization's (or mission's) success? Is leadership more about giving or taking? Being a king/queen or a servant? How do your answers to these questions reveal the way that you look at and treat your employees?

Management Theory: Some in management theory promote the idea that leadership is fundamentally about putting other people's highest needs, core interests, and central objectives before their own. About treating their employees as important ends-in-and-of-themselves who are worth their best efforts and attention. About helping people grow as individuals and assisting them in their personal development. About being a responsible and respectful steward of the organization and its human as well as other resources. About emphasizing mutual collaboration over command and control. In other words, about engaging in "servant" leadership. The following are some of the important dimensions that have emerged in management theory to capture the dimensions of a true servant leader: open-minded listening, demonstrations of empathy, a philosophy of support and healing, keen emotional sensitivity, benevolent persuasion, creative conceptualizations of situations, superior capacity for foresight, an attitude of stewardship, genuine dedication and commitment to the cause, and an aim of community building. Some also include the dimension of calling to reflect a spiritual investment in the growth of others and the willingness to self-sacrifice in its pursuit. Overall, servant leadership advocates an approach to running an organization that is not self-serving but rather one that is more about giving to and building up others. This view of leadership intersects with management theories that emphasize development-oriented behavior and overlaps with the idea of a transformational leader. Although not as widely tested as other frameworks, the notion of the servant-first leader has influenced many (but some argue not enough) organizations and those charged with their stewardship. Our story is by a manager who was influenced by the powerful as well as practical effects of servant leadership.

In Action [Case Study]: Servant leaders put the organization ahead of themselves. They believe that people are able to work together and achieve results when they have a leader who lets go of their ego and cares about the people and the mission before their personal glory. I unknowingly had the opportunity to witness this theory in action when I was a corporate trainer during a two-week management development session. The employees were divided among two groups. Robert lead group A and Sean lead Group B. Robert treated his people like soldiers in the army, they were under his command and expected to follow his rules. Everything was always about Robert. He cared mostly about looking good and promoting his career. Sean, on the other hand, treated his people like he would treat his best friends and seemed to genuinely care about their well being and growth. Group A and B often competed in training exercises and, even though the two groups were purposefully constructed to be equally matched, it was Sean's team that usually came out on top. Sean's people seemed to be very harmonious and cooperative and really put their all into the exercises. Robert's people were often fighting among themselves or running around the building trying to avoid another lecture by Robert on the right way to do things and did not seem fully committed to the tasks. *In retrospect I can see that Sean was a true servant leader who shared his values and power with his employees while Robert emphasized the division between power and peon and hence, Sean was definitely the more effective leader at creating a productive, cooperative atmosphere.* At the end of the training session, Sean received a better report from the corporate bigwigs, was granted a promotion, and actually received a good-bye present from every person in his group. Robert received none of these and my guess is that many of his people would never want to talk with him again. To this day I have been deeply influenced by this experience and have patterned much of my personal approach after Sean's servant-first philosophy.

Walking the Talk: Select a situation in your life where you were a leader. (1) **D**etermine whether you were a servant leader. (2) **E**valuate the degree to which these behaviors were effective from the organization's, your own, and your employees perspectives. (3) **A**nalyze specifically how you were able or not able to achieve the different dimensions of servant leadership and why this affected your employees and bottom-line performance outcomes. (4) **L**everage these insights to enhance your ability to approximate the ideals of servant leadership.

To better aspire toward the ideals of servant leadership, I will...

11.9 Building Trust

Ask Yourself: Is it important for you to trust your leader? Be trusted as a leader? What happens when there is little trust between a leader and their followers? How can a leader build trust within their organization?

Management Theory: We now turn our attention to the dreaded "T" word—trust. Trust can make or break leaders. Trust has been linked to people's willingness to grant a leader power, listen to their advice, cooperate with them, work hard, offer their support and respect, stay loyal and committed, and subjugate their best interest for the larger organizational objectives. There are many definitions of trust but they share several common characteristics. Trust is about creating confidence that you will act in a manner that will not harm people. It implies faith in your intentions, abilities, and behaviors to behave in accordance with commonly accepted or mutually agreed principles. It assumes interdependence insofar as you can impact another's well being. There is an element of even vulnerability in trust, whereas followers hand over power to you with the belief that it will be used wisely and justly and not to act opportunistically against their better interests. Management theory articulates several characteristics and related strategies for achieving leadership trust: integrity and being honest, competence and being able, consistency and being reliable, loyalty and being true, and openness and being accessible. It also suggests different types of trust that might be achieved. For example, trusting with your head by being able to count on someone as well as trusting with your heart by believing someone cares about your welfare. Trust has also been found to exist at different levels, from a superficial everyday trust based in fear or obedience, to a deeper trust that emerges over time in proven relationships, to a deeper still identity-based bond when followers inherently believe in the leader's good will and abilities so that they willingly defer to their best judgment and go the extra mile for them. Our case is by a manager who learned just how important trust can be in her success as a leader.

In Action [Case Study]: Trust is the most important component leadership. I would like to contrast two organizations that I worked for and how trust made all the difference. My former law firm was a shark tank. One of my clearest memories was when a senior attorney walked past my desk and I mentioned to my coworker that I do not trust him and his response was "I don't trust anyone in this firm." The fact was that even though we were a small office of twenty people and everyone had been here at least two years no trust exists between anyone. The president lacked in every dimension of trust and had no integrity whatsoever. We always joked that he was pulling illegal business transactions on the side. He was inconsistent with his behavior and actions; you never knew what was going to come out of his mouth or what his next move might be. There was absolutely no loyalty within the firm. I guarantee that if someone ever came in the office and offered everyone a job; each person would have walked out without looking back. The lack of trust was also evident in our deteriorating performance records. It seemed like with each day, we were slowly slipping to nonexistence. This was extremely unfortunate because there were great, intelligent employees there but the lack of trust literally destroyed the firm as it eventually disbanded. Now I am with a new firm as the supervisor of the legal department. When I first came on board my main goal was to be trusted. I recognized that I should be honest with everyone in the office even when it was not easy to do so. I only spoke whatever was true and played no politics among the group. My consistency gained me respect since I followed up on all my promises and always tried to save face for my employees. *My openness ensured my subordinates that I would say nothing but the truth and help with any work or personal matters. This trust had the whole group working fantastically together.* We now have the highest morale of any area in the firm and have been cited many times for outstanding performance. We also received a professional award that was never before gained by any attorney at our firm. Everyone stays late hours when needed and nobody ever complains. Not a single lawyer called in sick or took annual leave days this year, and I finally had to ask them to schedule their vacations. The turnover rate has been zero during my service.

Walking the Talk: Select a situation in your life where you were a leader. (1) **D**etermine whether you were trusted and the level of this trust. (2) **E**valuate the degree to which this trust had an impact on your ability to effectively lead your followers. (3) **A**nalyze specifically how you embodied or did not the different components of trust and why you chose certain strategies for pursuing it. (4) **L**everage these insights to enhance your ability to develop trust.

To better develop trust as a leader, I will...

11.10 Becoming an Empowering Leader

Ask Yourself: Are you an empowering leader? Are you sure? What exactly is empowerment and how is it executed? What are its potential advantages? How can managers become more empowering in their leadership style?

Management Theory: There is perhaps no management buzzword that is simultaneously so popular and so widely misunderstood than the concept of empowerment. Formally defined, empowerment involves the transfer of decision-making authority to its lowest appropriate level in the hierarchy. In this sense the term has been used in harmony with that of managerial delegation and sharing responsibility with subordinates. Yet empowerment is much more than just this. It is also the process whereby leaders increase the commitment and motivation of their followers by enhancing their roles and strengthening employees' positive orientation toward their work. Empowerment is about creating intrinsic feelings in followers rather than merely giving them externally based rewards or recognition. And contrary to popular beliefs that hording power and keeping others weak is the best path to leadership effectiveness, empowerment suggests that sharing ones power and strengthening others is a surer way to personal and professional success. Management theory delineates several dimensions in which managers can effectively empower others. First empowerment is about giving followers a sense of meaning that conveys the inherent value of their work and its significance toward achieving a larger purpose. Second empowerment is about instilling a sense of competence in followers so that they develop healthy levels of self-esteem and have confidence in their actions. Third empowerment is about conveying a feeling of control and self-determination in followers that they can make real choices and take initiatives in support of desired objectives. Fourth empowerment is about enabling genuine feedback regarding the consequences of followers' behaviors and showing them how they are making a real difference. Together, empowerment done right will effectively model and mentor desired behaviors, build an environment of psychological as well as emotional support, and ultimately foster employees' personal mastery of their jobs. Our story is by a manager who worked to change the ways after discovering some personal failings in the leadership related to a lack of empowerment.

In Action [Case Study]: I have always had difficulty depending on people at work, which is an important factor in becoming an empowering leader. I have a strange way of thinking that if I expect the worst there will be no disappointment to follow. Also I often get caught in a negative spiral of the busier I get, the less time I have to teach others the ropes. Plus I am a bit of a control freak when it comes to depending others to do a job that I know I could do well by myself. As I have become aware, however, this tendency only generates a self-fulfilling prophecy and the consequences of this behavior are clearly detrimental to myself, my staff, and my organization. Therefore I have embarked on a program to empower my people and give them a true sense of meaning. During the past two weeks I have taken the time to meet one on one with each of the employees in my department. Two central themes emerged from our discussions. First, a number of them felt that their jobs were boring with no real responsibility. They thought I made all the decisions and they were paid not to think too much. Second, quite a few people stated that I, as manager, played "favorites" by delegating what they considered some of the more interesting tasks to individuals in better standing with me. *Initially I was shocked to hear these comments, but now I find that they have some validity. My employees' feelings seemed to stem from my improper management of empowering and delegating techniques.* I went through the list of empowering guidelines and found that I ignored some methods such as fostering "mastery" in their work, was deficient in "modeling" behaviors that I expected them to learn and perform, and neglected proving an adequate sense of meaning and control to all members in team projects. To address their concerns, I have prioritized the sharing information and facilitating learning among all team members. I have made a promise to give star performers more opportunities to make real decisions and poor performers more feedback and support to develop their skills. As far as delegating is concerned, I made it clear to the employees that I will insist on input from all group members and attempt to develop some sort of consensus before making major decisions. Hopefully the star performers will feel more challenged and involved in the process and that poor performers will feel less alienated. Hopefully everyone will better understand the "whys" behind my decisions. Even though it is too early to tell whether they will have any lasting impact, I do sense a change of attitude in myself and my employees.

Walking the Talk: Select a situation in your life where you were a leader. (1) **D**etermine whether you were an empowering leader. (2) **E**valuate the degree to which these behaviors were effective in increasing the commitment and motivation of your followers. (3) **A**nalyze specifically why you embodied the different dimensions of empowerment and adopted appropriate strategies for achieving them. (4) **L**everage these insights to enhance your ability to empower others.

To better become an empowering leader, I will…

CHAPTER TWELVE
─────────────────────

Developing a Global Mindset

Chapter twelve examines management theories about globalization and the management skill of developing a global mindset. Globalization has fundamentally altered the business landscape. Not in a literal sense per se, but for all practical purposes it is a small world after all. More than ever organizations operate across national borders and information travels the far reaches of the globe at a faster pace than it once did between neighboring villages. In fact, one would be hard pressed to identify an organization that does not have an international competitor, supplier, customer, contributor, or stakeholder among its ranks. As such management can no longer be viewed as a local phenomenon but rather a transnational profession that challenges its members to understand, adapt, and learn from a seemingly countless variety of cultural contexts. Even if one artificially constrains their focus on the purely domestic arm or sphere of a business, they will almost certainly encounter an internally diverse set of employees who have been born in, educated by, or otherwise intertwined with globally relevant differences in, for example, ethnicity, race, gender, religion, values, language, communal norms, and socioeconomic background. There is simply no escaping the fact that the modern manager must execute the functions described in this book with a careful eye to their relevant cultural contexts. Therefore in this twelfth and final chapter we look at how organizations can adopt and perpetuate a global mindset so to respect, respond, and leverage a complex and multidimensional mixture of characteristics in this age of increasing diversity in the workplace environment.

12.1 Appreciating the Importance of a Global Mindset

Ask Yourself: How has globalization changed the way organizations do business? Manage? Compete? Approach pretty much every single topic mentioned in this book? Why is it important to adopt a global mindset? Do you have one?

Management Theory: There is little debate as to the ubiquity of globalization and its increasing effect on management. Multinational companies and technological advances are quickly turning the world as we know it into a global marketplace. Although this has greatly benefited many companies it has also created new challenges for their managers. The culturally savvy organization will recognize these differences and create an environment that is compatible with cultural beliefs and norms. However, as famously attributed to Will Rogers, what is common sense is not always translated into common practice. All too often managers seem to assume that a "one size fits all" approach will work when dealing with people from across the world. Cultural differences influence every dimension of performance at every level of an organization. If organizations do not sufficiently recognize and value global diversity, then they will be less likely to become proficient in recognizing key differences as well as less able to grow the needed competencies to succeed both within and across them. Without this sense of appreciation, they will not be as sensitive to nuanced customs and best practices. They will not be as willing or able to adapt their behavior to fit different cultural contexts. They will not be in as strong a position to make optimal use of the diverse knowledge, skills, and abilities of its global workforce and networks. They will not be as likely to capitalize on business opportunities that could affect the bottom line. They will not be as apt to construct a positive diversity climate and promote a fair and equitable environment. Overall a lack of managers' cultural appreciation can inhibit their companies from effectively competing in the global marketplace. Our story is by an international manager who confronted this issue head on in their dealings with foreign subsidiaries.

In Action [Case Study]: I am a manager in a multinational bank headquartered in London and that has a presence in every major financial market around the world. In turn, we are able to provide clients with different investment vehicles from around the world. One of the biggest differences I encounter when dealing with foreign subsidiaries is their lack of urgency when compared to American managers. In the New York office, everything needs to be done yesterday, while the many of the European offices seem to be content with the belief that "things will get done when they get done." *The clash between cultures causes frustration on both sides of the pond. The only way I have been able to avoid problems from mushrooming is by remembering my management theory and keeping a global perspective.* You cannot expect everyone else to adapt to your style, it just does not happen and if you try and push too hard it can be seen as rude and disrespectful. In situations such as these I try to appreciate the other cultural perspective. By respectfully explaining our deadlines to my counter parties in Europe and why problems need to be resolved sooner rather than later, I feel I have been able to accomplish more. At the same time I have tried to learn a thing or two from my overseas colleagues by taking things a little easier and better appreciating the joys of life by not rushing through lunch or taking my time walking through the park to work. Another barrier that sometimes comes up is age. At twenty-three years old, I am the youngest manager in my office. When interacting with some cultures my age is a benefit seen as more "with the times." In other cultures people do not want to talk with me and one Asian client told me to put my supervisor on the line immediately after asking my age. Although businesses may be breaking geographical barriers and moving into foreign markets, cultural difference will always be present. Appreciating peoples' differences will reduce friction between various peoples and help improve work-related performance. By creating a positive environment within the organization, it will contribute to a more satisfied workforce and the multinational company's bottom line.

Walking the Talk: Select a situation in your life where you encountered a different culture. (1) **D**etermine whether the cultures were different and in what way. (2) **E**valuate the degree to which you appreciated the power of these cultural differences in influencing peoples' behaviors and attitudes. (3) **A**nalyze why you were or were not able to see the potential value of cultural diversity and how you might improve this. (4) **L**everage these insights to develop a better appreciation for a global mindset.

To better appreciate the importance of a global mindset, I will…

12.2   Combating Parochialism and Ignorance

Ask Yourself: Are all of the worlds cultures basically the same? Any meaningful differences related to effective business practices? Will a management technique that works in one culture always have the same effect in others? Why do some organizations remain blind to the managerial implications of globalization? How can they get over their parochialism?

Management Theory: It might be hard for people who grew up on the Internet and were raised in an age of globalization to believe, but all too frequently organizations demonstrate a remarkable obliviousness to culture context. Some managers just do not seem to see the differences between cultures and the way that they affect management practice. This type of ignorance is referred to as "parochialism" and represents an assumption that peoples and practices from different cultures are all alike or, at the very least, that their difference are not important for effective management. Cultural diversity is ignored or downplayed, as such essentially eliminated as a criterion for determining how to best manage an organization. Parochialism may be evident when a firm markets a product with a name or color that is positive in one culture but carries negative connotations or even offensive messages in another. For example, advertisements using the word nova might signify a "bright star" in some places but translate into something that "does not go" (no-va) in others. Parochialism may surface when an office layout, client interface, or professional service is simply transported from one culture to another without thought as to how it might fit with regional norms and values; for example, adopting a highly individualistic leadership style in a more collectively oriented context. It may be observed when a management practice is instituted across a global company without recognition as to its appropriateness with local religious or political traditions. For example, instituting performance-based incentives and variable pay into a more traditional and conservative culture. Overall this ignorance of cultural differences can impinge an organization's ability to expand globally, attract and satisfy customers, and inspire loyalty and high performance in its workforce. Our story is by an international manager who struggled with and eventually helped overcome elements of their firm's parochialism.

In Action [Case Study]: Having succeeded in America, my company wanted to forge into the European and Asian markets. Being an American-born cosmetics company, the firm initially suffered from parochialism but, by learning what worked and what did not work, we were able to change many aspects of our corporate culture and succeed. However these lessons did not come easy (or cheap). For example, during our entry into Spain and England, we conducted launches that were basically identical to those done in the home market. *Although they were very successful in the United States, my firm noticed differences in reactions to the presentations of our product and experienced major difficulties with everything from sales style to language.* At first, my firm was baffled because through their American eyes, the reactions to the product and selling procedure should have been overwhelming. However, when planning launching strategies for future countries, we began to realize that there will always be challenges. I pushed my team to rethink their business strategy using more universal terms. Since the United States used ounces while Europe used milliliters, we developed "universal packaging" that included both measurements. Also, we stated the ingredients on the packaging in both English and French. In Germany, strict disposal laws regulated the design of the outer packaging of consumer goods. My team decided to eliminate the outer packaging of all of our product lines in order to be environmentally correct, which was the rage in these cultures, and at the same time, perpetuated the highly envied, utilitarian look. Even when our risqué advertisements were banned in Italy and China, we effectively manipulated the strong image of America's fashion brands to match local values, and the products were able to stand on their own. The corporate meetings of the satellite offices were initially conducted separately from the domestic ones. Recently, I directed my assistant to make sure that the meetings are integrated into one gathering complete with translations for all relevant languages and media-intensive presentations. Changing our strategy to a more globally sensitive one has had a positive influence on our corporate image. I realized that when an American company wishes to pursue global endeavors, "parochialism" could very easily surface, but if they view their business through global eyes, new standards of business would develop and ultimately a stronger company will emerge.

Walking the Talk: Select a situation in your life where you came face to face with a different culture. (1) **D**etermine whether the cultures were exactly the same or differed in any important ways. (2) **E**valuate the degree to which you were able to detect these cultural differences. (3) **A**nalyze why you were aware of or blind to these differences and how you could have become more sensitive to them. (4) **L**everage these insights to enhance your ability to overcome parochial tendencies.

To better overcome parochial tendencies, I will...

12.3   Combating Ethnocentrism and Arrogance

Ask Yourself: Is your culture's way of doing things always better than everyone else's? Can you learn anything important from other cultures? Why are some organizations so superior-minded when doing business with people from different backgrounds and traditions? What are the implications of this? How can they work to get over their ethnocentrism?

Management Theory: The previous section discussed cultural ignorance. An additional problem that organizations have to overcome is cultural arrogance. It is a sad truth that some people see their own culture as universally and unequivocally better than all others. Blanketly adopting a "my way is always right and your way is always wrong" attitude is called ethnocentrism. Adopting an approach that all the values and practices of one's home culture are by default superior to all others, in every situation, and for every task is clearly self-centered and naïve. Within each society there can certainly be found unique as well as useful predilections and preferences, and these represent potentially complementary managerial strengths and opportunities. Judging other cultural characteristics purely by the standards of ones own culture can lead a manager to dismiss valuable information or disregard potentially helpful ideas. It can also create barriers that prevent healthy and productive relationships based on mutual respect from forming. Ethnocentric interactions instead frequently lead to feelings of hostility, shock, and even discrimination. Thus ethnocentric management is a cause of much tension and failed partnerships between firms operating across international boundaries. Furthermore, ethnocentric attitudes make it harder to learn global best practices and develop a world-class organization. Whereas the parochial manager might unintentionally demonstrate insensitive behavior, the ethnocentric individual is purposefully closed-minded (and proverbially "ugly") in their approach. Our story is by a manager experiencing both the ugly and potentially hopeful side of an ethnocentric approach.

In Action [Case Study]: I own and operate an import-export company specializing in African artifacts. Representatives from a large multinational retail company came to visit my country to speak about us supplying local goods for their stores. *Right from the start, their ethnocentric attitude promoted a belief that there was only one right way to do things, their way, and this made us feel disrespected.* When we greeted them at the office and began to welcome in the traditional way of my people they seemed disinterested and pushed us to get right down to business. The visiting managers spoke only English and expected that all conversations be conducted that way. Fortunately our employees all speak a minimum of two languages and were able to adapt. Also the visiting managers frequently talked down to many of my staff and came across as very arrogant and aggressive. The behavior of their managers really surprised me because they were such a large company. You would think that they would at least pretend to respect our cultural heritage or learn a few phrases of the local dialect. In contrast my employees genuinely respect the different cultures of our clients. For instance, we are willing to try different cuisines from other cultures and change into local attire when visiting clients even though at the home office, when nobody was visiting, we would dress in African clothes. When making further inquiries about this potential client, I found out that all of the senior executives are locals with no foreign born people in upper level management positions. In the end we did not go into business with them even though the money was good. My staff and I did not make this decision easily but it did not seem right doing business with them. Plus we would rather have our artifacts sold by a company that showed some respect for our history. Everything worked out for the best when about six months later we entered into an agreement with a different firm. The money was about the same but more importantly they showed us respect, and we were confident that they would represent our culture in their stores the right way.

Walking the Talk: Select a situation in your life where you came face to face with a different culture. (1) **D**etermine whether the cultures were exactly the same or differed in any important ways. (2) **E**valuate the degree to which you were able to respect and learn from the other culture. (3) **A**nalyze why you were or were not biases in your attitude and how you could have become more open-minded to the rich opportunities found in cultural differences. (4) **L**everage these insights to enhance your ability to overcome ethnocentric tendencies.

To better overcome ethnocentric tendencies, I will...

12.4 Adapting to Individualism versus Collectivism

Ask Yourself: What do you care about more—your personal success or that of the overall group or community? For most people in your society is the "I" usually more important than the "we"? How about in other cultures? What are the implications for managing in an individualistic versus a collectivistic context?

Management Theory: The theoretical framework proposed by Geert Hofstede uses several dimensions of values and norms to understand cultural differences and their implication for management. The patterns which emerge from these varying dimensions come together to represent a "software of the mind" that influence how people in a given culture tend to see, act, and interact with each other. Each dimension therefore provides us with a general assessment of a cultural context and contains vital information about how managerial interventions are likely to be received. One of these dimensions is Individualism versus Collectivism. In some cultures such as the United States and similar societies, people tend to look first at the individual person and self; hence the central emphasis is usually on personal performance and satisfaction. Because the "I" tends to be more important than the "we," they usually emphasize characteristics such as achievement, freedom, autonomy, and initiative. Within highly individualistic cultures there is a predominantly independent construal of self, and they will consider personal interests as primary. In other cultures such as China and similar societies, people tend to look first at the larger collective and group; hence the central emphasis is usually on public performance and satisfaction. Because the "we" tends to be more important than the "I," they usually emphasize characteristics such as respect, social harmony, cohesion, loyalty, and cooperation. Within highly collectivistic cultures there is a predominantly interdependent construal of self, and they will consider communal interests as primary. The implications of this cultural characteristic are considerable. For example, personal bonuses and job assessments might be better accepted in more individualistic contexts whereas group rewards and more inclusive measurements of success might work better in more collectivist contexts. No particular location along this continuum is inherently better than the other, each has its strengths and vulnerabilities, the key is to recognize and adapt accordingly. Our story is by a manager learning about the importance of these differences and applying subsequent lessons when on an assignment in China.

In Action [Case Study]: There are no right or wrong cultures; there are only different cultures. Individualism verse Collectivism, especially should be considered when dealing with the mixture of east and west. *Chinese people usually act toward collectivism; whereas the US people usually act toward individualism. I learned this quickly after I started my service as a manager in our office in China.* I was anxious to make changes when I first arrived at the post. Our offices were not in good shape and it became evident that all of my predecessors had never made any efforts to negotiate with the landlord. I asked my assistant to contact our landlord so that we could speak with them about the situation. He made the right contacts and we were granted a meeting the following week. The landlord was very gracious and welcomed us into his office. I explained the situation to him and stressed the personal importance of this for my success within the company. I also spoke about how improved performance in our office could benefit him personally with more money and prestige. He was very polite the entire meeting and I thought it had gone well. However weeks and months went by and nothing changed. I asked my assistant to look into the matter. He informed me that our landlord had not taken kindly to my individualistic behavior and decided not to help us. It was obvious that I was insensitive to Chinese culture and made a huge mistake. Fortunately, I learned something from this experience and was able to make some amends. This was applied when the home office instructed me to look into better ways of motivating the local work force. My first thought was to institute a bonus system for the most outstanding performers. However I remembered my lesson from the landlord incident and did something different. We decided to reward the entire office staff equally for any performance improvements and announced that each employee would be a critical part of the team in raising the benefits of all workers. This worked out very well and we were able to achieve increased productivity and give out nice raises, which made the workers very satisfied. I received commendation from the headquarters for this effort. This supports the importance of knowing the cultural difference between individualism and collectivism and changing your management approach to fit it.

Walking the Talk: Select a situation in your life where you did business in another culture. (1) **D**etermine whether the culture was more individualistic or collectivistic. (2) **E**valuate the degree to which their style was similar or different to your own. (3) **A**nalyze why your traditional management approach did or did not work in this culture. (4) **L**everage these insights to enhance your ability to fit your style to the degree of individualism versus collectivism within a culture.

> To better adapt to more individualistic versus collectivistic cultures, I will...

12.5   Adapting to Masculinity versus Femininity

Ask Yourself: What do you care about more—material possessions or aesthetic pleasures? Do most people in your society adopt more of a "tough" or "tender" approach to business? How about in other cultures? What are the implications for managing in a quantity- versus quality-oriented context?

Management Theory: An additional dimension suggested by the Hofstede framework is Masculinity versus Femininity. Some refer to this as a distinction between "quantity of life" versus "quality of life" values. In more quantity-oriented cultures such as the United States and similar societies, people tend to prioritize work and the accumulation of money and possessions. As the saying goes, and as the perennially beeping Blackberry's attest, here people seem to "live to work" more than they "work to live." Therefore of particular emphasis are stereotypical masculine traits such as hard-driving competition, dominance, and assertiveness. Within these cultures people tend to be a more aggressive, bold, and objective in their approach to management, focused mainly on results and bottom-line performances and defining success in terms of material means. On the other hand, in more quality-oriented cultures such as many Scandinavian as well as Latino and similar societies, people tend to prioritize leisure and the enjoyment of aesthetic pleasures. As the long lunchtimes attest, here people seem to "work to live" more than they "live to work." Therefore of particular emphasis are stereotypical feminine traits such as emotional sensitivity, compassion, nurturing, and concern for the feelings of others. Within these cultures people tend to be a more laid-back, modest, and caring in their approach to management, focused mainly on process and personal relationships and defining success in terms of more holistic means. The implications of these differences are considerable. For example, getting right down to business might be more acceptable in more quantity-oriented contexts whereas taking the time to establish relationships, and making the effort to partake in aesthetic pleasures might work better in quality-oriented contexts. Our story is by a manager who learned to take this into account when traveling on assignment across Central America.

In Action [Case Study]: I am an international manager in a consumer goods company. Modern companies such as mine have an employee and customer base consisting of people from different countries with diverse cultures. The need for managers to understand those differences and adapt to them will give their business a competitive advantage. Four years ago I visited Central America with my husband for two weeks on a business trip. We spent all of our time in small communities and lodged in the equivalent of Bed and Breakfasts. Everyone we encountered from the business owners to the locals in town had very little concern for material possessions and genuinely seemed to enjoy life. Lunches were long and you could not get any work done when people were home with family or taking a "siesta." *We saw a culture that valued quality of life and emphasized relationships. As Americans we were very careful not to be "pushy yanks" when exploring business prospects or looking for information.* Whenever I met with a shop owner we did not get right down to business as you would in New York or London. Instead we spent a few hours sitting over drinks or just talking and getting to know one another. The conversations were frequently about nonbusiness matters and emphasized family and local beauty such as a mountain, sunset, or indigenous flower. These people really could teach us a thing or two about stopping to smell the roses! The locals were extremely friendly and once they commit to you will go out of their way to make the relationship work. They value family and community. For example, after the hard days work everyone goes to the local town center to talk to others in the community and hear music (traditional music not top 40!). It is a time for friends and family to keep up on the local news and events. In fact, my husband and I were stunned to find out that every inn we stayed at already knew all about us and why we were in the area. The shop owners and local people we encountered seemed very satisfied with what they did. Their concern for others and their strong community relationships, in my perception put them high on a quality of life standard as opposed to a high quantity of life standard. Knowing this I was able to successfully do business there.

Walking the Talk: Select a situation in your life where you did business in another culture. (1) **D**etermine whether the culture was more quantity- or quality-oriented. (2) **E**valuate the degree to which their style was similar or different to your own. (3) **A**nalyze why your traditional management approach did or did not work in this culture. (4) **L**everage these insights to enhance your ability to fit your style to the degree of masculinity versus femininity within a culture.

To better adapt to more masculine versus feminine cultures, I will...

12.6   Adapting to Power Distance and Uncertainty Avoidance

Ask Yourself: Do you feel that power in organizations should be centralized at the top or shared in an egalitarian manner? Do you generally like working in changing, uncertain situations or prefer more structured and stable environments? How about for most people in your society?

How about in other cultures? What are the implications for managing in a high-versus-low power distance society or high-versus-low uncertainty avoidance context?

Management Theory: We now consider the final two dimensions in the original Hofstede framework for understanding the effect of international cultural differences on management practice. First, power distance refers to the degree to which people accept and expect influence to be distributed unequally. In lower power-distance cultures people are more equal in stature within flatter, more decentralized hierarchies emphasizing participative leadership and fewer status differences. In higher power distance cultures work is often organized in taller, more centralized hierarchies with a larger disparity between officeholders and a more autocratic style of management with clear lines of authority and a greater respect for rank and job title. Second, uncertainty avoidance (be careful of the double-negative here) refers to the degree to which people are tolerant of ambiguous and unstructured situations. In low uncertainty-avoidance cultures people are not as fearful of the unknown and tend to be more comfortable in fuzzy, relativistic, dynamic situations found in less formal structures emphasizing flexibility, creativity, risk-taking, and empowerment. In higher uncertainty avoidance contexts there will usually be more formal clear-cut guidelines and procedures governing organizational action along with more emphasis placed on stability and security as well as a greater overall respect for rules and regulations. Even though these are distinct conceptual dimensions there are important ways in which they interact. When managing within dynamic, innovative cultures that are relatively low in both power distance and uncertainly avoidance (i.e., United States), there will be large contrasts between more traditional cultures that are relatively higher in these dimensions, such as Russia or France. Our story is by an international manager who considers this very issue with a focus on US-French business patterns.

In Action [Case Study]: When I was transferred from our bank's Paris to New York office, it was a shock to find out just how different the American and the French cultures and values were. Even though they are both Western countries with common roots in elected democracies they face large thinking disparities that managers must be aware of if they are to do business across them. America has lower power distance and uncertainty avoidance scores, while France has higher ones, which results in big discrepancies in the general attitudes toward work. *A high power distance and uncertainty avoidance make a country rely a lot on bureaucracies and rigid hierarchies, where there is little room for innovations and personal initiatives.* In France people accept the hierarchy at work, because if they question it, they can try to find a job elsewhere. In large French companies the hierarchies are very strong and they are based on education, network, and seniority. I saw an extremely rigid and clear hierarchy here where everybody is the superior of someone, and where it is difficult to move upward. Even in our back office of six people, everybody was the boss of another one! Such situation could be more or less easy to live depending on the personalities of people. In America my bank's structure is much more flexible, and with a good idea and personality you can go much further. With uncertainty avoidance there were also big differences. French managers require maximum technical information, and they are known for following instructions with extreme precision. Our French clients did not tolerate ambiguity of tasks, and refused to take responsibility for assignments that are lacking complete and precise requirements. If they receive a technical instruction that they consider being incomplete, they will not start working on the assignment until their version is acceptable. Most managers in France felt uncomfortable making decisions if comprehensive information was not available. In contrast, American managers would rather use their discretion and treat instructions as a general guideline rather than as exact directions to be followed. In order to stress importance of a particular request, I must repeat two to three times how important it is so the American managers would accentuate their attention and efforts complying with it. Technical instructions that French clients will find incomplete, will be welcomed by American clients without reservations.

Walking the Talk: Select a situation in your life where you did business in another culture. (1) **D**etermine whether the culture was higher or lower in both power distance and uncertainty avoidance. (2) **E**valuate the degree to which their style was similar or different to your own. (3) **A**nalyze why your traditional management approach did or did not work in this culture. (4) **L**everage these insights to enhance your ability to fit your style to the degrees of power distance and uncertainty avoidance within a culture.

To better adapt to contexts that vary in power distance as well as uncertainty avoidance, I will...

12.7   Managing amid Gender Diversity

Ask Yourself: At work do you only interact with just men or just women? Is this important? Why? How does gender influence the way in which organizations function? Are there better and worse ways of managing within a business climate of increasing gender diversity?

Management Theory: Different cultures vary in the standards that they apply and the opportunities that they afford to women. Therefore gender-based diversity issues transcend any particular culture or context and thus are truly a global phenomenon. Consider the fact that, despite the tremendous progress in recent times, women have still not achieved equal access, promotions, and pay in the workplace. Numerous public sources such as the World Economic Forum statistically documents that no country has altogether eliminated gender bias. This is important from a productivity and human resources perspective, given the increased percentages of women in the ranks of management, as well as from an ethical and social justice perspective. Yet even though research had found few if any performance-related differences between men and women, very real workplace challenges persist today. For example, although the proverbial glass ceiling has cracked to a greater or lesser extent in different cultures, it has not shattered. These asymmetries can negatively affect workers' motivation and opportunities for development and advancement, in addition to representing a form of discrimination. Fortunately all of the news on this front is not so grim. Many organizations have been making real progress on managing gender diversity through what has been termed family-friendly policies. For example, by instituting flexible or part-time work schedules, telecommuting opportunities, extended parental and family leaves, alternative career ladders, and onsite daycare organizations can better accommodate those employees who are primary caregivers for their family. This allows for a more effective use of employee talent and minimizes a key barrier facing professional women. Management research supports the notion that these types of initiatives, done well, are excellent investments that more than pay for themselves in increased productivity, satisfaction, attendance, and retention. Our story is by a manager whose organization is trying to become more "family-friendly."

In Action [Case Study]: Any manager who has traveled the globe knows that women are not treated the same way in different areas of the world and this no doubt is because of differences in history and culture. Even in this country there is a wide variety of ways in which women are treated and many companies have a long way to go in fully embracing women into their executive ranks. *As companies are finding that a diverse work force is beneficial to their organization, they are using "family-friendly" ways to recruit and retain talented female managers.* My firm is attempting several such programs. For example, we are offering job sharing programs where more than one person may share the same position and responsibilities while working part-time. The managers of my department job share. They have small children and want to be able to spend more time with them. While one manager comes to the office on Monday, Tuesday, and Wednesday, the other comes on Wednesday, Thursday, and Friday. We have another woman vice president with young children who makes extensive use of telecommuting. She comes to the office on Tuesday and Wednesday and works out of her home on Monday, Thursday, and Friday. This allows her to work a forty-hour week and still be there for her children when they need her. She has consistently received top job evaluations so this arrangement shows no signs of limiting her ability to manage her department. We also offer flexible work days and hours to accommodate different situations and lifestyles. I personally take advantage of flextime to vary my hours depending on my kid's school and extracurricular schedules as well as their doctor's and other appointments. A company's decision to offer family-friendly programs to their employees can play a large part in employees' perception of equality and loyalty. The organizational benefit is the ability to maintain and motivate a diverse work force that may have otherwise left to tend to children, elderly parents, or further their education. If it was not for these programs I do not know whether it would be possible for me to stay with the company.

Walking the Talk: Select a situation in your life where you interacted with someone of a different gender. (1) **D**etermine whether any work or management-related differences existed. (2) **E**valuate the degree to which gender influenced the interaction. (3) **A**nalyze what aspects of your management style and techniques would or would not work for this person in this culture and the reasons why. (4) **L**everage these insights to develop an enhanced management approach that effectively considers gender diversity.

> To better manage amid gender diversity, I will...

12.8   Navigating Time Orientation

Ask Yourself: How do you view time? At work does everybody whom you interact view time in the same way? How about those who live in or come from different cultures? How can time orientation influence the way in which organizations function? Are there better and worse ways of managing across contexts that vary in the way they view time?

Management Theory: Of particular importance to the global manager is the varying meaning of time across cultures. Although Dr. Einstein was referring to the physics of time in his formulas regarding relativity, the thrust of his insight (time is seen differently depending on ones point of view) is just as useful in the social domain of management. Fortunately there are a number of theories available to aid the modern manager in this respect. First, we can look at the relative emphasis of a particular temporal domain. For example, people in some cultures exhibit more of a "past" orientation through veneration of ancestors and focus on tradition, some adopt a greater "present" orientation with their pursuit of short-term results and the here and now, and others still are more "future" oriented in their high savings rates and long-term, forward-looking thinking. Second, we can look at the relative attitude toward its direction. For example, people in some cultures regard time as essentially linear and finite, putting a cash-value on this valuable resource, whereas others see time as more circular, interrelated, and repeating. Third, we can look at the relative approach toward grouping and executing tasks. For example, people in more monochronic cultures tend to process activities one at a time in a sequential manner—think relay race. By contrast people in more polychromic cultures tend to do multiple things simultaneously and tackle jobs in parallel— think rugby scrum. Monochronics are usually more singularly focused and engaged in distinct activities while polychronic managers are often found multitasking and juggling many projects (or customers, employees, etc.) at once. Taken together, it is clear that practically all of the managerially relevant processes in this book would be affected by such distinct outlooks. Our story is by a manager experiencing and adjusting to different cultures' time orientations while on an overseas assignment.

In Action [Case Study]: According to management theory, societies differ in the value they place on time. I worked for two and a half years in northern and central Africa. I came in brand new to the culture and customs. The biggest problem that I ran into in my job was time orientation. *I was brought up to think that "time is money" and that speed is of the essence. Now I was in a different world altogether.* This was particularly frustrating because nothing ever seemed to get done according to my schedule. It could take three weeks to receive a package from the United States or maybe a week to get an overnight telegram. Whether it was telephone meetings that did not occur at their scheduled time, or documents failing to be faxed or e-mailed by a certain deadline, it was clear that the local sense of time was quite different from mine. I mean just to order basic supplies for my office, I had to organize one of the two trucks in my entire village to take me to the nearest town, then I had to get the local boss to sanction the money, then I had to have the bursar write a check and have the boss sign the check, then navigate my way back to the office. This whole process could take a full week. However once I finally resolved the fact that I was not going to change this part of their culture I did the only thing I could do. I adapted my attitude toward their different time orientation. At that point things began to get a lot easier. Once I acclimated to my new culture's beliefs I started to become less stressed, my mood became more positive, and my working relationships with the local workforce improved substantially. Absenteeism however at my remote location was higher than back at the headquarters. Many times I would not make it back to the office in time but I was never reprimanded, this was their culture and time just did not matter. Whenever things got done, they got done.

Walking the Talk: Select a situation in your life where you interacted with someone from another culture. (1) **D**etermine whether any time-orientation differences existed. (2) **E**valuate the degree to which time-orientation influenced the interaction. (3) **A**nalyze what aspects of your management style and techniques would or would not work for this person in this culture and the reasons why. (4) **L**everage these insights to develop an enhanced management approach that effectively considers time-orientation.

To better manage amid time orientation diversity, I will...

12.9   Navigating Culture Shock

Ask Yourself: Is it easy for you to adapt to different local environments when traveling from one culture to another? How about when the cultures are very different? Do you ever find these differences disorienting, even shocking, and do they create barriers to your effective work performance? How should organizations best handle these types of cultural transitions?

Management Theory: Global organizations must contend with the challenges of simultaneously managing, as well as sending their people to and from, multiple cultural contexts. It is not always easy for evened seasoned managers to make the physical, mental, and emotional transitions that come with doing business in vastly different environments. Mostly anyone who has traveled internationally can relate to the strange and often disorienting feeling about finding oneself embedded in an unfamiliar atmosphere of diverse values, languages, and practices. In management theory, the concept of culture shock refers to the disconnect that people may experience when they confront environments different than they are used to. Research suggests that culture shock tends to unfold in a series of phases, each of which can be better or poorly managed. First the initial encounter with a foreign culture often brings feelings of adventure and exhilaration. Think of the eager tourist, newlywed couple, or new employee beginning an exciting new journey. In the second stage, the excitement begins to fade as the reality of facing so many different standards and expectations sinks in. This may cause an overload of new information that, exacerbated by the absence of typical familiarities, can reverses initial highs and cause distress akin to the feeling of homesickness. Finally, the expatriate often faces a key inflection point, a moment of truth where they can either adjust or not, sink or swim. This involves the choice between becoming socialized to and contributing effectively within the new culture or entering a downward spiral or poor attitude and performance that they become a liability both to themselves and to the organization. Managers can take steps to facilitate a positive transition, including developing employees' "cosmopolitan" outlook, building social support structures, and providing formal training programs to boost "cultural intelligence". Certainly the wider the gap between cultures the greater the potential culture shock and thus the more organizations must be proactive in managing it. Our story is by a manager supervising an unsuccessful adaptation to culture shock by an employee transferred from the United States to the Far East.

In Action [Case Study]: My company decided to expand operations and offered Bill, a high-tech worker in one of their California laboratories, a chance to work in Japan for three years. He was given a sizable salary increase and a housing subsidy as an extra incentive to work overseas. He was required to report back to us each month on his activities. I and one other manager from our office also made a number of short trips to Japan during Bill's stay there to keep track of his progress. Using Culture Shock theory, Stage I went by very quickly as the newness of the situation wore off and he settled into a very small apartment and adjusted to long working hours. As he slid into Stage II, the frustrations of trying to communicate all the time in a foreign language began to get to him. The work that he was doing on a parallel processing computing system was very challenging and so this initially kept him satisfied. After approximately three or four months, he entered into Stage III and not in a good way. *He began to complain about how isolated he felt and how everything was foreign for him.* Even though, he enjoyed the work that he was doing, he never felt that he was part of "the team." He was excluded from their meetings and after-hours entertainment. Rather than trying to adapt to his new environment, he tried to fight it. He would try to get my boss to make special arrangements for him but this is not well accepted in a Japanese company. He then cut his workday down to Western standards and allowed his performance to drop off. His Japanese associates responded by ignoring him that just increased his level of frustration. Bill never made it. He resisted the Japanese culture and resigned after less than two years overseas. Could this have turned out differently? Well we definitely should have given Bill more cultural training beyond what amounted to basic language lessons. There are so many traditions that one must know if they are to function successfully in a culture. For example in Japan, it is customary to give gifts to those whom you are indebted to or obligated to; legitimately, this practice serves as a time-honored gesture to strengthen already existing relationships and as a furtherance of social balance and harmony. When we spoke Bill never seemed to understand this practice and this could not have been helpful in his cultural transition. Without adequate training, it was impossible for him to manage culture shock well.

Walking the Talk: Select a situation in your life where you traveled from one culture to another. (1) **D**etermine whether you were able to successfully adapt to the new cultural context. (2) **E**valuate the degree to which you went through the various stages of culture shock. (3) **A**nalyze the reasons why you were or were not able to make the transition and how this could have been improved. (4) **L**everage these insights to develop better approaches for managing culture shock.

To better manage culture shock, I will…

NOTES

Introduction

1. Rynes, S.L., Bartunek, J.M., & Daft, R.L. 2001. Across the Great Divide: Knowledge Creation and Transfer between Practitioners and Academics. *Academy of Management Review*, 44 (2): 340–355.
2. Adler, N.J. & Harzing, A.W. 2009. When Knowledge Wins: Transcending the Sense and Nonsense of Academic Rankings. *Academy of Management Learning and Education*, 8 (1): 72–95.
3. Hambrick, D.C., 1994. Presidential Address: What If the Academy Actually Mattered? *Academy of Management Review*, 19 (1): 11–16.
4. Bennis, W.G. & O'Toole, J. 2005. How Business Schools Lost Their Way. *Harvard Business Review*, 83 (5): 96.
5. Novello, D. Five Minute University by Father Guido Sarducci. http://www.fathersarducci. com/video.html. Accessed May 1, 2009.
6. Jeffrey Pfeffer, J. & Sutton, R.I. 2000. *The Knowing-Doing Gap: How Smart Companies Turn Knowledge into Action*. Boston, MA: Harvard Business School Press.
7. Sternberg, R. 2008. Applying Psychological Theories to Educational Practice. *American Education Research Journal*, 45 (1): 150–165.
8. Gosling, J & Mintzberg, H. 2004. The Education of Practicing Managers. *MIT Sloan Management Review*, 45 (4): 19–23.
9. Kessler, E. H. 2007. Presidential Address—Making a Difference: A Professional, Scholarly, and Engaged EAM. *Organization Management Journal*, 4 (1): 111–115.
10. Kessler, E.H. 2006. Applying Theory to Practice: The Eastern Academy of Management White Paper Series. *Organization Management Journal*, 3 (3):160–163.
11. Kessler, E.H. & Bailey, J.R. 2007. Handbook of Organizational and Managerial Wisdom. Thousand Oaks, CA: *Sage Publications*.
12. Kessler, E.H. & WongJi, D.M. 2009. Cultural Mythology and Global Leadership. Northampton, MA: *Edward Elgar Publishers*.
13. Kessler, E.H. 2009. Business Honors Program, Pace University, Lubin School of Business.

AUTHOR BIOGRAPHY

Eric H. Kessler, Ph.D. is a senior Professor of Management at Pace University in New York City and founding Director of their Business Honors Program, which prepares students with the knowledge and skills for successful careers in global business leadership. He is a Fellow and Past President of the Eastern Academy of Management, the northeastern United States association of business management scholars, where he designed and launched the EAM White Paper Series initiative to better apply management theory to practice. He has served on numerous editorial and advisory boards and as the guest editor for several professional management journals, as well as with the United States National Security Education Program. Dr. Kessler has published or presented more than 100 scholarly papers in top academic outlets and conferences, won numerous research and teaching awards, and produced several additional books, including Handbook of Organizational and Managerial Wisdom (2007) and Cultural Mythology and Global Leadership (2009). He is a member of Phi Beta Kappa and has been inducted into national and international honor societies in Business, Economics, Forensics, and Psychology. He instructs courses on the doctoral, masters, and bachelors levels and has worked as an executive educator, policy analyst, and business consultant for public and private organizations. He has led numerous international field studies and his professional travels have taken him across the six populated continents of the world. Eric is an avid reader of history and philosophy, a sports and puzzle enthusiast, as well as the spinner of many a bad pun. He lives with his best friend/wife, two terrific sons, and faithful dog.

INDEX